D1389322

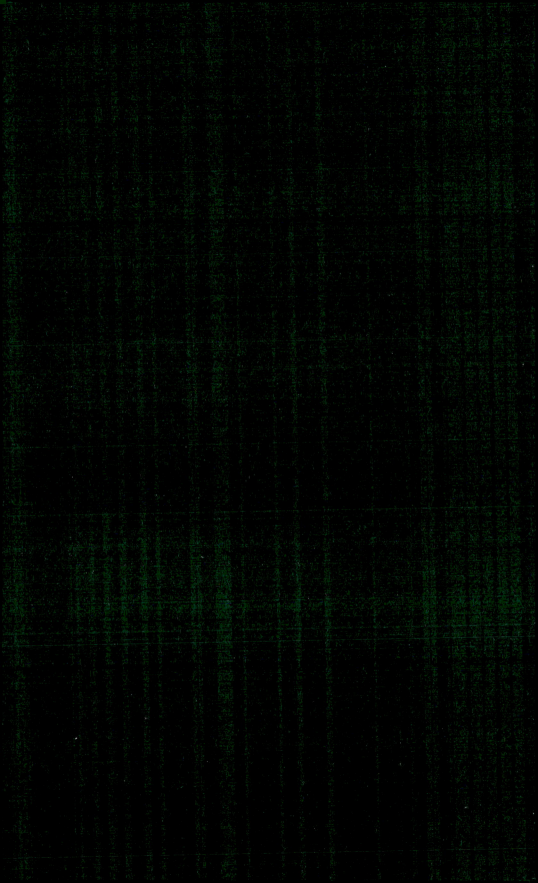

Do Let's Have Another Drink

GARETH RUSSELL

Do Let's Have Another Drink

The Singular Wit and Double Measures of Queen Elizabeth the Queen Mother

WILLIAM
COLLINS

William Collins
An imprint of HarperCollins*Publishers*
1 London Bridge Street
London SE1 9GF

WilliamCollinsBooks.com

HarperCollins*Publishers*
1st Floor, Watermarque Building, Ringsend Road
Dublin 4, Ireland

First published in Great Britain in 2022 by William Collins

1

Set in Minion Pro
Printed and bound in the UK using 100%
renewable electricity at CPI Group (UK) Ltd

MIX
Paper | Supporting
responsible forestry
FSC™ C007454

This book is produced from independently certified FSC™ paper
to ensure responsible forest management.

For more information visit: www.harpercollins.co.uk/green

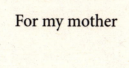

For my mother

CONTENTS

III: The Delightful Duchess (1920–1930)   37

IV: Queen (1930–1940)   65

AUTHOR'S NOTE

Do Let's Have Another Drink is the story of Elizabeth Bowes-Lyon told through 101 anecdotes: one, broadly speaking, for each year of her life. Having previously written a full-length life of one of Elizabeth's particularly tragic predecessors as queen, I should point out that *Do Let's Have Another Drink* is a different kind of biography and different, too, to other books I have written. Although it covers the entire length of Elizabeth's life, it is not exhaustive; that has been done elsewhere and, for those keen to read more, I have included recommendations at the end.

I have aimed to tell Elizabeth's life through anecdotes, short stories and punchlines. This is a skimming-stone biography, and a travel guide to a world that no longer exists. Stepping into the Queen Mother's rarefied universe, which continued to function like an Edwardian country house well into the 1990s, is a little like falling through the looking glass. Alongside many stories that made me laugh – she had a fantastic sense of humour – I encountered the occasional tear-jerker, particularly during her teenage years. I have done my level best to explore her enmities and feuds, particularly the truth about her behaviour towards Wallis Simpson, Nerissa Bowes-Lyon and Diana, Princess of Wales. To keep it of a digestible length, I try to explain, within the text, where the sources originate. Where that has not been feasible, I have included a brief set of footnotes. Each chapter focuses on a decade, beginning with an overview of what happened to Elizabeth in those years.

I hope this book helps too to preserve the memories of those who knew the Queen Mother later in her life. I am immensely grateful to those who shared their private recollections with me; I've tried to maintain a conversational – often very funny and partisan – tone – and if these are the kind of stories that can be told over dinner or drinks, I'll be pleased. Outside any quotations, all opinions are my own, as are any mistakes. It has been a hugely entertaining experience to write this book and I leave it with reluctance.

A note on Elizabeth's titles

Monarchy and aristocracy can be a labyrinth of titles, many of them redefined over the centuries. Different countries also have their own traditions as to how they use titles.

From the British perspective, there are five kinds of queen – regent, consort, regnant, dowager, mother. A queen regent is a king's wife or mother who is temporarily left in control of the government while he is abroad or ill, such as Queen Katherine Parr when her husband Henry VIII went off to war in 1544. A queen consort was Elizabeth Bowes-Lyon's role from 1936 to 1952, when she was married to a reigning monarch, King George VI, and so held her title by right of marriage to the head of state. A queen regnant is a woman who has inherited the throne; like most reigning monarchs in British history, a queen regnant's name is followed by a number if she is not the first of her name to be head of state. When George VI died in 1952, the crown passed to his eldest daughter, who became Elizabeth II – not to differentiate her from her mother Elizabeth but from Queen Elizabeth I, who ruled England, Ireland and Wales from 1558 to 1603. Since, historically, the title of a king has always been higher than that of a queen, the husband of a queen regnant is not referred to as a king, but as a prince or prince consort, hence Prince Philip and Elizabeth II.

When a queen consort becomes a widow, she becomes a dowager queen. If, however, the new monarch is the child of the dowager queen, she has the option to become the queen mother. The title of queen mother originated with the French monarchy from where it was imported to Britain in the seventeenth century by Charles I's wife, the French princess

2

Henrietta Maria who, when widowed, went by the title of *la Reine Mère* or the Queen Mother during the reign of her son, Charles II. Outside of the Anglican prayer books, the title had not often been used in court etiquette since Henrietta Maria's death in 1669, until it was revived for Elizabeth Bowes-Lyon in 1952.[1]

I

East or West, Home is Best (1900–1910)

When Elizabeth Angela Marguerite Bowes-Lyon was born in the summer of 1900, Queen Victoria was the British monarch. Elizabeth's childhood would be one of wealth, comfort and love, as the youngest daughter in a large family of the Scottish aristocracy. Her first memory was of sitting on her grandfather's knee at the castle of Glamis (pronounced 'Glams') on the east coast of Scotland. She was four years old when her grandfather died and his earldom – and three homes – passed to his eldest son Claude, Elizabeth's father and the possessor of a truly fantastic moustache.* Claude was also a superb cricketeer, who liked to maintain his skills out of season through unorthodox means such as bowling Christmas puddings down the Dining Room table to his English wife, Nina Cecilia Cavendish-Bentinck, a great-granddaughter of a former British Prime Minister. Had women been permitted to inherit the dukedom, Cecilia would have become the Duchess of Portland. Instead, the title passed to a cousin, who walked her up the aisle at her wedding to Claude in 1881. Cecilia could not have known that her youngest daughter would one day become a duchess with the added sparkle of an HRH.

---

* In ascending order, the aristocratic titles in Britain are baron, viscount, earl, marquess and duke, the female equivalents being baroness, viscountess, countess, marchioness and duchess. With her father's accession to the rank of earl in 1904, tradition meant that Elizabeth and her sisters became Lady Mary, Lady Rose and Lady Elizabeth. One of several uses of 'Lady' in British etiquette is as an honorific for the daughters of dukes, marquesses and earls, the higher three rungs of the aristocracy, while children of the lower two titles – viscount and baron – are prefixed with 'the Honourable', which is sometimes shortened to 'the Hon'.

Elizabeth did not seem to mourn her mother's lack of ducal status. She took great pride instead in the fact that her father became the fourteenth successive member of their family to hold the title Earl – of Strathmore and Kinghorne – since it was bestowed upon them by King James VI in 1606; indeed, there were stories tying their clan to the castle of Glamis since the adventures of their medieval ancestor, Sir John Lyon, who received it in the 1300s from his father-in-law, King Robert II.[1] From 1606, the earldom's heir has carried the title Lord Glamis.

Set in 65,000 acres of land, many-turreted Glamis was described in Elizabeth's lifetime as 'a castle not of this world, but … a castle of ghosts, and Queens, reaching to the stars. The air of ethereal unreality impresses one instantly.'[2] It had once belonged to Macbeth, a Scottish king who ruled from 1040 to 1057, and it became the setting for Macbeth's assassination of his cousin, guest and monarch, King Duncan, when Shakespeare wrote his play centuries later. In truth, Duncan was almost certainly killed in battle nearby.

There had been plenty of kings, queens, pretenders and rebels at Glamis in the centuries between Macbeth and Elizabeth Bowes-Lyon, who liked to amuse herself by recreating scenes from the castle's dramatic past. These included dousing her youngest brother with a pot of cold water from the ramparts, pretending it was boiling oil and her little brother a medieval knight besieging Glamis.

Glamis's traditions were maintained by the Bowes-Lyons. They extended to the absence of electricity until 1929, the wearing of lace caps by the women during daily chapel services, and Cecilia's ordering of bespoke seventeenth-century outfits for Elizabeth and her youngest brother. To their youthful chagrin, the pair were taught the minuet; they were encouraged to perform, in costume, this stately seventeenth-century dance before dinner parties for the endless stream of guests who came to shoot, hunt and socialise. One visitor thought that, as their mother accompanied the children on the piano, it was as if a Velázquez or Van Dyck painting had come to life. Another wrote of Glamis as a place where there was 'no aloofness anywhere, no formality except the beautiful old custom of having two pipers marching round the table at the close of dinner, followed by a momentary silence as the sound of their bagpipes died away gradually in the distance of the castle. It was all so friendly and so kind.'[3] The Bowes-Lyons' staff was headed by the butler, Arthur Barson, whom a young Lady Elizabeth introduced with, 'Nothing would go on without him – he keeps everything going!' Barson's fondness for a tipple, or three, of wine and whisky did not count against him, nor did the occasional liquor-induced whoops when he spilled food on the family or their guests.

The Victorian era came to an end a few months after Elizabeth's birth, when Queen Victoria died and was succeeded by her son, King Edward VII. Initially, there was no perceptible change in the way the aristocracy lived as they entered the Edwardian age. Modernity was not welcomed, certainly not by Elizabeth's grandmother, the Dowager Countess, after she broke both of her arms during an enthusiastic jaunt in her first motor car.

Claude and Cecilia, Lord and Lady Strathmore, with their children and fourteen servants (including boozy but devoted Barson), moved between their homes by overnight train and horse-drawn carriage to and from the local station. Theirs was a large family, ranging in 1900 from sixteen-year-old Mary to six-year-old Michael. The heir to the earldom was the eldest son, Patrick, named after a Bowes-Lyon uncle who became a Wimbledon tennis champion. Excepting Patrick and Fergus, the siblings were often given nicknames – Mary was 'May', John was 'Jock', Alexander 'Alec' and Rose 'Rosie', while Michael got 'Mick' or 'Mickie'. Elizabeth got 'Buffy', after mispronouncing her name 'Elizabuff' as she learned to speak. There were occasional holidays to Italy to visit Elizabeth's widowed grandmothers, both of whom unsurprisingly found grief more manageable in their respective villas overlooking Florence and the Mediterranean but, by and large, Elizabeth's childhood passed shuttling between England and Scotland.

With her tribe of siblings, Elizabeth spent a great deal of time at their parents' English country estate of St. Paul's Walden Bury in the county of Hertfordshire, where Elizabeth developed a liberal attitude towards the concept of 'owner's discount' as it pertained to anything that took her fancy in the larder. She was frequently caught clambering on a stool, trying to break in to get her hands on the clotted cream. Like most aristocratic families at the time, the Bowes-Lyons also had a London residence.

They rented Number 20 St. James's Square, an eighteenth-century town-house designed by the famous Adam brothers.[4]

The home at which they spent the least amount of their time was Streatlam Castle, a Georgian-era residence in north-eastern England that had come into their possession when it was left to Elizabeth's father after the death of his childless cousin, the art collector and former Member of Parliament John Bowes.[5] When Elizabeth's eldest brother married the Duke of Leeds' daughter in 1908, they were given Streatlam as their marital home.

Her parents' happiness, their social privileges, and their large family combined to create what Elizabeth called 'a marvellous sense of security' and a contentment that 'I suppose one took for granted as a child'. Their homes were decorated with inherited antiques and art, alongside stitched Victorian equivalents of *Live, Laugh, Love* signs, bearing sayings like *East or West, Home is Best*.

Born as the twentieth century dawned, Elizabeth was, in many ways, for good and ill, to carry the attitudes of her Edwardian childhood with her for the rest of her life.

1. Late to her own christening

Elizabeth was not noted for her punctuality. She was habitually late, a trait she shared with her father Claude, who was so lackadaisical about time-keeping that he did not file the proper forms for Elizabeth's birth with the local authorities until six weeks after the event. Faintly contemptuous towards the bureaucracy of modern life, Claude only went to get the forms when the vicar punctiliously insisted on them being in proper order for his own baptismal records. Claude was fined for this tardiness, a mild punishment that nonetheless solidified his view that the whole thing was ridiculous. On 21 September 1900, he recorded Elizabeth's 4 August birth in the parish of St Paul's Walden Bury.[6] The vicar's daughter, Margaret Valentine, noted that her piano lesson on that day had been interrupted by the news, brought over by a maid, 'to say that Lady Glamis had given birth to a baby girl'. Elizabeth's biographer Hugo Vickers has plausibly suggested that the family had relocated nearer to London for the birth to be within easy reach of the capital's superior medical services.[7] There were some nerves over this pregnancy, as it was Cecilia's first since the birth of her son Michael six years earlier.

When it comes to royalty – or the famous of any variety – very little in their lives is allowed to have a banal, accidental or commonplace explanation. Intrigue or conspiracy must play their part. In Elizabeth's case, her father's lack of interest in the paperwork led, in the 2010s, to a theory that Elizabeth must have been a changeling. Perhaps her father's child with somebody else. Maybe the illegitimate daughter of a French cook or a Welsh servant. Elizabeth was allegedly secretly adopted and passed off as a Bowes-Lyon to assuage Cecilia's grief at the death some years earlier of her eldest daughter, Violet. If the delayed paperwork was not enough, supporters of this theory point to the suspicious timings of the pregnancies, separated as they were by six to seven years. Cecilia was allegedly 'too old' at the time she conceived Elizabeth. She was thirty-seven.

A Scottish Dr Ayles, who allegedly attended Claude Bowes-Lyon on his deathbed when he confessed the whole deception, has also been identified as a primary source for this story. There is, however, no doctor registered with that surname for the year of Claude's death. Some proponents have even utilised Elizabeth's physical appearance later in her life to support their argument, since, as she gained weight, 'she did look like the daughter of a cook. You can hardly say she looked aristocratic.' For those who looked for further proof, Elizabeth's ability to talk comfortably with 'ordinary' people when she was queen was proffered absurdly to suggest her real mother was one of 'the servant class'.

Using Claude's slapdash paperwork and Violet's death as evidence that Elizabeth was a cook's surrogate changeling is the historical equivalent of adding two to two and getting 375. Violet Bowes-Lyon's death as a motivation is also questionable, since although it is true that Elizabeth's eldest sister had died of diphtheria at the age of eleven, she did so seven years before Elizabeth's birth. Moreover, had they been trying to cover up a secret adoption, the Bowes-Lyons would likely have been more rather than less careful with the paperwork. Even if the evidence for this theory was not already a cocktail of the improbable and the bizarre, it would be weakened further by comparing photographs of Elizabeth to her mother Cecilia, particularly as they aged, and noting the clear similarities between the two.

2. The Benjamins

On 2 May 1902, Cecilia gave birth to her tenth and final child, a boy christened David. With less than two years between them, Elizabeth and David occupied the Nursery together, where they often put on plays for their parents. Cecilia nicknamed them 'my Benjamins', an affectionate term for children born slightly later than their siblings. When David was older and home from boarding school, a guest repeatedly made sly insinuations about him by calling him a 'pretty boy'. After this visitor said it one too many times to be politely ignored, Lady Strathmore turned to her and said firmly, 'Yes, and he's a very nice one, too, which is better!'

Elizabeth described her mother as 'the pivot of the family'. A devout Christian – her late father had been a Protestant clergyman – Cecilia taught the children to say their prayers at the foot of their beds every evening, a habit that Elizabeth maintained for the rest of her life. The practice came with pieces of motherly advice such as, 'Say your prayers properly and don't mumble. You're talking to God.'

3. Bowes

Among the portraits at Glamis is one of Elizabeth's ancestor Mary-Eleanor Bowes, for ever captured in an enormous gown and a wig twice the size of her head. Born in London in 1749, she had been sole heiress to a vast fortune that included the estate and house of St Paul's Walden Bury. She married John Lyon, the handsome 9th Earl, described in high society as 'the beautiful Lord Strathmore'. To preserve the Bowes name, Mary-Eleanor's father stipulated that whoever married his daughter would have to take her surname if they wanted to have any access to her money. Beautiful Lord Strathmore, described as 'innocent and without the smallest guile, a sincere friend, a hearty Scotchman,' and a good drinking companion, was happy to accept this arrangement and the requisite petitions were submitted to Parliament. Since the Lyon name was one of the oldest in the British nobilities, various double-barrelled combinations were tried by Mary-Eleanor and John's descendants over the next century until they settled on Bowes-Lyon in 1865. However, Elizabeth signed herself 'Elizabeth Lyon', preferring, like most of her relatives, to use the older name rather than the double-barrelled.

4. The Monster of Glamis

In the summer of 1537, King James V of Scots had Elizabeth's ancestor Janet, Lady Glamis, executed as a witch. The King extracted the legally required evidence after authorising that her servants be tortured and then forced Janet's teenage son, John Lyon, to watch as his mother was burned to death outside Edinburgh Castle. Although she did not die at Glamis, Janet was one of many ghosts claimed by her former home. Cecilia and her friend, the Countess of Glasgow, reported sightings of Janet, as did Elizabeth's sister, Lady Rose, who believed she had seen Janet's ghost, 'the Grey Lady', near the castle chapel where the family met daily for prayers. Elizabeth's decision to dress up as the Grey Lady and jump out at her siblings may not, therefore, have been particularly well received on all occasions by Rose.

The novelist Sir Walter Scott, a guest at the castle in the late eighteenth century, described Glamis after sunset as being 'far too far from the living, and somewhat too near the dead'. Elizabeth's youngest brother claimed to have seen proof throughout his childhood that Glamis was haunted, as did their great-aunt, Lady Frances Trevanion. Glamis was allegedly one of the most haunted buildings in the British Isles. Its dead but not departed residents included a spectral drummer boy, possibly a remnant of the Ogilvy clan who had been butchered at Glamis during a fifteenth-century feud, and the blood-soaked 'Tongueless Woman', silenced then slaughtered in the Middle Ages to carry some since-forgotten secret into the grave. The castle has a haunted Hangman's

Chamber, built centuries earlier when the thanes* of Glamis had been tasked with administering the King's justice in that part of Scotland. Again, Elizabeth's sister Rose was a believer, telling a friend years later, 'When I lived at Glamis, children often woke up at night in those upper rooms screaming for their mamas because a huge, bearded man had leant over their beds and looked at them. All the furniture was cleared out a dozen years ago. No-one sleeps there today.'

Guests reported strange occurrences like clocks smashing to the ground at four in the morning, sheets being pulled off beds, or seeing figures looming over them from the shadows or by the fireplaces. An avid believer in the supernatural, Charles Lindley Wood, 2nd Viscount Halifax, reported numerous hauntings during his sojourns at Glamis, and the Archbishop of York's wife was so perturbed during her stay that she suggested to Claude that they arrange for an exorcism of the house. She was particularly unsettled by stories of the 4th Earl of Crawford, a medieval nobleman nicknamed 'the Bearded Earl' or 'the Tiger Earl' for his ferocity in life and who had been a regular guest at Glamis in the fifteenth century. He had overstayed his welcome by half a millennium, trapped there in punishment for having sold his soul to the Devil in a room of the castle following a quarrel with one of Elizabeth's ancestors. An Australian cook in the Bowes-Lyons' service swore she could still hear the Bearded Earl rolling dice with the Devil in the turret where he made the bargain: 'I've heard them rattle the dice, stamp and swear. I've heard three knocks on my bedroom door and no one there. And I've lain in bed and shaken with fright.'

The most famous spectre at Glamis haunted it in life rather than death and, if he existed, may still have been alive when Elizabeth was playing in its Nursery. The legend goes that sometime around 1821 – on a night which was cold, dark and storm-swept, as they must be in such stories – a child was born at Glamis, so severely disabled that the family pretended he had died at birth. A room was constructed in the castle in which the child could be kept safe but secret. Cruelly nicknamed either the Monster,

---

* An ancient title unique to the Scottish aristocracy, gradually replaced with 'earl' over the centuries.

or the Horror, of Glamis, he lived an unusually long life, during which he left his secret chamber only at night for walks and exercise. A visitor to Glamis in the 1960s was reportedly told, 'the Monster was immense. His chest an enormous barrel, hairy as a doormat, but it is said that his head ran straight into his shoulders and his arms and legs were toy-like. Shaped like an egg, he was immensely strong. He was the heir – a creature fearful to behold.'

Only four people knew the truth. The first was the Earl and the second was the Factor (estate manager) of Glamis. The other two were their respective eldest sons. The position of Factor at Glamis was almost as hereditary as the earldom and was held by only two local families between the 1760s and 1940s, while an initiation into the secret was a traumatic rite of passage for every heir to the earldom on his twenty-first birthday, when the Earl took him to wherever the Horror was kept behind Glamis's sixteen-foot-thick stone walls. As they entered the locked chamber, the Earl introduced his son to the Horror with the words, 'This, my boy, is your great-great-uncle. The rightful Earl.' The description of the relation-ship changed; the ritual did not. The same family friend from the 1960s continued, 'Silence, a horror-filled silence, as the young Lord Glamis recoils from the dull-eyed, uncomprehending creature behind the bars. The oaken door shuts behind them and the Monster goes back to his animal sleep. Before their twenty-first birthdays, several heirs lightheart-edly promised their friends that they would reveal the secret as soon as they knew it. None of them did.'

This conspiracy of silence extended even to their relatives. Elizabeth's mother Cecilia asked their Factor, Andrew Ralston, if the legends of the Horror were true, to which he replied, 'Lady Strathmore, it is fortunate you do not know it and will never know it, for if you did you would never be happy.' Ralston, despite serving the Bowes-Lyon family loyally for half a century, refused to sleep at Glamis. Even when the region was envel-oped in a snowstorm, he preferred to chance the one-mile journey home rather than spend the night at the castle. And, while the Strathmores allowed their children to tell stories about the castle's ghosts, Lady Rose said that when it came to the Monster, 'We were never allowed to talk about it when we were children. Our parents forbade us to discuss the matter or ask any questions about it. My father and grandfather absolutely refused to discuss it.'

Perhaps needless to say, all of this is hearsay, as is the frequently cited testament of an unnamed admiral who, at a dinner party table, insisted that the Horror of Glamis had lived to nearly his one-hundredth year, dying in 1921.[8] Who the Horror was is also contested. One version of the story states that his parents were Elizabeth's great-great-grandfather, the 11th Earl, and his third wife, Marianna. Another has it that the father might have been the 11th Earl's adult son from his first marriage, whose wife gave birth at Glamis to a son, Thomas; the boy tragically died at Glamis on the same day, 18 October 1821. Most stories identify this infant Thomas as the child who became the Horror. To complicate things further, there is a third possible timeline, based on alterations made to Glamis in the early 1680s and described in its accounts as 'things of considerable trouble', on the orders of Patrick Lyon, the 3rd Earl. This gave rise to the argument that the tragedy of the Monster in fact dates from the seventeenth, rather than the nineteenth, century and that whispers of it persisted, to be revived by the Victorians' fascination with Gothic mysteries.

There is a surprising amount of circumstantial evidence about just how many people linked to Glamis believed that the Monster had existed. It is very possible that the gossip was self-engendering, that it grew over the years until even various members of the Bowes-Lyon family believed in some variation of the legend, while the truth was that the poor man nicknamed the Monster of Glamis never existed or died as a baby in 1821, and that a myth mushroomed from that. Elizabeth's youngest brother, David, certainly thought so. Unlike their sister Rose, he dismissed the whole thing as a product of the nineteenth-century's obsessive love of melodrama: 'A frightful lot of rot was written about Glamis in Victorian days,' he told a friend in the 1950s. 'Most of them seized on the Monster as a peg and then thought up the most unutterable bosh.' Lending credence to David's scepticism is the fact that, during a fire at Glamis in 1916, no mention was made of trying to find, evacuate, or secure the secret chamber.

We do not know what Elizabeth truly thought about the legends of the Horror, since according to several of her friends (and several of her critics) she refused to discuss it. She was certainly a lifelong believer in ghosts, after spending much of her childhood in homes that she and her family believed to be full of them.* One of the oldest parts of Glamis is the stone-floored medieval room called Duncan's Hall, watched over by portraits of King James IV, the Scottish monarch who was killed leading an invasion of England in 1513, and his granddaughter Mary, Queen of Scots, who had spent the night at Glamis in the summer of 1562. While the hall's name alludes to the death of King Duncan I, it is more probable that it was Duncan's father, King Malcolm II, who expired while staying at Glamis in November 1034, an event commemorated by a chamber there called King Malcolm's Room.

As a child, Elizabeth always felt uneasy in Duncan's Hall. It was the only room at Glamis through which she ran or 'scuttled at top speed'. Lady Rose remembered, 'When my sister the Queen Mother and I were children, we would sometimes be sent downstairs to fetch something. We always raced through Duncan's Hall and the Banqueting Room. As for King Malcolm's Room, where Malcolm was murdered, there was a blood-stain on the floor which would *never* wash out. So my mother had the whole floor boarded over. The bedroom next to it had a door which always opened of its own accord at night. You could bolt it, lock it and even stick a chest of drawers against it – it was still open in the morning! So my parents took the wall down and put the door upstairs in another room.'

5. Clipping Lord Crawford

In October 1905, David Lindsay, 27th Earl of Crawford, and his wife Constance trundled towards Glamis in the novel conveyance of a motor car, in which they had driven from their home at Balcarres House. According to a family friend – although given what he said about them,

---

* She attended her last 'exorcism' in the summer of 2000, when she and a local vicar thought an old bedroom at Sandringham was disturbed by the spirit of King George VI or Princess Diana.

that designation might be stretching the word 'friend' to its limits – 'Lady Crawford looms like Medusa and is vast. She wears unsuccessful frocks of dullish colours, which are a bad background for her heavy massive jewels. She always looks untidy, if not dirty, which Lord Crawford, the most charming of men, frankly is.'

The Lindsays and the Lyons had been neighbours for generations. One of Crawford's ancestors, the aforementioned 'Tiger Earl', was among the Glamis ghosts. Lord Crawford suspected that when the subject of the hauntings came up at the dinner table, the Bowes-Lyons downplayed the satanic handshake that had trapped his predecessor's soul there, as they worried that discussing a deal with the Devil might have an impolite ring to the spectre's descendants.

The Crawfords arrived at Glamis just after the start of the pheasant and woodcock shooting seasons; grouse was also in season until early December. In pursuit of the latter, Elizabeth's father accidentally wounded Lord Crawford – although, as a supporter and collector of the arts,* Crawford was more stung by the family's 'phenomenal ignorance of the castle and its contents'. He heard Elizabeth's 19-year-old brother Jock ask his mother 'about the identity of a portrait which turned out to be a portrait of his own grandmother. They are nice boys, and Strathmore is a delightful man: by the way, he put two pellets in my wrist while we were driving some grouse this afternoon.'

---

* 'Art' might be stretching it a tad. Lord Crawford had an enormous collection of what has politely been called 'nineteenth-century erotica', but given that he amassed said collection in the nineteenth century, it might be more accurate to refer to it as a colossal stash of pornography.

II

War Wounds
(1910–1920)

At Christmas 1910, Elizabeth and David were left at St Paul's Walden Bury in the care of the newly married Mary and their 21-year-old brother Fergus, who took their youngest siblings to church, to parties, and on flower-picking expeditions in the local woods. Cecilia and Claude went to look after 23-year-old Alec, who was complaining of blinding headaches. 'Darling Sweetie Lovie Mother,' Elizabeth, aged ten, wrote on 13 December, 'I hope Alec is <u>much</u> better. <u>Please please</u> don't worry <u>too</u> much about him. We <u>do</u> miss you so! … I hope you won't mind lovie, dovie but I took your rain umbrella to church with me on Sunday because it was raining so hard.'

As 1910 gave way to 1911, Alec continued to suffer from migraines. By the middle of October, his parents were back at Alec's side, when Elizabeth wrote a similar letter to Cecilia, signing off by asking her, 'Do give Rosie, Father and Alec my love, and a lot of kisses.' Edwardian children were usually kept away from distressing news and, while Elizabeth knew Alec was ill, she had no idea just how bad things had become for him. The rest of her letter chattily informs her mother of how close they came to missing the train in Edinburgh and how foggy it was in Scotland that week.

Meanwhile, word was sent to Elizabeth's brother Jock, by then working at a bank in Boston, that he needed to get home if he wanted to say goodbye to Alec. Jock was only a year older than Alec and, since childhood, they had been so close that their grandmother Caroline called them one another's 'Companion Brother'. Jock booked passage on an ocean liner leaving America at the first available opportunity. It was still a few days off the British coastline when Alec died in his sleep on 29 October. Jock revealed several years later that he had suffered a breakdown following his brother's death.

Alec Bowes-Lyon's death was probably caused in the long term by a frontal brain lesion and in the short term by a seizure while he slept. Like his brothers, Alec had boarded school at Eton; like his father, he loved cricket. In his final year at Eton, Alec played for his school in the celebrated Eton–Winchester annual cricket match, where, it is said, he was hit on the head by a fast-bowled ball. In his three subsequent years studying at Oxford, it became progressively clear that such an accident – likely on the cricket pitch – had left Alec with permanent and deteriorating internal injuries.[1] He may have been suffering for longer than his parents and siblings realised; several of the family later noted how cheerful Alec tried to be when he was around them, even when he was in a great deal of pain.

Cecilia was devastated at burying a second child, and Alec's death marked the start of a decade that was to prove extremely painful for Elizabeth's family, as it was for millions of others thanks to the outbreak of the First World War in 1914. The events Elizabeth witnessed in the four years of the Great War were to indelibly shape her character.

6. The Countess of Rothes's trip to New York

In 1911, Elizabeth's tutors asked her to write a short essay titled 'A Recent Invention, Aeroplanes'. In her reflection on this eight-year-old technology, Elizabeth wrote, 'An aeroplane, to look at, is like a big, great bird. They are clever inventions. An aeroplane is usually shaped like a cigar, and has a propeller at one end, and on each side the great white wings, which makes it look like a bird. An aeroplane can fly very high and it makes a great noise. They are not quite safe, yet, and many, many accidents have happened.'

Compared to the safety of the ever-larger series of passenger ships being churned out in the shipyards of the United Kingdom, France and Imperial Germany, travel in aeroplanes seemed dangerous to the point of lunatic. However, in the spring of 1912, when Elizabeth was eleven years old, she and the rest of the world were reminded that these 'queens of the ocean' – floating palaces with room onboard for thousands – also remained vulnerable to the power of nature. On Monday 15 April, Freddy Dalrymple-Hamilton, a family friend who was hopelessly in love with Elizabeth's sister Rose and who had joined the Bowes-Lyons at St Paul's Walden Bury for a few days in the country, was on his way back into London when he saw news bulletins – then written in chalk on huge black billboards – announcing that the British luxury liner *Titanic* had sunk on its first voyage to New York, with the loss of hundreds of lives.

Cecilia's friend Noëlle Leslie, Countess of Rothes, had been on board the *Titanic* when it struck the iceberg. In the hours between her evacuation and rescue, the Countess of Rothes had helped steer and then row her lifeboat which, coupled with exposure in the ice field, caused her some ill health in the weeks immediately after. Back on land, the public's interest in the disaster seemed to grow rather than diminish, which did not help the Countess's attempts to put the ordeal behind her. She had been travelling on the *Titanic* with her maid Roberta and her husband's cousin, Gladys, both of whom also survived. Gladys was even less patient than the Countess with the increasing frequency of questions about the disaster. A journalist asked her, 'Is it true you crossed the ocean on the famous *Titanic*?'

To which Gladys replied, deadpan, 'Part way.'

7. Honey, jam, buns and tea

Elizabeth, dark-haired and blue-eyed, popped her head into the kitchens with a question. Having spotted a maid clearing away a barely touched chocolate cake from one of Cecilia's teas, Elizabeth had bolted downstairs to finish her quest before it disappeared into a locked larder. Elizabeth made clear her intentions with, 'May I come in and eat more? *Much more* of that chocolate cake that I liked to eat while it was upstairs?'

While Mrs Thompson the housekeeper proved a soft touch on Elizabeth's snacking agenda, the cook was less so, recalling, 'The little imp! I was forever chasing her out of the kitchen.' Elizabeth soon realised that it was better to ask for forgiveness than for permission, so she flung open the cupboards to help herself to a treat, while maintaining a steady stream of conversation with Mrs Thompson, who was offered little chance to interrupt, much less to say 'stop'. Sometimes the kitchen servants would turn around from their work to see Elizabeth swaying into view outside the window atop Bobs the pony. Her quick rap on the pane was followed by a request for a sugar lump for Bobs and, now that the jar was open, why not one for his rider too.

Elizabeth's brothers teased her about how much she enjoyed meal-times, and the snacks peppered liberally between them. In early 1913, one of them – either Fergus or Michael – found her diary. Many pages were empty as Elizabeth's interest in it was, at best, intermittent. Jokingly pretending to be Elizabeth, they forged the following entries:

January 1st
Overeat myself.

Thursday Jan 2nd
Headache in the morning. Very good tea. Christmas cake, Devonshire Cream, honey, jam, buns & tea. Eat too much.

Friday Jan 3rd
Not quite the same thing today. Breakfast very good. Sausages, kedgeree, Brown Bread, Scones & honey. Excellent lunch – beefsteak – 3 helps – jam and roley poley [pudding]. I eat a good deal.

Sat Jan 4th
I am putting on weight. My waist measurement today is 43 inches. Appetite good.

Sunday 5th
Appetite still good, after healthy breakfast went to church. Came back very hungry for lunch. Roast beef, chicken, Yorkshire pudding, Plum pudding, cheese, cake & oranges. Oh, my poor tummy. Just going to have tea. Am very hungry.

Monday Jan 6th

Quite an ordinary breakfast. No jam today! Rode Wonder [her horse] in the morning & came in simply ravenous for lunch. Omelette – two helps of roast chicken, finished up the bread sauce – five chocolate éclairs rium rium.* Chocolate éclairs for tea – as no one else liked them, finished them up. Wish I was allowed more for supper – always so hungry by the time I go to bed.

Tuesday Jan 7th

Barrel of apples arrived today – had one for breakfast.

10 am – eat an apple.

* 11 am – had an apple for [my] 11 o'clock lunch.*

* 12 – had an apple.*

* Roast pigeons and chocolate pudding & apples for lunch!*

* 3 pm – eat an apple.*

* 3.15 pm – David and I fought and have got bruise on my leg because he said I was greedy.*

* Eat two apples for supper.*

Elizabeth, whose sense of humour was similar to her brothers', refused to feel ashamed over her love for food. She stated quite firmly that one of her favourite smells was 'the delicious smell of toasting bread' and declared later, 'In times of distress, you *must* have chocolates!'

8. Goodbye to the German governess

By the spring of 1914, Elizabeth was the only one left in the Bowes-Lyon Nursery. She had wept when her brother David went to boarding school for the first time in September 1912. Until David's departure for Eton, brother and sister had shared their lessons – taught to read and write by

---

* *Rium* means 'to me' in Scots Gaelic.

their mother and then at home by a series of governesses.* Elizabeth's best subjects were History and Scripture (the study of the Bible); her worst, by a considerable margin, was Mathematics. Like all the British aristocracy at the time, regardless of where they were born, they were taught to speak with an accent later called Received Pronunciation or 'RP'. Sister and brother had occasionally escaped to an empty room near the stables, reachable by a rickety ladder, where they hid chocolate bars, oranges and apples purloined from the kitchens.

Cecilia was unmoved and unimpressed by her children's occasional claims of boredom, responding, 'If you find anything or anybody a bore, the fault is yours.' Manners were a major preoccupation; their nannies were permitted to smack the children across the back of their legs after any sign of rudeness.† In 1913, Cecilia hired a young German governess, 21-year-old Käthe Kübler, whom Elizabeth addressed as 'Fräulein' and who took over her lessons after a two-week trial period. Kübler wrote, 'With true German thoroughness, I drew up a timetable of her lessons and a plan of study, both of which were approved by Lady Strathmore.' This curriculum consisted of classes in Drawing, French, Geography, German, gymnastics, History, Mathematics, needlework, piano and Science. Lessons ran until four o'clock in the afternoon, after which Elizabeth and her governess usually went for a walk in the grounds or took out the pony and cart, sometimes with a picnic. The early summer of 1914 was so beautiful, weather-wise, that the picnics were a regular occurrence. While lessons were conducted in English, on their walks, cart rides and picnics, Kübler spoke German to Elizabeth, who quickly became comfortable conversing in the language.

On the last Monday in June, a maid came into Elizabeth's bedroom carrying a tray with towels, a jug of hot water with an accompanying

---

* Elizabeth and David had briefly attended a day school when the family was in London, but that was unsustainable given how much time they spent in Hertfordshire and Scotland.

† The lessons stuck. Decades later, when the actress Mia Farrow asked the Queen Mother what she thought the most important thing was to teach children, she answered, 'I think it's manners.' 'Really?' Farrow replied. 'Yes,' Elizabeth said. 'I believe that manners can get one through anything.'

basin, tea and biscuits. She then opened the curtains. Washed and dressed, Elizabeth went to her mother's room, also as usual, to read a chapter of the Bible together, before having her piano lesson with Fräulein Kübler. After which, she and her governess went down to break-fast, where Lord Strathmore was reading the conservative-leaning *Morning Post*. It carried the story that the Austrian Emperor's nephew and heir, the Archduke Franz Ferdinand, had been assassinated on an official visit to the city of Sarajevo, where half the population wished to remain part of his uncle's empire and the other half wished to unite with the neighbouring kingdom of Serbia. A supporter of the latter cause, Gavrilo Princip, had opened fire on the imperial motorcade as it drove through the city. The Archduke's wife was killed almost instantly; the Archduke bled to death not long after his entourage got him back to the local governor's mansion. By the next day, the loudest question in Europe was whether Gavrilo Princip had acted independently or if his mission had been encouraged by the Serbian government. Serbia was protected by her Russian allies, who had treaties with France and Britain; the latter was also treaty-bound to protect Belgian independence. Belgium was at risk from invasion by Germany, who might use it to get their armies quickly to Paris after they declared war on France to help their Austro-Hungarian allies, who were convinced – correctly – that the Serbian government had not so much encouraged as organised the assassination of the Archduke. When combined with long-festering tensions between the countries concerned, it was the world's most lethal game of domi-noes.

As Elizabeth and Fräulein Kübler entered the Dining Room, Lord Strathmore passed over the newspaper and said, 'Here, read this. It means war.'

Kübler did not agree with Lord Strathmore's gloomy assessment and, less than two weeks later, she went home to Germany to take her annual holiday and celebrate her parents' wedding anniversary. Cecilia marked Elizabeth's fourteenth birthday by taking her to the theatre in London to see a performance by a Russian ballerina, followed by comedians and jugglers. They had just received news that Elizabeth had passed the Oxford Local Examinations, a set of public exams in which Fräulein

Kübler had enrolled her.* When Elizabeth and her mother left the Coliseum theatre to go home to St James's Square, crowds were pouring into London's streets to celebrate the outbreak of hostilities against Austria-Hungary and Germany. Everywhere she looked, Elizabeth could see people 'shouting, roaring, yelling their heads off', amid their confident assertion that the war would be won by Christmas. She was to remember the scale and depth of that delusion for the rest of her life, along with the fact that Britain entered the First World War on her fourteenth birthday.

As returning to Elizabeth was impossible, Fräulein Kübler remained in Germany, where she trained as a nurse and joined the Red Cross. Elizabeth's strict schedule of lessons collapsed, and, within weeks, she was crumpling mountains of tissue, 'until it was so soft that it no longer crackled', so that it could be used as insulation in lining soldiers' sleeping bags for the Front. On 23 October, her cousin Charles Bowes-Lyon became the first member of the family to be killed in action.†

9. Old Year's Night

By Christmas, it was clear that the war would be neither as short nor as simple as the crowds had hoped in August. Elizabeth managed to exchange a few letters with Fräulein Kübler, until she soured on their correspondence after Kübler defended the Kaiser. Elizabeth announced to her new governess, Beryl Poignand, that she did not want to continue her German language classes and, instead, wished to learn Russian, in solidarity with Britain's Tsarist ally in the war. Miss Poignand did not speak a word of Russian, but the German was nonetheless dropped. The Bowes-Lyons' Christmas Eve toast that year was, 'To hell with the bloody Kaiser!'

---

* Elizabeth loathed exams and felt they were a waste of time that required weeks of work, the results of which boiled down to how one performed over the course of a few hours.

† This was a particularly cruel irony as, only five months earlier, Charles had survived the peacetime sinking of the Canadian passenger liner, the *Empress of Ireland*, when it was struck by another ship in heavy fog.

Glamis and St Paul's Walden Bury were converted into military convalescent homes on Cecilia's orders and Elizabeth was soon running errands into the village to buy tobacco for their wounded guests. There were a lot of patients from Australia, Ireland and New Zealand with whom Elizabeth liked talking – this was the first recorded example of her extraordinary ability to remember dozens of names and match them to the correct faces.[2] Although Elizabeth was too young to train as a nurse, her sister Lady Rose did and was assigned to work in a London hospital, where she was soon assisting at surgery. Their brother Michael decided not to return to Oxford to start his second year of study, instead volunteering for the army, as had his three elder brothers. In the excitement between enlisting and deployment, Jock and Fergus were married within days of one another, with Elizabeth as a bridesmaid at both weddings. Fergus married Lady Christian Dawson-Damer, the Earl and Countess of Portarlington's second daughter; twelve days later in Scotland, Fergus married the Honourable Fenella Hepburn-Stuart-Forbes-Trefusis. Hers, improbable as it may seem, was not the longest surname to which one of Elizabeth's siblings was partnered; Fenella lost the distinction by one letter to Lady Mary's groom, Sidney Buller-Fullerton-Elphinstone.

By the end of 1914, three of Elizabeth's brothers were in the trenches. Jock wrote home saying that any form of deep sleep was impossible and had been for weeks. Michael recorded seeing 'hundreds & hundreds of dead Germans everywhere'. A fourth brother, Fergus, who had been in the army from 1910 until he left for a job in banking a few months before the Archduke's murder, voluntarily returned to the military once war began. As of Christmas 1914, his unit was still in England, however they were expected to be sent to the battlefields in France soon. Elizabeth did not stay up on Old Year's Night (New Year's Eve) 1914. She, and the rest of the family, went to bed early.

10. The Mad Hatters

During the war, Elizabeth made friends with several other young aristo-crats whose families also had houses in London. Nicknaming themselves 'the Mad Hatters', Elizabeth and one of her closest friends from this stage of her life, Lady Lavinia Spencer, formed a trio with Lady Katherine Hamilton, Katie to her friends. Katie's elder sister, Cynthia, later married Lavinia's brother Albert,* meaning that both of Elizabeth's best friends as a teenager were Princess Diana's great-aunts.

The Mad Hatters enjoyed going to the theatre together, where Elizabeth developed a crush on the actor Henry Ainley. When her brothers at the Front found out about this, they all made sure to co-ordinate sending her telegrams asking if Ainley's stomach was as large as it looked in photo-graphs and constantly implying that he was decrepit. 'He is 35!' soon became Elizabeth's staple riposte, launched with increasing frequency, espe-cially after her brothers recruited Lady Rose to join in the teasing. Lavinia Spencer had a cousin who knew Ainley and promised to get his autograph for Elizabeth, who informed her governess, 'I am so pleased. I feel that it is quite worth sticking up for him all this time. Oh my sacred Aunt in pink tights, perhaps we shall even meet him, help, I shall die in a minute.' The Spencer cousin made good on the promise and sent a signed headshot from Ainley, which Elizabeth proudly displayed on her mantelpiece at Glamis.

She and Lavinia were also besotted with a chauffeur who worked for the Red Cross near St James's Square. They never had the opportunity to speak with him, but when he smiled at Elizabeth on a July afternoon in 1915, she described it as 'the most seraphic, glorious, delightful, beautiful, wonderful smile from the Beautiful One'.

The Spencer family were friends with the royals and, in the spring of 1916, Lavinia invited Elizabeth to tea at her family's London townhouse to meet the King's only daughter, Princess Mary, and her brother, Prince Albert. Strictly speaking, this was not their first encounter; Elizabeth had met Prince Albert before, at a children's party hosted by the Duchess of

---

* Cynthia and Albert's son 'Johnny', 8th Earl Spencer (1924–92), was Princess Diana's father.

Buccleuch (pronounced 'Bu-clue'). Noticing the Prince's shyness, Elizabeth gave him the glacé cherry off her slice of cake, in the hope that it would cheer him up. This charming act had been without romantic inspiration given she was four years old at the time. Lavinia's tea in 1916 would be Elizabeth's first meeting she could remember with the man who later became her husband. It wasn't exactly Romeo and Juliet. Elizabeth told her governess that she had met Prince Albert at Spencer House and concluded, 'he's rather nice'.

11. Miss Poignand's singalong

Elizabeth may have exaggerated her governess's tipsiness on the one occasion Beryl Poignand let her proverbial hair down during the war years; but, either way, fifteen-year-old Elizabeth was highly amused. They went into Dundee for an evening at the theatre where, according to Elizabeth, Miss Poignand threw herself with gusto into the singalong portion of events, becoming 'so, so loud that the manager came and asked her if she would kindly stop'. Noticing that 'the poor man had a red nose', Miss Poignand 'sang most aggressively at him … *Put a bit of powder on it*, which is a vulgar song. To crown all that, she drank three cocktails on reaching home, and had to be carried up to bed by Barson.'

12. Telegrams

Elizabeth and Cecilia went to Victoria Station in London with Michael, where he boarded a train to return to the Front after a few days' leave. On the platform, they spotted another officer saying goodbye to his mother, who was sobbing; Michael leaned out of the train carriage window to try to comfort her, saying, 'Don't worry! I'll look after him.' Eighty years later, Elizabeth still remembered that moment at Victoria, particularly the woman's grief at her son's departure: 'I can see her now,' she said, 'and do you know, he was killed the next day. It was so awful when one thinks about it.'

Michael Bowes-Lyon developed a bad case of what was then called shellshock and would now be recognised as post-traumatic stress disorder, as did his brothers Jock and Patrick. Given that fatalities were rising at a rate few had thought possible before 1914, Cecilia initially counted herself lucky that only Jock's finger had been amputated. Patrick was soon in worse shape, mentally and physically. Heir to the earldom and so handsome that a relative once said he looked like he belonged more on Olympus than at Glamis, he came home on crutches, where he soon began drinking heavily and suffered regular panic attacks and night terrors.

Fergus had a few days' leave around the time of his first wedding anniversary and his daughter's birth. On 1 October 1915, a message arrived at Glamis to inform Cecilia that Fergus had been killed at the Battle of Loos, the day after he returned from leave. The news was couched in a well-intentioned lie that her son's death had been quick. The truth, which the family only discovered later, was that Fergus had been picked as the officer to help lead a second attack on a German defensive position known as the Hohenzollern Redoubt. Fergus had suspected that another attack on the Redoubt was a mistake and some of those who served with him recalled him almost apologising to his men when the command came through. As he led the advance, shortly after four o'clock in the morning, an explosive landed at Fergus's feet, blowing off one of his legs; before he fell, he was struck by bullets several times in his chest and shoulder. He was caught by two sergeants and then carried back to the British trenches, where he died nearly seven hours after being wounded.

For the rest of her life, Elizabeth downplayed how much she did for her mother in the next few years, because to admit to it would have revealed how badly Cecilia was affected by Fergus's death. Intensely protective of her mother, who was a very private person, Elizabeth never really discussed Cecilia's battle with depression. She began to deputise for her mother at local events and took steps to shield her in private. Every morning, Elizabeth got up early to make sure she met the postman at the gates. She would then sort through the mail to see if there was another telegram from the War Office; if there was, she would open it, so that at least she could try to break the news to her mother as gently as possible.

Eighteen months after Fergus was killed, his brother Michael vanished while leading an attack on a French village occupied by the German army. Cecilia was in London, while Elizabeth received the news at Glamis and wrote to a friend, 'I don't know what to say, you know how we love Mike … he's all right, he must be.' Somehow, she had thought that nothing would ever happen to Michael and that he was so loved, 'but one forgets that doesn't count in a War'. She took the overnight train south to comfort her mother but, within a few days of arriving, Elizabeth's face and neck swelled, her temperature spiked, and she collapsed and took to her bed. Her family went back into mourning for a third dead son.

Nearly a month after Michael's disappearance, the Bowes-Lyons, still in London, received a morning telephone call from Cox's, a bank. Elizabeth fired off a letter to her governess Beryl:

> *I'm quite and absolutely stark, staring, raving mad. Do you know why? Canst thou even guess? I don't believe you can!*
>
> *AM I MAD WITH MISERY OR WITH JOY?*
> *WITH*
> *!*
> *!! JOY !!*
> *!*
>
> *Mike is quite safe! Oh dear, I nearly, nearly burst this morning, we had a telephone message from Cox's to say they'd received a cheque from Mike this morning, so we rushed round, and it was in his own handwriting … Isn't it too, too heavenly? I can't believe it, yes I can but you know what I mean, & how awful the last 3 weeks have been.*
> *Yours madly,*
> *Elizabeth*

Michael had been captured and taken as a prisoner of war to a camp in Germany, where he remained until 1918.

13. Old Billy-O

Whilst medical authorities observed increasing numbers of wounded soldiers suffering from shellshock, an understanding of the psychiatric effects of industrialised warfare was in its infancy and certainly had not yet reached Glamis, even in its wartime role as a soldiers' convalescent home. On 16 September 1916, Elizabeth and her younger brother were walking home from an afternoon's shooting in the grounds, something that would soon be unthinkable with survivors of the trenches nearby. As they returned, the siblings saw smoke on the horizon. Glamis was on fire. It seemed to have started accidentally in one of the older chimneys. Luckily, the nurses had taken some of the patients into the nearby town of Forfar for a trip to the cinema, which meant the castle was relatively empty. Sixteen-year-old Elizabeth ran inside and asked somebody to telephone the local fire brigades.

The four convalescents who hadn't gone to the pictures helped her, David and the maids, who 'rushed up and handed buckets like old Billy-o [but] the more water, the more smoke'. By then, the flames could be spotted in the village and dozens of people rushed over to help as they waited for the firemen to arrive. The day after the fire, Elizabeth wrote to her governess:

The little flames were sort of creeping through the roofs, you know, where the tiles are. It was too awful. Before 10 minutes the whole village was down! The [Forfar fire brigade] was absolutely no use, having only a hand pump. The Dundee one heard at 6 o'clock, & was here in 26 minutes! Wonderful. They had powerful engines, and by midnight most of it was out. But the danger was great, & we were so thankful when the water started. From 6.30 till about 10 o'c I stood just outside the drawing room door, sweeping down the water. The cistern upstairs burst and the flooding was dreadful.

Four soldiers who were harvesting on the farm helped very well, also people from the village. All the furniture on the top two floors had to be carried down, & I had an awful job trying to find a place. The drawing room was full, then King Malcolm's Room, then your room [and] *the Strathmore Room! Only the very top rooms (where the empty turret is) were absolutely gutted, and the most awful amount of damage by water. It was pouring into the Drawing Room all night, and the Chapel is a wreck. All the pictures with huge smudges, it's beastly. The Blue Room & Crypt were flooded, & the water didn't stop till 5 this morning. Everybody was splendid, & my word I do ache!*

You see, there was none of us indoors, and I had to direct every man bringing down the furniture, also it began to get dark, & I had to get candles. Mrs Stewart commanded everybody, & Mrs Swann was very flurried, just like a little partridge!! I can't tell you all the little incidents, but it was too dreadful, we thought the whole place would be burnt. Captain Weir, the Chief of the Dundee [Fire Brigade] *said that if the fire had been today (a strong wind is blowing) nothing on earth would have saved the castle. I can't tell you how unhappy we are, the flames were so awful … Oh Lor', I've swept the big stairs the whole morning, I am so tired.*

… PS Two firemen are staying. It broke out again this morning, and wants watching for a day or two.

If the relative novelty of a house telephone had helped her contact the two fire brigades quickly, it also introduced Elizabeth to well-intentioned and equally distracting calls from friends offering encouragement while she needed to focus on sweeping the burst cistern's water away from the Drawing Room or, by the next morning, the staircase. The first call came through from the Countess of Airlie, who 'telephoned to say would we come over if it got too bad'; she was followed by the famous Scottish mountaineer Sir Hugh Munro, then by more neighbours, and lastly by the Countess of Dalhousie, quite convinced Glamis 'was burnt to the ground'.

Elizabeth's actions on the day of the fire – especially her attempts to divert the water after the cistern burst, her organisation of the attempts to move the art and antiques, and her quick thinking to use the telephone to contact both local fire brigades – certainly saved Glamis from being gutted. She was immeasurably helped, as she pointed out in her letter, by the people of Glamis and by the weather. The damage was nonetheless considerable; it took several years to completely repair the castle. Fortunately, it was soon habitable again for the Bowes-Lyons, the recuperating soldiers and the medics.

14. 1917

Elizabeth turned seventeen, and the Great War three, on 4 August 1917. By then, it was clear that whichever side emerged victorious, the post-war world would be very different to what had gone before. The Russian monarchy had collapsed under the pressures of the war a few months earlier, the Tsar and his family had been moved to an internal exile in Siberia from which none of them would emerge alive. Crowns were trembling all over Europe. With anti-German feeling in Britain at such a level that even dachshunds were being kicked to death in the streets, the British Royal Family changed their dynastic name to Windsor, abandoning their admittedly seldom-used former name of Saxe-Coburg-Gotha.[3]

Elizabeth was miserable that summer. Her niece Patricia died in June of acidosis, aged eleven months, while the casualty lists from the Front seemed unending. Elizabeth wrote later, 'I remember quite well thinking when I was seventeen that I could never be happy again. I mean everybody was unhappy. Because one knew so many people. Every day somebody was killed, you see. It was a real holocaust. It was horrible. I remember that feeling quite well.' She found it very difficult saying goodbye to the soldiers who recovered at Glamis – 'I hate doing it' – because of course the cruel irony was that once the men were well enough to leave, they were sent back to the Front, where many of them were either injured again or killed – 'It's so dreadful saying goodbye.'

Not long after her seventeenth birthday, Elizabeth fell ill for the fourth time in a year. It again resembled influenza until her heartbeat became erratic. She was soon struggling so badly with her balance that the doctor ordered her to take bed rest, and she did not recover her health until the autumn, just in time to hear that their neighbour Patrick Ogilvy had been killed, aged twenty-one, at the Battle of Poelcappelle in Belgium, and St

Paul's Walden Bury had been damaged by bombs from the Zeppelin air raids.

15. Armistice at Glamis

There was a happier fire at Glamis on 11 November 1918. Earlier that day – famously, at the eleventh hour of the eleventh day of the eleventh month – the Great War ended with victory for Britain and her allies. That victory was pyrrhic, with millions of people dead and revolutions sweeping through countries on the winning side, like Ireland, Italy and Russia, just as powerfully as they did through vanquished Austria, Germany and Hungary. Decades later, when she was in her nineties, Elizabeth reflected on the young men who used to visit Glamis and St Paul's Walden Bury with her brothers: 'I think of my twenty best friends in 1914. Only five came back.'

The true long-term consequences of the war were a matter for another day. According to Elizabeth, when news reached Glamis that the Kaiser had been deposed, Germany had surrendered and it was all over, those who could 'went straight to the village to celebrate and I think they drank too much. Seats got broken up to make a bonfire and all that sort of thing.' The people of the village joined in, with dancing and singing at the bonfire well into the night, all celebrating what Elizabeth called 'this wonderful moment'.

III

The Delightful Duchess (1920–1930)

Elizabeth began the 1920s as Lady Elizabeth Bowes-Lyon and ended them as Her Royal Highness The Duchess of York. The journey between the two commenced with her experiences as a debutante on the London social scene.

Described by contemporaries as 'an exceptionally beautiful dancer' who had 'taken London by storm', Elizabeth thoroughly enjoyed her time as a 'deb'. Her childhood stood her in good stead for this. She emerged from it an extrovert, comfortable in conversation and with meeting new people. As a child, Elizabeth had chatted happily with her parents' guests, such as the Earl of Rosebery, a former Prime Minister and leader of the Liberal Party. A neighbour in London noticed that Elizabeth had 'the ability to listen and make everyone feel special'. A family friend, Sir Alec Douglas-Home,* recalled that, at Glamis, 'She moved around the tenant farmers talking to them about their animals, the crops, their dogs and the farm life. I think if you lived in a certain part of Scotland you couldn't avoid being to a certain extent a philosopher, competing with the elements, understanding the animals and the rhythms of life. It laid the foundation of her ease of manner with a lot of different people.' Being one of the youngest in a large group of siblings had also increased Elizabeth's ease in speaking to people older than herself.

The Season, as it was known, originated from a time when the upper classes had returned to their London houses after spending much of the

---

* Later leader of the Conservative Party (1963–5) and Prime Minister (1963–4).

autumn and winter hunting in the countryside. During the Season, there were charity balls like the Royal Caledonian, co-chaired by Elizabeth's mother, there were polo, cricket and tennis matches (which was how the Wimbledon tournaments initially developed), horse race meetings at Ascot and for the Grand National, lunches and regattas. The debutante component to the Season launched the young women of the upper classes into high Society's ballrooms and dinner parties, with the goal of introducing them to potential husbands from a similar background. By contemporary standards, the ideal debutante experience should culminate with an engagement notice in *The Times*. And it should begin by being presented to the King and Queen, which meant wearing formal court attire, including a train, while curtseying deeply to the monarch and his wife. This was known as the debs' 'coming-out' – which, as the Dowager Duchess of Devonshire noted decades later, now has a very different meaning.*

The most famous location for the coming-out presentations in 1920s Britain was Buckingham Palace; however, as the daughter of a Scottish earl, Elizabeth 'came out' at the Palace of Holyroodhouse, the Royal Family's official residence in Edinburgh. She judged 'it was really quite fun'. The next day, there was a garden party, after which Elizabeth and Cecilia caught the overnight train to London in time for the Royal Air Force Ball at the Ritz, where the King's second son, Prince Albert, asked Elizabeth to dance. It was four years since they had last met at Lavinia Spencer's tea. According to a letter Elizabeth wrote a few days later, she again thought the Prince was very nice, but she was far more enthusiastic about the next two days, which she spent with her family, including her youngest brother David, watching the Eton versus Harrow cricket match ('That was really great fun. I loved it').

Throughout the Season, there was a round of socialising for Elizabeth to enjoy. Some events were annual traditions, such as Queen Charlotte's

---

* Quite interestingly, the two terms are linked. The gay community in 1920s and 1930s New York organised parties in the era of early ballroom culture, where they used the language of the contemporary debutante season to celebrate a new gay person's arrival or acceptance into the ballroom demi-monde. Hence how 'coming out' came to be associated with gay people, long after the debutante season had faded into oblivion.

Ball, a London ball first hosted in 1780 by King George III to honour his wife's birthday. At that inaugural Queen Charlotte's Ball, Queen Charlotte herself had stood by her enormous birthday cake while the debutantes of the 1780 Season curtseyed to her. The event was such a great success that it was repeated every year, even after Queen Charlotte's death in 1818. Although Queen Charlotte herself would henceforth be a permanent declines-with-regrets, her birthday party kept going, with each new wave of debutantes continuing to genuflect to a multi-tiered cake. Never keen to sacrifice a good party for something as trivial as a death, an aristocratic lady was often asked to be a surrogate for Queen Charlotte to ceremonially cut said cake. Recalling the Season aged eighty-six, Ruth Sebag-Montefiore, who as Ruth Magnus made her debut in the 1930s, considered, 'It was a joke. It *really* was a joke when you think about it. Curtseying to a cake. But it was one of those things.'

Parents typically threw a party to mark their daughter's coming-out. Elizabeth's first was the Earl and Countess of Powis's ball for their daughter, Lady Hermione Herbert, at which Elizabeth was asked to dance, several times, by 'a nice young American' called Sam Dickson, who worked at the US embassy. Elizabeth thought Dickson had 'such nice eyes. He was so funny', although he became jealous when Elizabeth danced with Lord Erskine, who in turn seemed irritated when she danced with Dickson. 'Whenever I danced with the American, he looked furious and whenever I danced with him, the American looked furious!' she explained to a friend. 'It was awful ... I have suddenly taken to blushing again. I do hope it will go soon, it's such a bore.' The day after the party, Dickson had a 'huge bunch of red roses' delivered to Elizabeth at her parents' house. Elizabeth was impressed. Red roses in such abundance were still a rarity after wartime privations.

At the Season's dinner parties, the debs were placed next to eligible bachelors. It was dealer's choice if they ended up next to a Hooray Henry (rich, stupid, loud), a Chinless Wonder (rich, stupid, stupefyingly dull), NSIT ('Not Safe in Taxis', debutante code for a sex pest), a VSIT ('Very Safe in Taxis', debutante code for gay), or someone genuinely charming and interesting (rare, though not impossible). To navigate the socialising rapids, Elizabeth and the other debs deployed games, which simultaneously helped them while measuring the eligibility of their male equivalents. The Alphabet Game was a staple for dinners or lunches. The deb would pick a topic in her head that started with 'A', then see if that interested the chap she was sitting next to. For example, 'I say, have you ever been to Austria?' If that didn't work, you moved on to 'B'. Maybe 'Do you keep bees?' or 'Do you know the Blandfords?' No luck there? They might try, 'Goodness, have you seen how they've redecorated Claridge's?' The farther along the alphabet you went, the duller the gentleman and the more despairing the deb. Nobody wanted to end up like Lord Harlech's poor daughter Katharine, who tenaciously made it all the way to 'R' with a Chinless Wonder to her left. He turned out to be an enthusiastic coin collector and leapt gleefully into her suggested conversation about Roman London. Romance did not blossom, but he was so touched by her consideration that he continued to send her postcards until just before his own death, seventy years later.

There was an air of stilted reality to most socialising in the years immediately after 1918. On the one hand, there was an attempt throughout British society to recapture something of the rhythm from the years before the war. This was understandable, yet, to a certain extent, hopeless. Too much had been lost and too many families destroyed for things to immediately go back to normal, even more so after the Spanish influenza pandemic swept the war-ravaged world, killing somewhere in the region of 35 million people. Within Elizabeth's milieu among the upper classes, there was also a post-pandemic tension between those who wanted to return to the pre-war status quo and a new generation of young people, who preferred to shrug off many of the restrictions that had governed their parents' lives. In London's Roaring Twenties, the latter set were popularly nicknamed 'the Bright Young Things', their number including 'flappers' who danced maniacally then spent the rest of the evening affecting a martini-fuelled ennui. Elizabeth was not one of them. This was the first of many times in her life when she was associated with a more traditional outlook. Her mother's friend, the Countess of Airlie, loyally insisted, 'Lady Elizabeth was very unlike the cocktail-drinking, chain-smoking girls who came to be regarded as typical of the nineteen-twenties. Her radiant vitality and a blending of gaiety, kindness and sincerity made her irresistible.' Often, she would be collected from Society parties by her family's aged coachman with his long-lived horse. It happened more than once that Elizabeth would have to pop her head out the window to ask what the delay was. She had to accept their coachman's good-natured response, 'It's quite all right, Milady, but the horse has stopped for a little sleep.'

A childhood acquaintance, who became one of the Bright Young Things and subsequently came to dislike Elizabeth intensely, noticed that, when she moved through London Society, she was already 'afraid of meeting the wrong people'. Unbeknownst to her, they included her saturnine host at the evening where her future husband fell in love with her.

16. Lord Farquhar's Ball

On 2 June 1920, Elizabeth attended a magnificent ball at the Grosvenor Square townhouse of Horace, Lord Farquhar, a consummate charmer and equally accomplished liar. Seventy-six-year-old Lord Farquhar had schmoozed his way between the worlds of old and new money through his directorship at a London bank, from where he offered excellent financial advice first to King Edward VII and later to his son, George V. Armed with the prestige of royal connections, he proceeded to dispense seemingly enriching advice to many members of the aristocracy. Secretly, he tipped off auction houses about aristocrats in financial difficulties, so they could make an early offer on their heirlooms at a good price. In return, those firms decorated Farquhar's home gratis. Both before and after the First World War, his lavish generosity made Farquhar a leading figure in British high society. It was only after his death in 1931 that Farquhar's clients – many of whom were his friends – realised that he had been fleecing them for years and that his glittering parties had been paid for with their money.

By the time of their ball in June 1920, the Farquhars were still at the apex of aristocratic society, their connections and their respectability seemingly unassailable. Along with dozens of fellow debs, Elizabeth danced around the Farquhars' ballroom at 7 Grosvenor Square. One of her partners was Captain James Stuart, the Earl of Moray's younger son and a recipient of the Military Cross for gallantry for his service during the war. One of the recurring themes in testimonies from those who knew Captain Stuart was how handsome he was. Two of Elizabeth's friends, Alec and Helen, were engaged to one another. Alec teased, 'You won't let James cut me out, will you, Helen? He's so attractive that there would be every justification for it,' while Helen remarked, 'I wonder he isn't spoilt with all the women making such fools of themselves over his good looks.' Elizabeth was very attracted to 23-year-old Captain Stuart. Her maid Mabel believed, 'He was an absolute heart-throb, and they fell for each other in a big way.'

After leaving the army, Stuart had briefly studied Law at Edinburgh, before dropping out to serve as an equerry* to Prince Albert, known to his family as Bertie. During the war, Bertie had served in the Navy and then in the newest branch of the British military, the Royal Air Force, where he became the Royal Family's first fully qualified pilot. The family hoped that Stuart's confidence would help ease Bertie's anxiety as he began to socialise more after the Armistice, hence why Stuart had accompanied the Prince to the Farquhars' ball. When Stuart and Elizabeth had finished dancing, Bertie leaned over to his equerry and said, 'Who was that lovely girl you were talking to? Introduce me to her.' Evidently, Bertie did not remember Elizabeth from their dance a few months earlier at the Ritz.

Described by a socialite as 'the hardest-working member of the royal family (but the least articulate)', Bertie was tall and thin, a heavy smoker, and an excellent tennis player obsessed with physical fitness. He had lived in such awe of his father that, aged about six or seven, he developed a strong stammer. The King's inflexible attitude to the rules he set for his children may also have caused young Bertie's gastric problems, although these might more likely be the fault of one of his nannies, who preferred Bertie's elder brother, withheld food from the younger prince as a form of punishment, surreptitiously pinched him to make others think he was prone to tears and melodrama, and generally belittled or ignored a child whose confidence was already in desperate need of stimulus. She was

---

* A military officer who assists members of the royal family with official functions.

dismissed after another of the Nursery servants felt brave enough to report the abuse to Bertie's mother Queen Mary, by which point quite a bit of physical and psychological damage had been inflicted.

Two days after the Farquhars' ball, the King created Bertie the new Duke of York, the traditional title for the second sons of the monarch since the late fifteenth century. Nervous about besmirching this ancient title by any inappropriate behaviour or associations, Bertie had broken off contact with an Australian socialite called Sheila Chisholm, with whom he had been besotted.* Sheila was married to a Scottish peer, Lord Loughborough, who was an alcoholic more interested in gambling than spending time with his wife. Sheila had once woken up to find him sitting on the edge of her bed with a loaded pistol and the announcement that he had made such a mess of their finances that the only option left was to kill her and then himself. She managed to keep him talking until he set the gun down and she removed the bullets. Sheila was in love with neither Bertie nor her morbidly egotistical husband, but instead with Prince Sergei Obolensky, a strikingly good-looking war veteran who had escaped his homeland after unsuccessfully leading a monarchist battalion against the Communists during the Russian civil war. To complete this ménage of sexual and romantic frustration, Prince Obolensky – miserably married to Tsar Alexander II's daughter, Princess Catherine – was not particularly interested in his wife, nor in Sheila.

Bertie's investiture as Duke of York indicated that he had promised his father that he planned to marry and 'settle down', in contrast to his glamorous eldest brother, the Prince of Wales, who thought Bertie rather pathetic for giving up on Sheila to win their father's approval. There was absolutely no question over the nationality of the future Duchess of York. In the political atmosphere after the Great War, Bertie would become the first British prince legally to marry a commoner since the future King James II eloped with his pregnant mistress in 1660.[1] Contrary to the popular assumption that royalty could only wed each other, throughout the Middle Ages British royals had frequently married non-royals. St Edward the Confessor, Harold

---

* The British stereotype of referring to an Australian woman as a 'Sheila' stemmed from Sheila Chisholm's fame in British newspapers in the 1920s and 1930s.

II, King John, the fathers of Richard II and Henry IV, Edward IV, Richard III and Henry VIII in England had all married their or their families' subjects, nearly all of them, admittedly, aristocrats; as had Scotland's Duncan I, Macbeth, Lulach, Donald III, David II, Robert II, Robert III and Mary, Queen of Scots. However, after the House of Hanover inherited the British thrones in 1714, they had imported and prioritised the German upper classes' preoccupation with 'fully equal' marriages and the British royals continued the practice until the First World War euthanised it.* During the war years, the novelist H. G. Wells famously wrote a public letter to *The Times* in which he severely criticised the King and Queen for their failure to publicly repudiate their many German cousins: 'The European dynastic system, based on the intermarriage of a group of mainly German royal families, is dead today,' Wells observed. 'It is freshly dead, but it is as dead as the rule of the Incas. The British Empire is now very near the limit of its endurance with a kingly caste of Germans. The choice of British royalty between its peoples and its cousins cannot be definitely [sic] delayed. Were it made now, publicly and boldly, there can be no doubt that the decision would mean a renascence of monarchy and a tremendous outbreak of royalist enthusiasm in the empire.'

Wells was correct, if slightly overstating the case; polemic and precision are not always the happiest match. The last time an immediate member of the Royal Family had married a German was decades earlier when Queen Victoria's youngest, Princess Beatrice, wed Prince Henry of Battenberg. Since then, the Battenbergs had sided with Britain during the Great War, serving in its armed forces, and changing their Germanic name of Battenberg to its anglicised form, Mountbatten. If shaky in detail, Wells's point nonetheless stood in principle and it was emphatically backed up by David Lloyd George, the Prime Minister from 1916 to 1922, when he strongly advised George V to encourage his children to marry British citizens rather than foreign royalty. The world had changed.

---

* Years later, Bertie and Elizabeth's youngest daughter, Princess Margaret, said that she was extremely glad of this change in custom because, had she lived a century earlier, she would have been married off to a minor German prince in a triple-barrelled territory that nobody had ever heard of. This was true. That she made this remark in conversation with a minor German princess was somewhat less tactful, however.

Obedient to his father's policies, Bertie seems to have considered only British options for matrimony. He had briefly harboured romantic feelings for the Marquess of Londonderry's scathingly amusing daughter, Lady Maureen Vane-Tempest-Stewart, before she disappointed her parents' dreams of a royal wedding by falling in love with the Earl of Derby's younger son. It was at the Farquhars' ball, after Lady Maureen's engagement, that Bertie noticed Elizabeth for the first time. Within a few weeks, as they bumped into each other at more and more parties, Bertie's feelings for Elizabeth became romantic. He confided this to his mother's lady-in-waiting, the Countess of Airlie. As a close friend of Cecilia's, Lady Airlie passed on the news that 'he had fallen in love' with Elizabeth Bowes-Lyon.

17. Princes to spare

Over the next few months, Bertie became a frequent guest at Glamis, travelling over from his family's Scottish estate, Balmoral, to spend days with Elizabeth and her friends. He was accompanied by his equerry Captain James Stuart, who had just broken off his engagement to Elfie Finlayson, daughter of a Glaswegian industrialist. With the end of Stuart's betrothal to Elfie and his frequent visits to Elizabeth, rumour initially had it that the Duke of York and his equerry were guests at Glamis because of Stuart's romantic interests, rather than Bertie's. Both men enjoyed sing-alongs around the piano, a Bowes-Lyon favourite, and the generous snifters of port with which Cecilia plied any and all guests before they left for the railway station. Captain Stuart was somewhat less enthused by Elizabeth and her friends' penchant for practical jokes, retaliating by pelting them with mud on an afternoon stroll after they had snuck into his room while he was at dinner to create an 'apple pie bed', a technique deploying a fake fold in the sheets whereby the aspiring sleeper cannot stretch out their legs. Bertie found the whole atmosphere at Glamis blissfully relaxed and happy, particularly in contrast to his father's soul-crushing protocols at Balmoral.

At some point, Bertie's interest in Elizabeth became too evident to ignore. Although Elizabeth liked him, she was not interested in him romantically and she hoped to avoid a conversation where she would have to hurt his feelings. Helen Gascoyne-Cecil, who had 'debbed' with Elizabeth, noticed that many of the guests tried to wander off ahead, or fall behind the pair, to give the Prince a chance to express his feelings. Helen refused to do so, feeling that 'Elizabeth's signals of distress were so obvious that it would have been beastly to go away.'

He was not the only man interested in her. Among those to profess their love to Elizabeth were Lord Frederick Gordon-Lennox, heir to a staggering total of four dukedoms (Richmond, Lennox, Gordon and Aubigny) and himself later a famous racing driver, Lord Gorell ('I fell *madly* in love'), and Lord Gage, a well-meaning tweed-clad old soul in a young man's body, who announced that he was 'desperately fond' of Elizabeth. He admitted much later, 'I loved her madly but really madly. You've no idea what a *wag* she was, so full of witty teasing and captivating jokes.' Probably unbeknownst to the Bowes-Lyons, Lord Gage was the lover of another of Elizabeth's alleged suitors, Henry Channon, whom Gage once called 'the best wife a man could possibly have'.[2] Channon, nicknamed 'Chips' by his friends, who included Elizabeth's brother Michael from their studies together at Oxford after the war, was the son of a Chicago banker. He was theatrically unpatriotic; as a child, he had resented the national holiday to commemorate the anniversary of George Washington's birth because '[I] hated anything then that savoured of America or Americanism'. After Oxford, Channon moved to London, where he became a naturalised British subject and later a Conservative Member of Parliament. His diaries are today more famous than his political record; they are an invaluable insight into life in the British upper classes between the two world wars. To describe them as free from bias would be like describing a marathon as free from leg pain, yet it is Channon's memorable, often cruel, turn of phrase which makes the diaries memorable. Despite confessing to being 'a little in love' with Elizabeth at this stage, he described one of her elderly relatives in the following terms: 'dripping with jewels and bowed down by age, she looks like a ferret that has got loose in Cartier's'.

Bertie was not even a gold medallist in the niche category of princes interested in Elizabeth. That summer, she began her lifelong friendship with the King of Serbia's nephew, Prince Paul of Yugoslavia.* Paul had studied at Oxford, where he had shared accommodation with Elizabeth's brother Michael and, later, a bed with Chips Channon. Prince Paul adored Elizabeth, so much so that there were rumours that he planned to marry her.[3] Their friendship endured longer than any putative romance and Paul instead proposed to Princess Olga of Greece, with Bertie as best man, sponsor, or *koom*, at their wedding in Belgrade.

During one weekend in the country, Elizabeth's friends began bowing and curtseying to her while they addressed her as 'Your Royal Highness' or 'Ma'am'. This wasn't due to Bertie's interest in her, but rather because of a headline in that morning's *Daily Star* newspaper which ran SCOTTISH BRIDE FOR PRINCE OF WALES. HEIR TO THRONE TO WED PEER'S DAUGHTER. AN OFFICIAL ANNOUNCEMENT IMMINENT. The journalists had not directly named Elizabeth. They did not need to, since their descriptions of the 'anonymous' peer's estates matched nobody but Claude Bowes-Lyon's, whose sole unmarried daughter by that stage was Elizabeth. It hardly took a genius to figure out who they were describing, hence her friends' teasing with their curtseys and bows, all of which Elizabeth smiled through. At least one of the friends thought the smile did not extend to Elizabeth's eyes and 'she has something on her mind'.

The *Daily Star*'s headline was an early iteration of the long-running rumour that Elizabeth was never in love with Bertie, and that she only accepted his proposal after she had made an unsuccessful attempt to start a romance with his eldest brother, the heir to the throne, who was known to his family as David. This version of events was seemingly confirmed by David himself, five decades later, by which point he and Elizabeth detested one another. 'To put it politely,' he said, the caveat immediately advertising that politeness was already dead in the water, 'she wanted to marry *me*.'

The Elizabeth–David theory is part of a wearying trend in history that can only ever attribute a woman's attitudes to who she was once in love with, and that her dislike of a man is probably linked to a romantic

---

* The Serbian royal family became the royal house of the new state of Yugoslavia when their former kingdom unified with Croatia, Bosnia and Herzegovina to form Yugoslavia after the collapse of the Austro-Hungarian Empire.

rejection by him or to him standing in the way of another romance. In Elizabeth's case, the narrative holds that she never forgave David for choosing another woman, that she 'settled' by picking Bertie, and that this all explains why, fifteen years later, she came to hate David and his wife, Wallis. This ignores the fact that Elizabeth and David barely knew each other before she married his younger brother, and that she was perfectly civil, even friendly, with most of David's girlfriends before Wallis. One of them, Freda Dudley Ward, commented after ice skating with Elizabeth, 'If I ever had to live in a bungalow in a small town, this is the woman I would most like to have as a next door neighbour to gossip with.'

Far from wanting to marry the future king, Elizabeth did not want to marry anybody in the Royal Family. She confided to a friend that if she married a prince, for the rest of her life 'privacy would have to take second place to her husband's work for the nation'. Elizabeth was encouraged in these doubts by her father, a royalist without much interest in the royals, who had once declared, 'If there is one thing I have determined for my children, it is that they shall never have any sort of post about the Court.' She was not sure she liked Bertie enough to make these sacrifices for him and, when he proposed in the spring of 1921, she said no.

18. Dickie, Diamond, and dancing the night away

Immediately after rejecting the Duke of York, Elizabeth decamped to France for a few weeks. Her host was Diamond Hardinge, a notoriously clumsy debutante who liked her lunchtime bread rolls to be baked in the shape of frogs. Diamond's father was British ambassador from 1920 to 1922 and, with the embassy as their base, the two friends enjoyed the glitz of Jazz Age Paris.

They attended 'a tremendous ball' at which Elizabeth, who turned twenty-one that August, tangoed with an exile from the Russian Revolution, 'Constantine Somebody', she wrote. 'I never found out his other name! It was so funny, one is suddenly hurled in the air, & then bounced on the floor till one is gaga, ooh la la! Very painful.' They were taken on sightseeing tours by the chic Lady Anastasia Cheetham, whose unhappy marriage to a British diplomat was on a downward trajectory as vigorous as that of the hollowed-out barrel Elizabeth and Diamond clambered into at the Neuilly fairground flume. This was a particularly risky move to undertake with Diamond, whose balance was so abysmal she could throw herself on the ground and miss. Luckily, the pair descended the flume with spirits, and bones, intact.

Prince Paul of Yugoslavia stopped off for two nights to see them, breaking his trip back to Britain from Belgrade on board the Orient Express. He took Elizabeth to dinner with the visiting Earl and Countess of Dalkeith since, as an unmarried debutante, it was considered improper for Elizabeth to dine out with a man who wasn't a relative. The Countess of Dalkeith, previously Mollie Lascelles, was less than a year older than Elizabeth; before her marriage, Mollie had been one of the Mad Hatters, nicknamed 'Midnight Moll' for her adventurous love life, which had included a fling with Elizabeth's beau Captain James Stuart. 'It was such fun,' Elizabeth wrote of their Parisian dinner, with just a touch of poison in her politesse, 'and delicious seeing Mollie again – although it felt very odd being chaperoned by her!'

There was more gossip to enjoy when Elizabeth and Diamond partied at Acacia, a nightclub co-owned by the British fashion designer, and war veteran, Edward Molyneux. The club's other owner was the American gossip columnist Elsa Maxwell, an outspoken critic of homosexuality in her columns, which was a tad ironic as it was Elsa's Scottish girlfriend, the soprano Dorothy Fellowes-Gordon (everyone called her 'Dickie'), who arranged for Elizabeth and Diamond to be added to the guest list. Also among the revellers were Edward Molyneux's lover and investor Harold Nicolson, a millionaire's heir from Illinois who claimed to have fallen in love with Elizabeth at first sight, and a Hungarian socialite who turned up wearing a cape made entirely of gardenias.

Elizabeth returned to London to don her family's tartan for the Royal Caledonian Ball, yet also to the news that her mother Cecilia had been diagnosed with cancer. Elizabeth realised, too, that Bertie was still besotted. He sent several invitations to join him at tennis and asking if she had enjoyed her time in France. At the end of the summer, his mother, Queen Mary, announced that she would like to visit Glamis, despite regally declaring to her lady-in-waiting, 'Mothers should never meddle in their children's love affairs.' Queen Mary's self-invitation to their home was not a request that Elizabeth's parents could politely refuse.

19. Dear old Anne Boleyn

All her life, Elizabeth used affectionate terms of RP endearment to describe things she loved or for which she had acquired a fondness. Buckingham Palace, for instance, was 'dear old BP' and Anne Boleyn, long-dead second wife of King Henry VIII, was referred to as 'dear old Anne Boleyn'. Anne, of course, famously did not make it to the old stage in life. In the syntax of Received Pronunciation, 'dear old' means less a state of age and more an expression of affection, for something that's always been there – or that feels that way.

In mid-July 1922, four hundred years after Anne Boleyn had made her debut at the English court, Elizabeth crossed the drawbridge to spend a few days at the Boleyns' beautiful former home, Hever Castle, in Kent. Encircled by a moat, the castle dates from the thirteenth century, although by the time Elizabeth arrived there with her sister Mary, Lady Elphinstone, and Mary's husband Sidney, it belonged to the Astors, the Anglo-American millionaires who once owned so much of Manhattan Island that they were nicknamed 'the landlords of New York'. Elizabeth's hosts for the weekend were John Jacob Astor V and his wife, Lady Violet Elliot-Murray-Knynynmound (trying say that after a double gin).

Elizabeth took great delight in being shown the secret door in the walls of the castle's Morning Room, which opened to reveal 'a priest hole' where the pious Waldegrave family hid on-the-run priests at a time when Catholicism was illegal in England during the late sixteenth century. From there, she was taken up the thirteen stone steps in a spiral staircase that looked exactly as they did when a young Anne Boleyn ran up and down to her bedroom on the floor above.* She was shown a lock dating from

---

* It is now generally believed that the room traditionally described as Anne Boleyn's Bedroom was too small and that she slept in the much larger room next door, where two of her prayer books are now kept on permanent display.

Henry VIII's reign and a hidden Catholic Oratory with an eighteenth-century icon of the Virgin Mary. Above the fireplace in the castle Library, Elizabeth saw a wildly flattering portrait of the first Astor to make his riches, Johann Jakob Astor, a German emigrant who became America's leading fur trader, then a shipping owner and property investor. She was fascinated to see a sword carried by an owner who had pledged loyalty to Bonnie Prince Charlie, the popular nickname for the Catholic prince who had returned to Britain in 1745 with an army in his unsuccessful attempt to restore his family to the throne lost by his grandfather, James II.

Supporters of the Bonnie cause were known as Jacobites and they had been particularly strong in Scotland. Like Hever's owners at the time, Elizabeth's ancestors had been Jacobites; they had even opened the gates of Glamis to host Bonnie Prince Charlie's father, Prince James, during his equally futile bid for the crown. Elizabeth learned to sing Jacobite laments around the piano as a child. Once, when shown a portrait of Oliver Cromwell, the anti-monarchist general who had briefly turned Britain into a republic after he deposed Prince James's grandfather, Elizabeth murmured, 'Yes, *such* a difficult time for my family,' as if these were events within her living memory, rather than in the 1650s.

Elizabeth stayed in a wing jutting out of the back of Hever Castle and connected to it by a moat-spanning covered corridor. Carefully designed in a mock-Tudor style to complement the rest of the estate, it had been added on the Astors' orders to offer their never-ending stream of weekend guests the comforts of a Billiard Room, a Music Room with fireplace, and bedrooms with all the mod cons. Elizabeth's host, John Jacob Astor V, had been born in New York to a former Republican senator, the one-time richest man in the United States, who declared that America was no longer a place for a gentleman and emigrated to the United Kingdom. He became a naturalised British subject in 1899 and, looking for a country estate near London, bought Hever, into which he invested a huge amount of money. Sprawling out towards a fountain-sporting loggia overlooking Hever's new man-made lake were Italian-style gardens, through which Elizabeth could walk on stone pathways to admire a lavender garden or the many pieces of ancient Roman and Greek sculpture, imported by the Astors.

Mary Spencer-Churchill, Marchioness of Blandford, was also a guest at Hever that week. Born in 1900, she was almost exactly Elizabeth's contemporary. She had come out as a debutante at the same time, an experience that ended with her wedding to the Duke of Marlborough's eldest son. Mary's first child had been born in 1921 and Elizabeth felt sledgehammer pressure from friends and family to accept a proposal, set the date, get married and start a family.

The Astors' guest book for Hever contains two entries indicating that Elizabeth wandered, unknowingly, into a trap that changed her life. Among Elizabeth and Lady Blandford's fellow guests was 51-year-old Evelyn Cavendish, Duchess of Devonshire, who a year earlier had returned to royal service as one of Queen Mary's ladies-in-waiting. It seems highly unlikely that this was a coincidental invite, especially since Queen Mary herself visited the Astors the week before they hosted Elizabeth.

A few months earlier, Elizabeth had rejected a second proposal from Bertie. He had proposed in the immediate aftermath of his sister's wedding, to which Elizabeth had been invited as one of the bridesmaids. Elizabeth was not one of the bride's close friends and so the request from the Princess was likely another piece of manoeuvring by the Queen to keep Elizabeth in Bertie's orbit. It is unclear whether Elizabeth genuinely did not realise that the royal wedding would be a prelude to another proposal or if she simply hoped to avoid it. Far less ambiguous is her distress at having to say no to Bertie for a second time. The day after he asked her, she wrote to him:

> I am so terribly sorry about what happened yesterday, & feel it is all my fault, as I ought to have known. You are one of my best & most faithful friends, & have always been so nice to me – that it makes it doubly worse. I am too miserable about it, & blame myself more than I can say. If you ever feel you want a talk about things in general – I hope you will come and see me … I do wish this hadn't happened.
> Yours, Elizabeth.

Queen Mary was undeterred. From her visit to Glamis in late 1921, when Elizabeth had acted as hostess while helping her mother with her battle against cancer, the Queen came away convinced that Elizabeth would be the perfect addition to the Royal Family. Queen Mary has a reputation for being cold, aloof and intimidating, something that she acquired in her lifetime; Chips Channon thought that, standing still, she resembled a Swiss mountain and, in motion, a battleship at full steam. Privately, Queen Mary was far more complex and interesting. When a German cousin gave birth to the illegitimate child of a married palace servant, Queen Mary defied customs at the time by backing her trauma-tised female relative to the hilt.[4] The oft-repeated anecdotes that Queen Mary refused to pay her tailors' bills on time or repeatedly asked fami-lies she visited about their heirlooms until they felt pressured into 'gifting' them to her are untrue, seemingly born from chatter around London dinner-party tables and accepted as fact the more often they were repeated.

However, Queen Mary was every bit as firm – sometimes even as ruth-less – as the popular image of her would suggest. She demonstrated this quite clearly in the months after her visit to Glamis. Having concluded that Elizabeth was 'the one girl who could make Bertie happy', Queen Mary moved to weed out the competition. Not long after Glamis, Captain James Stuart was allowed to resign his position as Bertie's equerry upon unexpectedly receiving an extremely lucrative job offer in the oil industry. It came via a family acquaintance, Sir Sidney Greville, a major share-holder in a company with oil fields in Oklahoma, where they offered to take Stuart to learn the proverbial ropes. Their timetable was tight, unusu-ally so, since it required Stuart to resign royal service then cross the Atlantic in January, one of the worst months for a voyage, when storms were more common than calm. Waves and gales would toss cocktails in faces and hurl passengers from their feet as the ships' slow lurch forward with the swell, then back up again, sent wicker chairs sliding, chandeliers jittering and stomachs churning in the Palm Courts and ballrooms of even the largest luxury liners.

It was only once he reached his temporary accommodation in an apartment on New York's East 55th Street that Stuart began to suspect that this career change had been part of a wider plot to get him out of Britain – and away from Elizabeth. Sir Sidney Greville's sister was one of Queen Mary's ladies-in-waiting and, by the time a train was bearing him towards the Oklahoma oil fields, Stuart was certain he had been played. 'That bitch Queen Mary,' he fumed years later, 'that cow, she ruined my life! I was in love with the Queen Mother and she with me, but Queen Mary wanted her for the Duke of York.'

James Stuart features in Elizabeth's story as 'the one who got away', a narrative that Stuart himself encouraged and which he likely believed. Elizabeth's maid Mabel thought, 'It was obvious when you saw them together that they were madly in love.' Although there can be no doubt that Elizabeth and Captain Stuart had very strong feelings for one another, it was not an unblemished relationship. Stuart, with timing so brutal it has to be read as intentional, proposed to Elizabeth's friend Lady Rachel Cavendish the day before Elizabeth's wedding and married her on Elizabeth's birthday. He proved persistently unfaithful to his wife, a situation that some generously blamed on him being denied the happiness of marrying his 'true love'. Yet he had done the same to Elizabeth. When they were apparently blissfully in love, he had, at least twice, had a secret fling with Elizabeth's friend Mollie Lascelles. When Elizabeth found out, she was deeply hurt. She did not speak to Mollie until they were reunited by Prince Paul for their dinner in Paris. Had Elizabeth married James Stuart, there is precious little evidence that he would have remained faithful to her for much longer than he did to Rachel Cavendish.

With the competition catapulted across the Atlantic, Queen Mary went to Hever Castle to stay with friends who were preparing to host her quarry at a long weekend in which she was joined by Mary's lady-in-waiting. Whatever was said to Elizabeth by the Astors and the Duchess of Devonshire is unknown, but it proved a turning point and the pressure was augmented by Elizabeth's mother. Cecilia, having recovered from her hysterectomy, made it perfectly clear that she thought Elizabeth had made a mistake in rejecting Bertie. She wrote, 'I do hope he will find a nice wife who will make him happy. I like him so much and he is a man who will be made or marred by his wife.' Within a few months of the Hever visits, Queen Mary's plan had worked.

Elizabeth thus became the second future queen to retreat to Hever Castle in order to ponder her options, and she remained fascinated by Anne Boleyn for the rest of her life.* Anne had a sense of humour so darkly irrepressible that on the night before her execution she made a joke to her attendants about the daintiness of her neck; four hundred years later, when helicopters were introduced as a mode of transport for British royals, Elizabeth announced, 'The chopper has made more difference to my life than it has to any queen's since dear old Anne Boleyn's.'

20. Cocktails with Fenella

According to her diary, on her way back from the dentist on 15 January 1923, Elizabeth 'called on Fenella – told her the news, & had a cocktail'. Over this drink with her brother Jock's wife, Elizabeth told Fenella that she had accepted Bertie's proposal, his third, the day before.

In the aftermath of Hever, there had been signs that Elizabeth's feelings for Bertie had changed. He found her favourite music on gramophone records, they played tennis together often and seemed more relaxed in each other's company. One evening at the fashionable London hotel of Claridge's, mutual friends noticed a new ease between them as Bertie teased Elizabeth about her perpetual tardiness. Her mother saw how often they were laughing together, and 'lately I noticed that she liked dancing & talking to him more than anyone else'.

As soon as Bertie told his parents that Elizabeth had said yes, the Royal Household released the news, prompting speculation that the royals had issued the announcement before Elizabeth had a chance to change her mind. The next day, Elizabeth was preoccupied with answering letters from friends congratulating her on her engagement and explaining that there were 'hundreds of reporters clamouring' outside her parents' home

---

* The two queens have also each been played by the same actress – Helena Bonham Carter played Anne in the 2003 British television mini-series *Henry VIII* and Elizabeth in the Oscar-winning movie *The King's Speech* (2011), while Natalie Dormer played Anne in the first two seasons of *The Tudors* (2007–2009) and Elizabeth in the 2012 movie *W./E.*, about the life of Wallis, Duchess of Windsor.

in London. Among her thank-yous was one to Queen Mary 'for your most kind letter, welcoming me as your future daughter-in-law. I do hope I shall make Bertie very happy, as he deserves to be, and my greatest wish is to be a real daughter to your Majesty. I shall look forward intensely to my visit to Sandringham on Saturday, and I do hope you will think I shall make Bertie a good wife, we are both so happy, and it is all wonderful. I remain, Your Majesty's humble & obedient servant, Elizabeth Lyon.'

As the engagement announcement appeared in newspapers across the empire and the world, Elizabeth told her brother David, 'I could hear a door clanging behind me – never to open again.'

21. The Old Ikon

About 140 miles from Windsor, the Sandringham estate in the Norfolk countryside had been bought privately by Bertie's late grandfather, Edward VII, king from 1901 until his death in 1910. Bertie loved it almost as much as had his father and grandfather. When they went to Sandringham, Bertie's parents resided in the relatively cramped quarters of a smaller house in the grounds called York Cottage, since King Edward's widow, Queen Alexandra, still lived in 'the Big House', as the red-brick residence at the heart of the estate was known.

On the Saturday after their engagement, Bertie brought Elizabeth to the Big House to introduce her to his grandmother. Elizabeth noticed that the door was guarded by an enormous Russian Cossack. Inside, Bertie bowed to Alexandra and Elizabeth sank into her deepest curtsey. It had been sixty years since Queen Alexandra – then Alexandra of Denmark, and described as the most beautiful princess in Europe – had arrived in Britain to harbours and streets thronged with cheering crowds ahead of her marriage to Queen Victoria's eldest son. Alexandra's husband, although intelligent and charismatic, was also extravagant and promiscuous, with the result that there had been several scandals during which his popularity with the British people fluctuated. Alexandra's never did.

By the time Elizabeth met her at Sandringham in 1923, Queen Alexandra was living an increasingly reclusive life. She had struggled with her hearing and her mobility ever since a rheumatic fever that had nearly killed her when she was pregnant with her third child. She had been so admired for her sense of style that, after the fever stiffened her right knee, it became the trend to mimic her new style of walking – to the extent that 'the Princess Alexandra Limp' briefly became all the rage at London balls and garden parties in the late 1860s, as perfectly healthy socialites fashionably hobbled across parquet floors and croquet pitches.

As she aged, the widowed Alexandra hid the signs with heavier and heavier make-up; she was particularly embarrassed by her deafness, worrying that people were talking about her behind her back. By the 1920s, she could only hear – and even then, faintly – with the help of an enormous ear trumpet. Her eyesight was failing and she hardly ever left Sandringham. T. E. Lawrence, better known later by his sobriquet Lawrence of Arabia, saw Queen Alexandra around the same time as Elizabeth and described her memorably, if not exactly kindly, as 'a mummied thing, the red-rimmed eyes, the enamelled face, with the famous smile scissored across all angular and heart-rending'. He continued: 'I nearly ran away in pity. The body should not be kept alive after the lamp of sense has gone out. There were the ghost of all her lovely airs, the little graces, the once-effective sway and movement of the figure.'

After Alexandra, Elizabeth curtseyed to the woman sitting next to the Queen. She was Alexandra's younger sister, the Dowager Empress Marie of Russia. Marie, whom Bertie called Aunt Minnie, had been evacuated with her two daughters and their husbands by a British warship not long before the Crimea fell to the Communist armies. Had there been a delay, the Dowager Empress would undoubtedly have been executed, just like her sons, Grand Duke Michael and Tsar Nicholas II, shot by revolutionaries within weeks of one another.

Diminutive in stature, rigid in posture, and in better health than Alexandra, the Dowager Empress extended her hand for Elizabeth to kiss. The Cossack outside the door was Marie's devoted bodyguard, the remnant of a time when she had been married to the most powerful man in the world. In the Russian monarchist community, the Dowager Empress was nicknamed 'the Old Ikon', a living relic of a way of life that had gone for ever. Seventy-nine years later, when Elizabeth had become the embodiment of a depleted generation, her last public audience was granted to a historian studying Marie's family; Elizabeth was by then the only person left alive who could clearly remember her.

22. Belfast

Moments before Elizabeth and Bertie disembarked via a gangplank at the Northern Irish port of Larne, their warship's mooring rope swayed in the wind and took out the top hats of the entire welcoming committee, who had been waiting on the pier to greet them. The same gust looked, just for a moment, as if it had intended to pitch Elizabeth into the water along with the hats now bobbing away from their owners, out towards the champagne cork popped from the warship's bridge mid-Irish Sea for a thirsty Elizabeth and Bertie.

The Duke and Duchess of York's first visit to Northern Ireland took place in July 1924, fifteen months after a million people had lined the rain-spattered streets of London to cheer them on their wedding day. Since then, Elizabeth had started her royal work as patron of various charities and attended official functions as Duchess of York, including her first state banquet, held at Buckingham Palace to honour the visiting King of Romania. Elizabeth was popular with most of the public and certainly with the press, where she was nicknamed 'the Smiling Duchess', 'the Delicious Duchess', 'the Delightful Duchess'. Privately, despite this applause, Elizabeth was intensely worried about making a mistake in Northern Ireland. She had to be buoyed up by her husband, who had already conducted several royal tours before his marriage.

Northern Ireland was only three years old on the day Elizabeth stepped off the swaying gangplank. While the southern twenty-six counties of Ireland had won *de facto* independence in 1921, after a considerable struggle, the north-eastern six had remained part of the United Kingdom. There had been a great deal of violence throughout Ireland, on either side of Partition, and when Elizabeth reached their accommodation she noticed that a police officer had been stationed on watch from every window in the house. The Yorks and their entourage stayed for several days at Clandeboye, the Georgian country home of the Marquess of Dufferin, which became the royal couple's base for their trips into Belfast, Northern Ireland's capital city.

The Belfast population was predominantly unionist,* and so the Duke and Duchess received a rapturous welcome from cheering crowds. Elizabeth was joined by one of her closest friends, fellow Mad Hatter Lady Katie Hamilton, whose father the Duke of Abercorn served as Governor of Northern Ireland, a largely ceremonial post with no great practical power. Katie was unimpressed by the Belfast crowds; she described their clamouring to get closer to Elizabeth as 'hideous. Their manners were appalling.' Elizabeth disagreed, and it was during this Belfast tour that she began to take more active control over her role. As she left Belfast City Hall, she was thoroughly unamused when her handlers tried to hurry her past the crowds and towards the waiting limousine. She felt that by rushing her, her retinue had not left her enough time to shake hands or talk to many of the people who had waited outside for hours to see her. It was not to happen again, she ordered, since 'When I do a thing I do like to do it well and feel people are satisfied.' She even managed to keep a poker face through one of her favourite moments of the Northern Irish visit when, during his wildly enthusiastic welcome speech over an official dinner, the mayor's gesticulations ended with his sleeves catching fire over a disobedient candelabra.

A train bore the Yorks north-west across the length of Northern Ireland to the city of Derry, where Elizabeth and Bertie pretended not to notice the posters calling for an end to the union with Britain. Even what to name this stop on their tour reflected the minefield of Northern Irish politics. The original city of Derry had been burned down in the early seventeenth century on the orders of an Irish rebel leader called Sir Cahir O'Doherty. To secure the necessary funds to rebuild it, city officials had appealed to London-based guilds of merchants, with the incentive of adding their city's name, London, to the old name, Derry, to form the portmanteau Londonderry. Over the centuries, the fact that this new name had been the consequence of a Jacobean version of commercial branding faded from memory. It was assumed that 'London' had been

---

* Along with 'loyalist', supporters of Northern Ireland remaining part of the UK.

added in enforced tribute to the British Empire's capital, for which reason many nationalists* understandably refused to call the city Londonderry, while some unionists – also mistakenly believing it was a politicised name – refused to call it Derry. Nearly everyone in the city itself, regardless of political views, called (and continues to call) it Derry. Eventually weary of offending somebody by calling it Londonderry/Derry, Northern Irish journalists later decided they may as well offend everybody by half-jokingly referring to it as 'Stroke City'.

Londonderry's population in 1924 was the demographic inverse of Belfast's unionist majority and nationalist minority. There had thus been some who thought sending the young royals there at all had been a mistake, given the security risks, and a compromise seems to have been reached whereby they would not stay overnight. According to Elizabeth, 'Arrived at Derry at 11. Considering that more than half are Nationalists, we had a marvellous welcome.' Having initially been the one reassuring her, Bertie wrote to his father, 'I am so lucky to have her help as she knows exactly what to do and say to all the people we meet.'

They then went south once more, this time as guests of the Marquess and Marchioness of Londonderry at their loughside estate, Mount Stewart, one of the most splendid private homes in the United Kingdom. Lord and Lady Londonderry had dreamed of being Bertie's parents-in-law until their eldest daughter, Lady Maureen, rejected him. There were no hard feelings and, after a dinner in which Elizabeth sat between her host and the Archbishop of Armagh, she and Bertie danced at Mount Stewart until two o'clock in the morning. En route to England on a warship, they celebrated with another couple of bottles of champagne.

23. Drinky-poos

Elizabeth enjoyed cocktails, but eventually decided that she disliked their name. Feeling 'cocktail' was too harsh a word, she suggested, 'Can't we call them "drinky-poos" instead?'

---

* Along with 'republican', meaning those in favour of an all-Ireland republic.

'I bought it in Windsor – it belonged to the Queen Mum!'

In the name of historical research, I whipped up several batches of her favourite drinky-poo – gin and Dubonnet – the making of which did not require me to become a skilled mixologist. It is one part gin to two parts Dubonnet – which, by way of context, is a fortified wine that was initially developed to treat malaria in early nineteenth-century France. While I have come to have a fondness for them, it must be said that after one gin and Dubonnet you'll need a taxi, after two you'll need an ambulance, and after three you'll need a priest.*

24. Naindikwa

Elizabeth stretched her feet in the Ugandan countryside. Wearing khaki shirt and slacks, and a red neckerchief, she seemed 'a little pathetic', according to one of the accompanying hunters. 'I don't think I look too

---

* My friend Paul, who gamely tried the batches I cobbled together at a Christmas party while writing this book, has since nicknamed them the 'Dubonnet and Clyde', because they robbed him of an entire day of his life as he grappled with the hangover they inflicted upon him.

bad in my trousers,' she concluded of the first occasion she had appeared in public in anything other than a dress. Since setting off from their camp at Naindikwa earlier that morning, Elizabeth's feet had blistered so badly in her boots that eventually the whole party had to stop for a couple of hours until she could put her socks and shoes back on.

Rather than admit a blister-inflicted defeat, Elizabeth breezily lied to her mother back home in Britain, 'I walk nearly twenty miles a day sometimes, & feel most frightfully well ... I love this life.' That latter part, at least, was true. Elizabeth had fallen in love with Kenya, which was then part of the British Empire, and Uganda, a self-governing protectorate, almost from the moment she and Bertie disembarked from the passenger liner *Mulbera*, which had carried them from Marseilles to Mombasa. It was the first time that Elizabeth had left the British Isles since her childhood holidays to Italy and the first time in her life that she had left Europe. The *Mulbera* brought them across the Mediterranean to the Suez Canal, then into the Red Sea where, in a letter to her mother, Elizabeth appreciated that 'though it is hot enough to wear thin clothes, there is always a little breeze & plenty of electric fans. The evenings are too lovely, with a huge moon. I am not sure whether you will get this message very long before Xmas, so I will wish you a very merry one darling.'

25. Lilibet

Elizabeth was four months pregnant with her first child when her grandmother-in-law died. As Elizabeth's friend Chips Channon noted in his diary entry for the day of Alexandra's death, 'The Kingdom is plunged into grief, no one had any idea how loved the old Queen was. People are weeping in the streets.' Elizabeth attended Queen Alexandra's funeral, after which her public appearances were cut back as her pregnancy progressed.

Elizabeth and Bertie were overjoyed at the pregnancy. As he told his parents, 'We always wanted a child to make our happiness complete.' Only two and a half years passed between the Yorks' wedding and the pregnancy, which had not prevented pressure on Elizabeth to conceive and speculation as to why she hadn't. The fact that Elizabeth was not expecting a child within weeks of her wedding prompted untrue rumours, at the time, that Bertie was impotent and untrue rumours, later, that the children were conceived through artificial insemination, even though this was not available in Britain until the late 1930s when its technology was woefully ineffective.

Rather than giving birth in one of the royal residences, Elizabeth chose her parents' London house, 17 Bruton Street, the townhouse in Mayfair that they had started renting after the lease expired on their place on St James's Square. It was a difficult labour. The baby, described by Queen Mary as 'a little darling with a lovely complexion', arrived via Caesarean just before three o'clock in the morning on 21 April 1926. Bertie wanted her christened Elizabeth after his wife, Alexandra to commemorate his late grandmother, and Mary in honour of his mother the Queen. As she learned to speak, Princess Elizabeth could not pronounce her first name, instead rendering it 'Lilibet', which became her nickname within the family.

When Lilibet was only a few months old, her parents left her as they conducted a six-month tour of Australia and New Zealand on behalf of the bronchitis-felled King. Newspapers at the time praised the Duchess of York for leaving her baby to support her husband on his duties. The prevailing wisdom in the 1920s was that taking an infant on such a trip would have been selfish, as children need the stability that comes from routine. Knowing all this and believing it, too, did not make the moment of separation any easier for Elizabeth. She sobbed so hard at leaving Lilibet that she had to ask the chauffeur to drive their car around Victoria Station several times until she could compose herself, hide any signs that she had been crying, then step out to the platform, people and press with a smile on her face.

IV

Queen
(1930–1940)

With her experiences as a debutante, the love that grew in her marriage, and the birth of her first child, Elizabeth would look back on the 1920s as the happiest time of her life. She developed an excellent relationship with her husband's parents and his siblings. Bertie's elder brother David told a friend over supper 'how bad-tempered his father is. How the Duchess of York is the one bright spot there, they all love her and the King is in a good temper whenever she is there.' George V's obsessive adherence to punctuality even yielded to his daughter-in-law's flamboyant tardiness. His children were stunned when she came down to dinner a few minutes late, a faux pas for which he would have sharply criticised them, but which elicited a chivalrous 'You are not too late, my dear. I think we must have sat down two minutes too early' for Elizabeth. The King told Bertie, 'The better I know and the more I see of your dear little wife, the more charming I think she is and everyone falls in love with her.'

There were difficulties for Elizabeth in adjusting to life as a Windsor. Some were comparatively mild irritants, such as the evenings in which her father-in-law, to his delight, found himself funny. As the joke lumbered towards its crescendo, George V would punctuate his delivery with staccato jabs of enthusiasm to his listener's arm as he flailed around in self-induced glee. On more than one occasion when Elizabeth sat next to him at a dinner at which George had regarded himself as king of comedians, she emerged with her arm black, blue and yellow. There were more deliberately unpleasant moments, including the King's anger when Elizabeth, bedridden with tonsillitis, cancelled two days' worth of engagements during a visit to New Zealand. In a surprisingly unguarded moment in a letter to a relative, she referred to her royal father-in-law as 'a narrow-minded autocrat'.

She and Bertie had an active social life, including dances at Claridge's, where fellow revellers noticed how much in love the couple now seemed. They hosted parties of their own, including one at which Elizabeth waltzed with their guest Fred Astaire, the famous American dancer then winning rave reviews for his performance in a West End musical.

Elizabeth was arguably the most popular member of the Royal Family at this point in her career, a status which surprised, and sometimes even alarmed her. An unsettling incident occurred in 1928 when she attended her brother Mike's London wedding. As she walked into St George's Church on Hanover Square for the service, an eyewitness recorded in her diary, 'there was a terrific crowd of stampeding women who nearly mobbed the Duchess of York who, surprised, looked tiny and nervous. The police had difficulty in protecting her, for she would have been torn to pieces by the adoring mob, who wanted to touch or kiss her.'

The 1930s was to be much more difficult for Elizabeth and, as had the 1910s, the decade began with the loss of a brother. Jock Bowes-Lyon died, aged forty-three, from pneumonia, having struggled with poor health since the trenches of the First World War. Pregnant once more, Elizabeth went to Glamis to care for her mother, who called the death of her fourth child 'more than I shall ever bear'. Elizabeth stayed north for most of her final trimester and her second child was born at Glamis on 21 August 1930.

Princess Margaret Rose was the first member of a British royal family to be born outside England since King Charles I's younger brother Prince Robert, Duke of Kintyre, in 1602, and the King was so pleased to have a granddaughter born in Scotland that he wanted a name historically associated with Scottish princesses. He thus rejected Elizabeth and Bertie's preference for Anne, in favour of Margaret, and Elizabeth accepted her father-in-law's choice. In a letter to the Archbishop of Canterbury, Elizabeth wrote of her second daughter, 'I am glad to say that she has got large blue eyes and a will of iron, which is all the equipment that a lady needs!' There were rumours, confidently repeated and wildly untrue, that the new princess was deaf and mute, which persisted for several years until she was heard to speak in public.

The Great Depression, one of the worst recessions in history, began in the United States in 1929 and spread throughout the world. It pulverised the British economy for the first half of the 1930s, leading to mass unemployment, mounting hardship and political radicalisation. Exhausted and infuriated by their democratically elected governments' seeming inability to fix any of the problems caused by the Depression, millions of voters were attracted to hard-line alternatives. There was a rise in support for Communism throughout Europe, likewise for fascism, which in 1934 took power in Germany as Hitler was elected chancellor. There was already a fascist government in office in Italy.[1] Both were expansionist and pro-war. Elizabeth initially thought the Nazis were absurd; she did not realise, until it was almost too late, just how serious a threat they had become, nor how dangerous was the spike in support for fascism in Britain.

At the depth of this politically fraught decade, Elizabeth became queen. Her father-in-law George V died at the start of 1936, shortly after celebrating his Silver Jubilee as king, and he was succeeded by his eldest son, who took the name Edward to reign as King Edward VIII, although in private his family continued to call him David. Ten months later, he relinquished the throne to marry socialite Wallis Simpson. With Edward's abdication, Bertie became King George VI, deliberately taking his late father's name in order, desperately, to suggest some sense of continuity between the old king and the new. This was despite having a younger brother already called George, the Duke of Kent.

Almost nobody expected George VI to be a successful king, as becomes very clear from reading not just the press coverage of the Abdication crisis but also the private letters and diaries of people whom Elizabeth and Bertie considered close friends.

26. The King's Speech

In the 1980s, Elizabeth received a letter from David Seidler, a British play-wright, with some questions about her late husband's struggle with his stammer and speech impediment. Through his research, Seidler had discovered that Bertie had benefited greatly from treatment by an Australian therapist called Lionel Logue, whom Elizabeth first contacted on her husband's behalf in 1926. According to Seidler, when, in response to his letter, 'the Queen Mother asked me to wait and not tell this story during her lifetime, because the memory of these events was still too painful, I realized the depths of the emotions involved.' Seidler respected the Queen Mother's request, particularly impressive since neither she nor Seidler expected that she would live for another twenty years.[2] The result-ing film, *The King's Speech*, eventually won Seidler the Academy Award for Best Original Screenplay in 2011 and Helena Bonham Carter was nominated for an Oscar for her portrayal of Elizabeth, with Bertie played by Colin Firth and the therapist Lionel Logue by Geoffrey Rush.[3]

Although certain liberties were taken with the historical details, as they inevitably must in costume dramas, *The King's Speech* captured much of Logue's therapy sessions with Bertie, including Elizabeth's role in arrang-ing the first meeting, her encouragement of her husband to seek professional help, and her gratitude to Logue. Two decades later, she wrote privately to Logue, 'I think that I know perhaps better than anyone just how much you helped [him], not only with his speech, but through his whole life & outlook on life. I shall always be deeply grateful to you for all that you did for him. He was such a splendid person and I don't believe he ever thought of himself at all.'

27. Just in case

Publicly, Elizabeth never deviated from devoted platitudes of loyalty to her father-in-law. Half a century after his death, she was still praising his 'great kindness' to her. There is no reason to suppose that this was a complete lie, and she sincerely respected his leadership through the First World War. However, it was nowhere near the whole truth, and her low opinion of George V's capabilities as a father is revealed in Elizabeth's private papers. Shortly after Princess Margaret's birth, Elizabeth composed a letter to her husband with parenting tips for their daughters, which she wanted him to read if anything happened to her. Her first instruction to Bertie from beyond the potential grave was, 'Be very careful not to ridicule your children or laugh at them. When they say funny things it is usually quite innocent, and if they are silly or "show off" they should be quietly stopped, & told why afterwards if people are there.'

Her next two pieces of advice pulled no punches regarding George V: 'Always try & talk very quietly to children. Never shout or frighten them, or otherwise you lose their delightful trust in you. Remember how your father, by shouting at you, & making you feel uncomfortable lost all your real affection. None of his sons are his friends, because he is not understanding & helpful to them.'

28. How do you solve a problem like Marina?

In 1934 and 1935, Elizabeth and Bertie acquired two new sisters-in-law as his younger brothers married. Elizabeth got on very well with the second addition to the Royal Family, fellow Scottish aristocrat, the Duke of Buccleuch's sister Lady Alice Douglas-Montagu-Scott, who had come out as a debutante at the same time as Elizabeth. Alice wed Prince Henry, Duke of Gloucester, an 'immensely kind, potentially irritable' whisky enthusiast, noted for the piglet-like squeals of his 'very infectious' laughter, which according to a dinner companion seemed 'orgasmic, so much pleasure does he get from it, so sudden and enjoyable does it seem'.[4] The Gloucesters' wedding was small and their marriage was happy. Their two sons, the princes William and Richard, arrived three years apart and their parents were devoted to them. Chips Channon mused in his diary, 'Alice, of course, is now Duchess of Gloucester, a lovely title. She has done little to capture the imagination of the public and hardly exists as a royalty of national character. But I hear the King and Queen like her the best of their daughters-in-law.'

That last detail may reflect Channon's growing disenchantment with his erstwhile friend Elizabeth, whom he increasingly resented for abandoning him after she married. What Channon did not know was that King George V detested him, which made a continuing friendship difficult on Elizabeth's part. Having given way on her daughter's name to please her father-in-law, she was hardly likely to pick her tepid friendship with Chips Channon as her hill to die on.

Channon remained close to the youngest of the Windsor brothers, Prince George, Duke of Kent, a good-looking and charismatic bisexual pilot who had beaten a drug addiction after first being introduced to narcotics by an ex-girlfriend. In 1934, Prince George became the only one of his siblings to marry foreign royalty. Enough time had passed since the war for the Duke of Kent's engagement to Princess Marina of Greece to prove popular with the public.[5] From 1934 until her death in 1968, Princess Marina was hardly ever off the 'Best Dressed' lists in British magazines. Her parents-in-law distrusted her chic Parisian wardrobe and blood-red nail polish.

'I'm afraid the King doesn't like painted nails. Can you do something about it?' Queen Mary told her.

'Your George might not, but mine does,' Marina replied.

Daughter of a Romanov grand duchess and granddaughter of Greece's King George I, Princess Marina was far more confident than either Elizabeth or Alice when marrying into the House of Windsor, and so she was less inclined to toe the line with the in-laws.

Chips Channon revelled in *schadenfreude* to see Elizabeth's position unsettled by Marina's popularity. Elizabeth, 'the Delightful Duchess' of York, was suddenly the stuffy traditionalist, thrown into the shade by the glamour of Princess Marina, who was greeted by cries from the crowds of 'Don't let them change you!' Channon wrote in February 1934 that 'The York household is jealous already of Marina, Duchess of Kent – it is time that Elizabeth of York had a little competition. She has had it all her own way for ten years.' With Marina's arrival, Elizabeth experienced the first rotation in a cycle that has since been applied to nearly every woman who has married into the Windsor dynasty. The names change, the narrative remains the same: a new bride is going to modernise the monarchy because she is a breath of fresh air. This lasts until the next wedding, whereupon the bride who was formerly the breath of fresh air becomes characterised either as jealous and vindictive or a characterless dullard, inevitably resentful of the beauty, popularity, loveliness, intelligence, charm or charisma of the new royal bride, who is *such* a breath of fresh air and will really blow away the cobwebs.

The relationship between the duchesses was not helped by the fact that Marina took repeated pot-shots at Elizabeth's 'inferior' ancestry. Over a century earlier, during the dissolution of the First Reich,* through a process that lasted from 1801 to 1806, a series of German princely families had lost their status as independent rulers; these families were the 'Serene Highnesses' and henceforth under the jurisdiction – and rank – of the German reigning families who kept their power. These demoted minor princely dynasties were referred to as the Mediatised Sovereign States and, for a century or so after, the devotees of 'pure' royal marriages begrudgingly regarded plucking a bride from a mediatised family as the last acceptable frontier of royal spouses, a sort of bargain basement of backwater bluebloods. Discussing her sister-in-law Elizabeth, Marina giggled that Bertie had married somebody who was 'not even mediatised'. The long yellow brick road into the arcane genealogy of the defunct First Reich necessary to explain Marina's insult here indicates just how few people outside her circle cared about it, even then. Marina referred to the non-royal Elizabeth and Alice as 'those common little Scotch girls', which allegedly was the polite version, as others recall Marina referring to them as 'common little Scottish tarts'. One or both of those remarks made its way back to Elizabeth, who correspondingly resented Marina for years. 'The Queen Mother adored Princess Marina the moment she died,' a friend joked. 'When she was alive, she hated her!'

It was an early example of Elizabeth's Olympian ability to hold a grudge, and a dress rehearsal for the one she nurtured for her final sister-in-law.

---

* Also known as the Holy Roman Empire, it lasted from 800 to 1806.

29. Wallis from Baltimore

Several months after King George V's death, his eldest son sped through the grounds of Windsor Great Park with driving, and love, goggles firmly in place. One protected him from the sunshine, the other from even the faintest glimpse of reality. The new King had decided to surprise Bertie and Elizabeth at Royal Lodge, their house in the grounds of Windsor Castle. From inside, the Duke and Duchess of York heard David, or King Edward VIII as he had been since January of that year, barrel up the driveway in his new American station wagon. After Elizabeth sent instructions to the Nursery to have her daughters ready to meet their uncle, she forced a smile onto her face, where it would remain, with a remarkable facsimile of sincerity, for the next hour. She and Bertie went to greet the King, who hopped out of his car and introduced them to his passenger, Wallis Simpson, the chic American wife of a London-based shipbroker. Since Elizabeth and Bertie had offered so many polite excuses for avoiding Wallis's company over the past few months, the King reasoned: why not bring her to them? After all, nothing smooths over awkward encounters like a total lack of warning.

From a down-on-its-luck 'old money' family from Maryland, Wallis was the witty and elegant embodiment of an impending constitutional crisis. Even though she was still married to somebody else as of mid-1936, Edward VIII was determined to wed her. The British monarch is also hereditary Supreme Governor of the Church of England, a branch of Protestantism which did not, then, permit divorcees to remarry. Wallis, who had been divorced once before, would therefore be problematic from the Church's perspective as a queen consort, and it was the Church's highest-ranking bishops who would be expected to crown Edward VIII and his wife at the coronation, timetabled for May of the following year.

Wallis Simpson was one of the first major examples of Elizabeth's policy of ignoring something difficult in the hope that it would go away: her 'ostriching', as a courtier put it. Even she could not keep pretending nothing was amiss when the problem was helped out of the car by the

King and introduced. 'Her justly famous charm was highly evident,' Wallis wrote magnanimously.

I was also aware of the beauty of her complexion and the almost startling blueness of her eyes. We returned to the house for tea, which was served in the drawing room. In a few moments the two little Princesses joined us. They were both so blonde, so beautifully mannered, so brightly scrubbed, that they might have stepped straight from the pages of a picture book. Along with the tea things on a large table was a jug of orange juice for the little girls. David and his sister-in-law carried on the conversation with his brother throwing in only the occasional word. It was a pleasant hour; but I left with the distinct impression that while the Duke of York was sold on the American station wagon, the Duchess was not sold on David's other American interest.

Elizabeth's and Wallis's dislike of each other, even hatred at times, has become legendary, a Bette Davis and Joan Crawford of the British monarchy. Although some of their friends piously claimed that neither truly disliked the other, this was an outright lie. Wallis was an excellent mimic, as Elizabeth discovered when she walked in on Wallis performing an unflattering impression of her before a group of laughing guests. As Edward VIII brought them more frequently into each other's company, Wallis realised that, to quote one of Bertie's equerries, beneath Elizabeth's 'graciousness, her gaiety and her unfailing thoughtfulness for others, she possessed a steely will' and a capacity for icy disdain.[6]

Chips Channon, who knew Wallis well, left perhaps the fairest assessment of her in his 1936 diaries. Its benefit lies in Channon's intelligence and in being written before hindsight coloured opinions of Wallis:

She is a woman of mixed motives and character. She is kind, warm-hearted, gay, witty, shrewd, glamorous and loyal. On the other hand she is somewhat frivolous and calculating. She has the American flair for High Society and is completely dazzled by it. When she first came to London she knew nobody and was miserable. Her first friends were not as grand as she would have liked, but whilst she quickly threw them over as she soared in the social scale she always found time to be kind to them and render them services, although she no longer saw them. She was dazzled by English life, pleased to call duchesses by their Christian names, and her reaction was very like that of any other American who arrives in London and is taken up. She is an excellent judge of character. She takes an exaggerated interest in food and drink and is interested in the culinary arts. She made the King supremely happy and he was a different being when she was in the room. On the other hand, she had no knowledge of this country, never having been out of London, until she went to stay in the houses of the Great where she was treated almost as an empress, and after all she only lived in London for about three or four years.

Elizabeth believed that Wallis hated 'this dear old country' and took to referring to her as 'That Woman', rather than by her name. Wallis and Edward VIII loved to joke about Elizabeth's weight gain, saying that she looked like an overweight frump, nicknaming her 'Cookie' and her eldest daughter 'Shirley Temple'.

30. That's Mummy now

Elizabeth and Wallis were subsequently presented by their respective critics as the Machiavellian brains behind the Abdication crisis, the name given to Edward VIII's announcement in December 1936 that he was relinquishing the throne so that he could legally marry 'the woman I love'. Either Elizabeth or Wallis is usually cast as the villain who shamelessly manipulated a weak-willed man, one who apparently would never have dreamed of hurting anybody's feelings until his scheming wife forced him to do so. The evidence supports neither scenario. Both women were quite seriously unwell as the crisis came to a boil. Elizabeth was bedridden with another bout of influenza that developed into pneumonia, while Wallis could not get out of bed for much of the latter half of November, when a friend confided to his diary that she was 'so ill (it is a form of nervous exhaustion)'.

In his ten months as king, Edward VIII had managed to win the approval of many left-leaning political figures, some of whom were traditionally sceptical of the monarchy. During a visit to the mining communities in Wales, he famously said 'Something must be done' to alleviate the poverty exacerbated by the Great Depression. (Years later, when his famous quote was brought up to him at a dinner party, the former king asked, 'About what?') Many of his supporters, including the Conservative politician Winston Churchill, thought that the admired King Edward should be allowed to stay on the throne and marry Wallis after her divorce was finalised. There was even talk of a compromise in the form of a morganatic marriage, whereby Wallis would legally be Edward VIII's wife but not his queen. A different, lesser title could be used – Duchess of Lancaster was considered at one point – and any children they had would not be in line to the throne, which would one day still therefore pass to Bertie or his eldest daughter.

A variety of factors ensured that crowns were denied not just to Wallis but, in the end, to Edward VIII as well. The first, which is sometimes underplayed in modern accounts of the crisis, was the sincerity of the Church's discomfort at the situation and what they feared Edward's actions said about the Sacrament of marriage. The Archbishop of Canterbury became a strong supporter of the plan to see Edward VIII surrender either the throne or Wallis, allying himself with Prime Minister Stanley Baldwin and even, incredibly, with Edward's Private Secretary, Alan Lascelles. Known to friends as Tommy, Lascelles had served Edward when he was Prince of Wales, a role from which he had emerged convinced that the Prince would make a terrible king. He thought Edward VIII's work ethic was non-existent, his interest in government minimal, his charm convincing yet superficial, and his selfishness on a planetary scale. In Lascelles's scorcher of a summation, his new king was 'a child in the fairy stories who had been given every gift except a soul'.

As Edward VIII reached the decision to stand down as king, he failed to communicate his plans to his family. Four days before the announcement, Bertie, who would become king the moment his brother signed the Instrument of Abdication, still could not get in contact with him. Phone calls were not returned, letters went unanswered, and requests to meet were ignored. Even the Duke of Kent, the brother to whom the King was closest, was temporarily ignored. Finally, on the evening of Monday 7 December, the King summoned Bertie and told him that he would succeed him that Thursday. Bertie asked his driver to take him to Marlborough House, the London residence of his widowed mother, where, the minute he saw her, he 'broke down & sobbed like a child'. Lying in her sickbed on Thursday, Elizabeth became queen as she listened to her brother-in-law's radio address relinquishing the throne. Before he boarded a warship for temporary exile in France and Austria, Elizabeth sent a letter to the ex-king to tell him that she prayed, '"God bless you" from my heart. We are all overcome with misery, and can only pray that you will find happiness in your new life.' Having renounced all titles on his abdication as king, a new title – Duke of Windsor – was created for him on his brother's orders, as he went from His Majesty The King on 10 December to His Royal Highness The Duke of Windsor on the 12th.

Elizabeth was so unwell that she did not get out of bed until twelve days after becoming queen. Under normal circumstances, she should probably have rested for longer. However, Bertie – or King George VI, as he had become – needed her. They went to Sandringham for Christmas, where Elizabeth cancelled the new tradition of the monarch recording a Christmas Day radio address to his subjects, correctly guessing that Bertie was not up to it. She told the Archbishop that she and Bertie 'feel our responsibilities very deeply, and though quite prepared for a difficult time, are determined to do our best'. They spent that Christmas taking stock of the situation, adjusting to the shock, and steadying George VI's nerves.

Chips Channon worried, 'I do not think that the Socialists nor – say – the miners in South Wales will ever have the same great affection for the present monarchs, or would refer to George VI as "Our King" as they did Edward VIII, during his short reign. I sincerely hope I am wrong and that the present King and Queen will eventually be as loved as George V. But the spirit of the world is changing and I much doubt whether they are strong enough.' Channon also had doubts about how successful Elizabeth would be as her mother-in-law's replacement:

she is well bred, kind, gentle, and slack. *She may well have deep-rooted ambition, but no surface trace of it. She is fundamentally lazy, very lazy and charming, always charming, always gay and pleasant and smiling. She has some intelligence and reads a lot, but she is devoid of all* eye, *and her houses have always been banal and hideous. Like all the Lyon family, particularly [her brother] David, she is superficially treacherous. She can never resist a slightly spiky remark about the person she has just left; but it means nothing, and in the long run she is loyal and kind. She will never be a great Queen for she will never be up in time! … She has few friends, only the Allendales, the Plunkets, and some respectable and dull Scotch people to whom she has ever been loyal.*

That last point touched on another concern – that, with her background, Elizabeth would be a puppet for the aristocracy, 'a class whose importance is every day lessened … there is something "tin-y" about the present King and Queen: they are disarming, almost pathetic, not unpopular, but so obviously puppets and not the real thing. The monarchy in a sense ceased with George V and Queen Mary.'

Princess Elizabeth, ten years old and suddenly first in line to the throne, saw an envelope addressed to *Her Majesty The Queen*. She pointed at it and said to her six-year-old sister Margaret, 'That's Mummy now.'

31. Send in the cavalry

One of Elizabeth's longest-lasting friendships was with the playwright Noël Coward, who said later that he thought a statue of Wallis Simpson should be erected in every village in Britain to thank her for sparing them Edward VIII as their king. In the 1930s, there were credible rumours that Coward was in love with Elizabeth's brother-in-law, the Duke of Kent, and that playwright and prince had been an item before Kent's marriage to Princess Marina. Elizabeth subsequently dispelled any doubt that she knew Coward was gay when, one evening, they passed the tall soldiers of the Household Cavalry in their gleaming breastplates, lined up on either side of the staircase. Catching Coward staring, Elizabeth whispered with a smile, 'I wouldn't if I were you, Noël. They count them before they put them out.'

32. An unstable throne

George VI's temper could be explosive, particularly in the early years of his reign, when he was terrified of embarrassing his family or his office. Sitting on their backless chairs and holding one of their first courts at Buckingham Palace, he and Elizabeth appeared magnificent. Until she noticed that her husband-king seemed to be slipping in his chair. Wearing the thigh-high boots of a field marshal's uniform, George VI kept trying to balance himself as he seemed, inexorably, to be sliding forward. It was as if his chair was staging some kind of rebellion, as Bertie tried to keep his dignity while acknowledging the seemingly endless stream of bows and curtseys flowing towards him and his Queen.

Standing nearby was thirteen-year-old Andrew, Lord Bruce, heir to the Scottish earldoms of Elgin and Kincardine, and to the chiefdom of Clan Bruce. He was serving as Page of Honour to Queen Elizabeth and watching her husband slide forward in his chair rather than settle backwards. The Lord Chamberlain whispered to the pages to see if they knew what on earth was happening to the King. Young Lord Bruce realised, 'I think the chair's the wrong way round.' The cleaner had put the chair in facing backwards, so it had acquired an incline that kept slowly tipping George VI towards his guests. It was too late to do anything. They had to carry on. Elizabeth's smile was plastered on as the presentations continued and she reached out to gently touch her husband's wrists, a loving code that said without words 'Keep it together'. Under his breath, heard only by his wife and his closest attendants, the sliding King's language became as colourful as the rainbow.

33. HRH

The 1937 Coronation, at which Bertie was crowned first as monarch and Elizabeth second as his consort, had taken place on a May afternoon at Westminster Abbey. A guest wrote:

> *the sun shone through the windows and the King, abashed, looking young (all the royal family look phenomenally young), almost boyish suddenly reminded me of his brother 'over the water'; and I thought, as many others, too, must have been thinking, of that sad, more glamorous wistful Edward VIII alone with Wallis Warfield (as she now is called), no doubt listening on the radio to the Coronation service of his brother, which ought to have been his own … [Elizabeth] advanced towards the altar. Once again the golden canopy was brought forward, and for a brief moment the four chosen duchesses held it over her. The second service was shorter and soon she mounted the throne.*

As the shock of the Abdication wore off and she had time to think about the way it had been handled, Elizabeth's feelings towards her eldest brother-in-law hardened into something very close to hatred. It was David who had given her husband less than seventy-two hours' notice that he was going to become king. It was David who had kept from them any helpful details about his plans, yet told people who leaked it to the press. And it was David who, from what he thought would be a temporary exile, kept badgering Bertie to give Wallis the designation of Her Royal Highness, allowing the initials HRH to be added to her title to confirm to the world that she was a senior member of the Royal Family.

David argued that by denying the title to his new wife, Bertie was withholding from Wallis something to which she had a legal right. From her new home at Buckingham Palace, Elizabeth retaliated that since Wallis had been considered unsuitable to be queen, how on earth could she be judged fit to be an HRH? While legal opinion held that Elizabeth was wrong on this count, the King agreed with his wife. He pointed out that, in his

Abdication document, Edward VIII had explicitly 'renounced all rights and privileges of succession for himself and his children – including the title of Royal Highness in respect of himself and his wife. There is therefore no question of the title being "restored" to the Duchess – because she never had it.' David countered that, thirteen years earlier, there had been a debate about whether Elizabeth should herself be given the title, when some of the more pearl-clutching snobs in court circles, and even in the wider Royal Family, had wondered if she deserved to be addressed as Her Royal Highness and curtseyed to, given that neither of her parents were royals. The Royal Household had responded then with a statement that 'in accordance with the general rule settled, that a wife takes the status of her husband, Lady Elizabeth Bowes-Lyon on her marriage has become Her Royal Highness the Duchess of York'. These rules, set in place for Elizabeth, meant Wallis too deserved to become Her Royal Highness The Duchess of Windsor, as wife of His Royal Highness The Duke of Windsor.

This logic proved as appealing to Elizabeth as a weak gin and tonic. She would not budge. On several occasions, she expressed disgust at the idea that anyone would feel the need to curtsey to 'That Woman' if she got the HRH. Nor could there be any question of David being allowed to return to Britain to carry out occasional duties as a member of the Royal Family, as he had hoped. One was either fully in or fully out, and Bertie must have no rival.

The new Queen made it perfectly clear that she did not want members of the Royal Family to go to France for David and Wallis's wedding, which therefore turned into a much quieter affair than the former king had hoped. His siblings' failure to attend particularly hurt. When the couple returned for a private visit to England three years after the Abdication, David proposed bringing Wallis to Buckingham Palace, perhaps in an effort to heal the rift. Elizabeth felt no such urge to see the grudge become a bygone. She wrote to Wallis directly 'before they came, saying that I was sorry I could not receive her. I thought it more honest to make things quite clear.'

Elizabeth launched a cold war against the Duke and Duchess of Windsor's supporters in London high society. To celebrate the Coronation, the Marchioness of Londonderry organised a magnificent ball at her family's London residence and sent the proposed guest list to the Queen before issuing invitations. Elizabeth approved every name except that of Wallis's confidante, Emerald Cunard, replying, 'I know that you will not mind my telling you that Lady Cunard is really the only one that we do not want to meet just now. The bitter months of last autumn and winter are still so fresh in our minds, and her presence would inevitably bring so many sad thoughts, that we should prefer not to meet her. I can say this to you as a friend for so long, and feel sure you will understand our feelings. (Private, of course.)'[7] A feud usually needs a surrogate and other socialites, like Lady Astor, took the initiative on the Queen's behalf by scotching invitations to anyone who had been strongly sympathetic to the ex-king; for a time, this meant a drop in the number of parties for Chips Channon and Winston Churchill.

The Queen's dislike was reciprocated by most of Wallis's and Edward's friends. A disgruntled Channon recorded that, at a party for the 1937 Grand National, 'no one has a good word for the Queen, who they say is "sugary", and "insincere" (which she is), and badly dressed in Pont Street numbers with dyed furs, and stockings, everything to match like a middle-class matron.'

34. Beaton, Hartnell and Winterhalter

Perhaps it was therefore no wonder that the high-society photographer Cecil Beaton dreaded his commission to make several new official photographs of Elizabeth. 'She looks horrid in photographs,' he lamented. When he arrived at Buckingham Palace for their shoot, the Queen was nervous, too, and it took some persuading on Beaton's part to convince her to try a different lipstick and wear eye shadow for the first time. They struck up a rapport and Elizabeth confided to him that she thought she had looked very ugly in her Coronation photographs, which 'went all over the world'. 'In fact,' she admitted to Beaton, 'it is so distressing to me that I always photograph so badly.'

She need not have worried. Cecil Beaton's studies of Queen Elizabeth in the late 1930s were some of the best-received royal portraits of the twentieth century. Shot on various locations throughout Buckingham

Palace, Beaton correctly guessed before Elizabeth that they had a hit on their hands. 'To my utter amazement and joy,' he wrote, 'the Queen looked like a dream, a porcelain doll, with a flawless little face like luminous china in front of a fire. Her smile as fresh as a dewdrop, her regard uncompromising and kindly, altogether a face that reveals what the owner is – someone with the best instincts, strict in her likes, gay, sympathetic, witty, shrewd, wistful and so well educated that she makes one full of admiration.' The photos were so successful that many British royal photographs have subtly paid tribute to their aesthetic in the years since, including Paolo Roversi's 2022 portrait of Catherine, Duchess of Cambridge, for the National Portrait Gallery.

Part of the success lay with Elizabeth's wardrobe, which consisted of an ankle-length garden party dress with parasol and a tulle ballgown with diamond tiara and necklace. While Beaton was photographing her in the latter, the Superintendent of the Royal Household walked in to check on progress and said, 'Your Majesty, it's lovely. It's just like a Winterhalter picture.'

Franz Xaver Winterhalter was a German artist who had died in 1873 and whose portraits captured an idealised version of nineteenth-century royalty and aristocracy. Dressing them in yards of fabrics, Winterhalter imbued living royals with the aura of fairy tales. Or tulle-trapped cupcakes, depending on the viewer's sympathies. His portrait of Empress Elisabeth of Austria with diamond stars pinned into her hair is still famous, as are his paintings of France's Empress Eugénie surrounded by her ladies-in-waiting and of Bertie's grandmother, Alexandra. Winterhalter's works positioned his subjects between dream and reality and, after the trauma of Edward VIII's abdication, George VI hit upon the idea of evoking Winterhalter's aesthetic for Elizabeth. She was never going to be chic and fashionable, in the way Wallis or Marina were. She could be magnificent instead. The monarchical makeover was entrusted to her new couturier, Norman Hartnell. The King asked Hartnell to visit him at Buckingham Palace, where he took the time to show him their Winterhalter collection. Hartnell understood the assignment: 'His Majesty made it clear in his quiet way that I should attempt to capture this picturesque grace in the dresses I was to design for the Queen.'

While the dresses for the Beaton shoot were among Hartnell's most famous pieces, he received his biggest commission thus far from Elizabeth when she and George VI accepted an invitation to make a state visit, their first as King and Queen, to France. Paris was, as Hartnell and Elizabeth well knew, the fashion capital of the world, where the Duke and Duchess of Windsor were quite popular, and the trip was not only important to Britain's diplomatic efforts to remain close to her French allies, but also a public test of the shy and allegedly awkward new King. Elizabeth must not let the side down.

35. The Kaiser sends his condolences

Hartnell's original designs for the French visit never saw the light of day. 'I have been dreading this moment ever since I was a little child,' Elizabeth wrote as the overnight train carried her, Bertie, and Glen their golden retriever north for Cecilia's funeral, 'and now that it has come, one can hardly believe it.'

Cecilia's death, aged seventy-five in June 1938, was in many ways a release for a woman who had suffered so many bereavements. 'I have had so many great sorrows,' she confided to a friend in 1931, a few months after burying a fourth child. Her passing was not a complete surprise; she had missed a granddaughter's wedding after suffering a mild heart attack. The Queen had continued with her engagements throughout her mother's final few days, including visits to a naval depot and a young mothers' charity, both of which she nonetheless tried to leave a little early. She was at Cecilia's bedside when she passed away in the small hours and she accompanied the coffin back by train to Glamis, where the funeral took place in the pouring rain. Cecilia's hearse, pulled by two horses, was escorted by those who had worked on the Bowes-Lyon estate for years. Arthur Barson, the Bowes-Lyons' elderly butler, was given a place of honour with the family, 'his battered old face full of grief, making apologetic & deprecatory noises at being given the place to which his long & faithful service so amply entitled him', according to a member of the congregation.

Among the telegrams of condolence Elizabeth received on her mother's death was one from Kaiser Wilhelm II, the deposed German emperor who had been living on a small country estate in the Netherlands since losing power at the end of the Great War. Elizabeth had never met the former emperor and, considering that she and Cecilia had once raised toasts of 'To hell with the bloody Kaiser', she was not exactly thrilled to hear from him now. To give Wilhelm credit where it is due, as the years passed he had attempted to re-establish contact with his British cousins and, by contemporary standards, he did the kind and proper thing in sending his condolences to the Queen. Many in the House of Windsor were delighted at these signs of rapprochement with the Hohenzollerns, none more so than Queen Mary, who still dreamed of living long enough to see the German monarchy restored. She invited the Kaiser's grandson, Prince Friedrich-Georg von Hohenzollern ('Fritzi'), to tea when he visited London. Queen Mary, and those who shared her views, thought that the new Nazi government in Germany consisted of criminals, morons and monsters who would, like most revolutionary radicals, eventually destroy each other. Once that happened, there seemed to be little chance of Germany reinstating the weak republic which the Nazis had buried at the first available opportunity. Instead, a coup would depose the weakened and bloody Nazis to restore the monarchy and its pre-1918 constitution, as 'Fritzi' acceded to his grandfather's throne as Kaiser Friedrich IV.[8]

Elizabeth shared neither this confidence in, nor sympathy for, a restored monarchy in Germany. During an official visit to Berlin in 1929, she and Bertie had been given a tour of the imperial family's former homes and, on seeing what had once been their private quarters, she thought it 'was most interesting & rather sad'. She was careful not to write down her full feelings, instead rounding off a letter to her friend Sir D'Arcy Osborne with the words 'I will reserve my opinions (if you care to hear them) of our late enemies until I meet you again.'

Nazi Germany was the reason why the King and Queen's visit to France could not be cancelled, despite Cecilia's death. Given the international situation, the friendship between Britain and France needed to be advertised in unambiguous terms. Preparations were reorganised for later in the summer by the two governments, while the Queen mourned her mother in Scotland. She wrote to a friend a week after Cecilia passed away:

It is a curious thing, but I have always been terrified of my mother dying, ever since I was a little child, and now that it has come it seems almost impossible to believe. But she has left so much behind her, and her influence will be strong with us, her children, all our lives. At Glamis this week we congregated in her sitting room & found comfort even in that. Her perspective of life was so wonderful, each event was given its true importance, and that is a rare gift. I was thinking today of how incredulous, slightly amused and so touched she would have been if she could have heard some of the appreciative things that her friends have said of her this week. She was modest to a fault, very proud & sensitive, and her judgement was never at fault ... I am writing too much about her, but I know you won't mind. I have climbed one or two mountains, & spent my days amongst them, and feel very soothed – they are so nice & big & everlasting.

36. The toilet-trapped Duchess

The King's shoulder slammed into the stubbornly locked door of a train loo as they tried to free the Dowager Duchess of Northumberland. After several moments of trying to jimmy the lock herself, the Duchess, Elizabeth's chief lady-in-waiting for just over a year, had to cry for help. The door defeated every champion sent against it, including the King, as the train hurtled through the French countryside. Just before they reached the station at Amiens, it gave way and the Dowager emerged onto the platform, dignity firmly intact, as if she hadn't just been shaken about like a cocktail, behind a head-to-toe-in-Hartnell Elizabeth.

Still in mourning for Cecilia, Elizabeth nonetheless could not go to Paris wearing black. The government felt it would send a depressing message. Nor could she wear Norman Hartnell's original designs, most of which were so colourful that they would be interpreted as an insult to her mother's memory. Having had its first revolution in 1789, monarchy had come and gone in France like the Spring collections. There had been revivals, or rebranding, in 1804, 1814, 1815, 1830, 1848 and 1852. There had been failed talks of another in the 1870s and the 1910s, and there would be again in the 1950s. Through his research, Hartnell discovered that, in centuries gone by, the queens of France had not worn black for mourning. They had worn white. Every one of Hartnell's dresses for the trip was thus remade in white. They were a sensation; Christian Dior said later that Elizabeth's wardrobe in 1938 contained some of the most beautiful pieces of clothing he had ever seen. A Parisian newspaper ran the headline, TODAY FRANCE IS A MONARCHY AGAIN, as the streets of the towns and cities were jammed with cheering crowds.

The government in London were relieved, and hoped forlornly that this testament to Anglo-French friendship would give Germany pause for thought. Duff Cooper, the future British ambassador to Paris, thought that the royals' rise in popularity throughout 1938 had steadied the couple's nerves, which he noticed when he sat next to the Queen at a dinner: 'I got on with her better than ever and found her more than ever charming,' he told his wife. 'There is nobody to whom I enjoy talking so much.'

37. Queen Elizabeth

On 27 September 1938, the Queen arrived at the John Brown and Company shipyard in Scotland to launch a luxury liner named in her honour. The 83,000-ton *Queen Elizabeth* would be the largest passenger ship built until 1996 and she was timetabled to make her first commercial voyage from Southampton to New York in 1940. Four years earlier, when Elizabeth's mother-in-law christened the *Queen Mary*, she had been accompanied to the ceremony by her husband George V, and George VI was expected to do the same for the *Queen Elizabeth*. There was a great deal of excitement about the launch. The *Queen Mary* was already a commercial success, fully booked on most of her voyages, during which she had captured the Blue Riband award for the fastest crossing of the Atlantic. Press attention and public interest was enormous, as there was a sense that these ships symbolised Britain's recovery from the worst years of the Great Depression.

When the Queen stepped out of her car at the shipyard, she was followed by her two identically dressed daughters. The King had decided to stay in London as the government waited to see if war would break out in Europe. The next day, Adolf Hitler's ultimatum to the Czechoslovakian government was due to expire. The German Chancellor had announced his intention to incorporate the Sudetenland, part of Czechoslovakia, into Germany and the President of Czechoslovakia had until 28 September to give Hitler what he wanted – or he would take it by force. The British Prime Minister, Neville Chamberlain, was about to fly to negotiations in the German city of Munich, where he hoped to broker a deal that would prevent a war over the issue. The Sudetenland's population was predominantly German, many had wanted to be a part of Germany since the 1870s, and there were many who felt Nazi Germany was therefore justified in trying to take the province. As some cynics in the West argued, who wanted to go to war over the borders of Czechoslovakia, a landlocked republic that had only existed for nineteen years? Was it, they asked, even really a country with a coherent sense of identity? Why should anyone care if Hitler tried to dismember it, a little?

The King and Queen hoped desperately to avoid another war. It had been German incursions into a small neutral country that had brought Britain into the Great War in 1914. Then it had been Belgium, now it looked very much like it would be Czechoslovakia. Elizabeth, who had endured one brother killed, another held for years as a prisoner of war, and three psychologically brutalised by the trenches, was at this stage an ardent Appeaser. Appeasement, a British foreign policy directive whereby it was hoped to prevent a war by giving the Nazis some of what they wanted, is now rightly notorious, a byword for diplomatic cowardice. Broadly speaking, there were two types of Appeasers in 1930s Britain. The first category, into which Elizabeth arguably falls, were those who, remembering what had happened in the first great war, were determined that it should not happen again. Their support for the policy fell away at different points of Nazi aggression; for some in 1936, for others in 1938 or

1939. The second, and far more insidious, group were those who promoted Appeasement less because they feared another war and more because they sympathised with Hitler. Many were pro-German, others were part of the British fascist movement, and practically all of them were virulently anti-Semitic.

Elizabeth's speech as she prepared to launch the *Queen Elizabeth* was captured by the Pathé newsreel cameras, and you can hear the worry in her voice. As the ship's enormous prow looms over her and her daughters, Elizabeth is much more sombre than she usually was during her public appearances. The breeze off the Clyde can be seen ruffling her fox-fur wrap as the Queen barely looks up from the notes for her speech, which was the first time most people had heard her voice. Many in Britain felt later that this moment, between the King's last-minute absence and the Queen's words, was also the first time they felt that there was a real chance of another terrible war in their lifetimes.

'This ceremony,' she began, 'to which many thousands have looked forward so eagerly, must now take place in circumstances far different than those for which they had hoped. I have, however, a message for you from the King. He bids the people of this country be of good cheer, in spite of the dark clouds hanging over them – and, indeed, over the whole world. He knows well that, as ever before, in critical times they will keep cool heads and brave hearts. He knows, too, that they will place entire confidence in their leaders who, under God's Providence, are striving their utmost to find a just and peaceful solution to the grave problems which confront us. The launching of a ship is, like the inception of all great human enterprises, an act of faith. We cannot foretell the future but, in preparing for it, we show our trust in a Divine Providence and in ourselves. We proclaim our belief that, by the Grace of God and by man's patience and goodwill, order may yet be brought out of confusion and peace out of turmoil. With that hope and prayer in our hearts, we send forth this noble ship.'

The *Queen Elizabeth* began to move too early towards the water and so the Queen quickly pressed the button to let loose the bottle of Australian red wine that smashed over the bow before it slid beyond reach. Two years later, the *Queen Elizabeth* made her maiden voyage on schedule, with no luxuries on board, all of them having been moved into storage as the largest ship in the world, painted in camouflage grey to avoid Nazi submarines, began her five-year service as a British military troop transport.

38. Have you read *Mein Kampf*?

Elizabeth crossed the Atlantic for the first time herself in May 1939 on board a 22,000-ton Canadian passenger ship, the *Empress of Australia*. Accepting that war was now probable rather than simply possible, the King and Queen were going to Canada to increase ties between it and Britain. From Canada, they would travel to America in the hope that a royal visit would stimulate pro-British sympathies and undermine the isolationist lobby, who wanted to keep the United States out of another European war.

It was wonderful publicity for the *Empress of Australia*'s owners that one of their ships had been selected to carry the King, the Queen and their entourage on the first leg of their tour. It was a slightly less pleasant experience for the King's Private Secretary, Tommy Lascelles, who had already made the transatlantic trip twice that year. The first had been when he was sent ahead to inspect the proposed sites, safety and accommodation for the tour. The *New York Herald Tribune* informed its readers that Lascelles' mission was so top secret that he had kept to his cabin on board the *Queen Mary* until he reached New York. Unfortunately, his failure to mingle with his fellow passengers was less a result of dramatic royalist subterfuge and more to do with the powerful wave of nausea that crashed over Lascelles about six minutes after they left Southampton, and which left him ashen-faced on his bed as his stomach did somersaults until they passed the Statue of Liberty. 'I have no doubt that the North Atlantic is the foulest and dreariest spectacle on this earth,' he lamented.

The Atlantic continued its vendetta against Lascelles on the *Empress of Australia*, by delivering more seasickness via choppy weather on the first two days of the voyage and on the third by wrapping the ship in a blanket of fog so thick that she had to slow almost to a halt. She took three days longer than planned to reach Canada. As Lascelles told his wife in a letter home:

> the fog began on Tuesday – it came down like a blanket, as thick as I have ever seen; and for three days we sat motionless on the Atlantic (which was luckily as placid as a pond), seeing nothing except for a brief half-hour after tea on Friday, when the curtain rolled back as if by magic, and revealed a handful of really formidable icebergs all round us. Then down it came again … the ship could nose her way forward at the pace of a rowing boat, with her siren, and those of the two escorting cruisers, roaring in a head-splitting symphony every two minutes. Our three fog-marooned days were really very curious. Michael* said he got the feeling we had all been dead quite a long time. It was rather like that – a strange sensation of being suspended right outside the world, with no dimensions. Space was limited to the grey wall outside, and time was non-existent – we might have been there three days or three months.

Spirits were not lifted by the trivia-spouting courtier who, over dinner, informed them how interesting it was that they had also passed so many icebergs, considering that they were now very close to the spot where the *Titanic* had gone down. To which Elizabeth allegedly replied, 'How reassuring.'

Elizabeth saw a silver lining in the delay, in that it gave Bertie a chance to rest nerves increasingly frayed by his fear that they would be at war by the end of the year. 'The foghorn moans hoarsely every minute or so,' she wrote to Queen Mary, 'such a melancholy noise, & I much hope that we shall get better weather soon. The ship is quite comfortable, the food is good, but there are too many stewards & liftboys & messengers about – one falls over them at every turn. But they are so obliging & eager to do anything that we haven't the heart to send them away, poor things. We felt

---

* Michael Adeane, Lascelles's deputy and later successor as Private Secretary to Elizabeth II from 1953 to 1972.

very sad leaving you all on Saturday – it was nice that you all came to see us off.'

Having run out of reading material because of the delay, Elizabeth went to find something in the ship's first-class Library, on the shelves of which she spotted a suspiciously hefty edition of Hitler's political testament, *Mein Kampf*. Published early in his career, it had been translated into English shortly before he won his first major election. It was so rambling and repetitive that the British edition cut out almost half of it, including most of the anti-Semitic and expansionist passages. The Canadian and American editions of *Mein Kampf* in contrast translated it almost word for word. As the *Empress of Australia* crawled past the icebergs and through the fog, Elizabeth told her mother-in-law, 'I am starting to read the unexpurgated version of *Mein Kampf* – it is very soap box, but very interesting. Have you read it, Mama?'

As she slogged through Hitler's testimony, Elizabeth was fascinated and appalled in equal measure. When the Nazis first came to power, she had laughed at them, mocking their salutes and the unison goosestepping on display at their rallies. She had giggled and joined in at dinner party impressions of Hitler and Mussolini. The unexpurgated edition of *Mein Kampf* left her in no doubt that she had been laughing at something that was not funny. It is possible to overstate this as a Rubicon moment; Elizabeth had been increasingly disillusioned with Appeasement following the Czechoslovakian crisis. Hitler had not stopped at the Sudetenland. Instead he had annexed the whole country, and there were fears he was planning to do the same to Poland.

The unedited *Mein Kampf* provided a confirmation of the Queen's fears rather than a revelation. It shocked her enough that after reading it, she sent copies to several fellow Appeasers, with a half-joking apology that Hitler was such a bad writer that 'you might go mad'. Nonetheless, the full text was important, she urged, since 'even a skip through gives one a good idea of his mentality, ignorance and obvious sincerity'. Too many, including Elizabeth, had been willing to believe that Hitler's bombast was bluffing and posturing to get what he wanted, rather than the sincere goals of a brutal dictator. *Mein Kampf* revealed what he had always been, had they been willing to pay attention.

Five days after picking up *Mein Kampf*, the Queen was still on the ship. She wrote to her eldest daughter, at home in Britain with her grandmother and little sister:

My darling Lilibet, here we are creeping along at about one mile per hour, & occasionally stopping altogether, for the 3rd day running! You can imagine how horrid it is – one cannot see more than a few yards, and the sea is full of icebergs as big as Glamis, & things called 'growlers' – which are icebergs mostly under water with only a very small amount of ice showing on the surface. We shall be late arriving in Canada, and it is going to be very difficult to fit everything in, and avoid disappointing people. It is very cold – rather like the coldest, dampest day at Sandringham – double it and add icebergs, & then you can imagine a little of what it is like … I do hope that you are enjoying your Saturday evenings with Mr Marten* – try & learn as much as you can from him, & mark how he brings the human element into all this history – of course history is made by ordinary humans, & one must not forget that. Well, my darling, I am longing to see you both again, & I send you lots & lots of kisses and some pats for Dooks [their corgi] – Your very very loving Mummy.

Four days later, with the sun having broken through, the *Empress of Australia* reached Canada, where the King and Queen were greeted by crowds judged larger and more enthusiastic than at their coronation.

39. Hot dogs on the Hudson

Tommy Lascelles did better by rail than by sea, becoming the first British person to be knighted on American soil as the royal party crossed by train into the United States. The royals were more nervous about the American reception after their success in Canada. American isolationists were

---

* Later Sir Henry Marten, he was recruited from Eton by the King and Queen to give History lessons to Princess Elizabeth to help prepare her for one day succeeding to the throne.

displeased and suspected, correctly, that President Roosevelt had invited the King to the United States to increase support for his administration's interventionist foreign policy. Furthermore, many Americans sympathised with the ex-king and his American wife, and the US press thus tended to characterise George VI as a mean-spirited bully, addled by jealousy of his brother and egged on by his 'excessively ambitious' wife, who was herself demented with envy of Wallis. As one magazine put it, 'As for Queen Elizabeth, by Park Avenue standards she appears to be far too plump of figure, too dowdy in dress, to meet American specifications of a reigning Queen. The living contrasts of Queen Mary (as regal as a woman can be) and the Duchess of Windsor (chic and charmingly American) certainly do not help Elizabeth.'

By the end of the tour, a Washington newspaper ran a headline bidding farewell to Elizabeth or, as they called her, the QUEEN OF HEARTS. The visit was a triumph in terms of its own aims, with tens of thousands thronging the streets of DC to see the visiting royals. Elizabeth's ability to talk easily to people proved a huge public relations boon to this mission on the eve of the war. Editorials appeared in the *New York Times* arguing that if British political values were destroyed by her enemies, America's too would be damaged, a stance that the anti-isolationists were keen to encourage. The King and the President got on very well and the First Lady, Eleanor Roosevelt, commented on the Queen: 'My admiration for her grew every minute she spent with us.' They joined the Roosevelts on the presidential yacht and at their New York country estate at Hyde Park, where the Queen was able to place a transatlantic call to her daughters. 'It was such fun talking to you both on the telephone today,' she wrote that evening, 'and directly after we had spoken we went off for a picnic luncheon. There were a lot of people there, and we all sat at little tables under the trees round the house, and had all our food on one plate – a little salmon, a little turkey, some ham, lettuce, beans & HOT DOGS too! ... Everyone was so kind & welcoming, & one feels really at home here.'

With Tommy Lascelles shuddering at the thought of completing his tenth, eleventh and twelfth thousand nautical miles in five months, the royal party went back to Canada to travel home on another Canadian ship. This time, the owners were keen to maximise publicity for their newest and glitziest flagship, the *Empress of Britain*. From her suite on board, Elizabeth reflected that 'Our chief emotion is gratitude.' A few years later, she looked back on those two months with the conclusion, 'That tour made us.'

40. Who is this Hitler?

As the countdown to war continued, so did the London social calendar. In 2014, Betty Morton could still remember being a debutante and missing a date in 1939, an opportunity unintentionally denied her by Elizabeth's attendance at the same ball. 'It was a bit awkward because if the Queen came into the room, you all had to stand up, when you'd be sitting with some *delicious* young man,' Morton reminisced. 'However, she was very sweet and said we could all sit down again, but you couldn't leave the room [while the Queen was there], so if you'd got a date with somebody else when she walked in, you couldn't leave!' Other debutantes remembered sitting in their cars, queued along the Mall to Buckingham Palace while they waited to be formally presented, as crowds of people peered through the vehicles' windows to compare the debutantes. Twenty-two-year-old Ruth Magnus was less than thrilled to hear, 'Oh, that one's not as pretty as the one in the other car!' A clique of four debs including Katharine Ormsby-Gore and Princess Alice's niece Elizabeth (the future Duchess of Northumberland) had been pre-emptively banned from that year's Queen Charlotte's Ball on the suspicion that they would get a fit of the giggles while curtseying to the sacred cake. 'They thought we were a disruptive influence,' Katharine explained later. 'They were right.'

Everywhere in Britain that summer, life continued much as normal, with millions hoping Germany would not invade Poland. 'Who is this Hitler, spoiling everything?' eight-year-old Princess Margaret asked her governess. Although Appeasement was dead and discredited to all but its most zealous champions, its acolytes resented Elizabeth's sudden lack of support and blamed her anti-German friends for 'dripping poison into the Queen's ear'.

On the morning of Sunday 3 September 1939, Elizabeth looked down and thought that this is 'my last cup of tea in peace!' She sat next to her husband 'with tears running down my face' as they listened to Prime Minister Chamberlain's broadcast, containing the fateful words, 'This country is at war with Germany.' The King and Queen went into a drawing room in Buckingham Palace, where they knelt down and 'prayed with all our hearts that Peace would come soon – real peace, not a Nazi peace'.

On the first day of the Second World War, the King addressed the country by radio, beginning: 'In this grave hour, perhaps the most fateful in our history, for the second time in the lives of most of us, we are at war. Over and over again we have tried to find a peaceful way out of the differences between ourselves and those who are now our enemies. But it has been in vain. The task will be hard. There may be dark days ahead and war is no longer confined to the battlefield.' He quoted a poem, 'The Gate of the Year, or, God Knows', by Minnie Louise Haskins, which was apparently brought to his attention by his thirteen-year-old daughter, Princess Elizabeth. Sixty-three years later, its words meant so much to the Queen Mother that they were included in the order of service for her funeral.

> And I said to the man who stood at the gate of the year:
> 'Give me a light that I may tread safely into the unknown'.
> And he replied:
> 'Go out into the darkness and put your hand into the Hand of God.
> That shall be to you better than light and safer than a known way.'
> So I went forth, and finding the Hand of God, trod gladly into the
>   night.
> And He led me towards the hills and the breaking of day in the lone
>   East.

V

The Most Dangerous Woman in Europe (1940–1950)

The six years of the Second World War, from 1939 to 1945, were the most important of Elizabeth's time as queen. The King sought her advice on most matters pertaining to the war; as she put it later, 'The King told me everything. Well one had to, you see, because you couldn't not, in a way. There was only us there. So obviously he had to tell one things. But one was so dreadfully discreet, that even now I feel nervous sometimes, about talking about things. You know, you knew something and you couldn't say a word about it, [even] when you heard people talking absolute nonsense.' The Queen's popularity, and her refusal to evacuate during the Nazi bombardment, proved such a significant boost to British morale that Hitler paid Elizabeth the compliment of her life by dubbing her 'the most dangerous woman in Europe'.

Most of the men on Elizabeth's side of the family were involved in this war effort as they had been in the last, which caused her a shudder during a visit to the Black Watch regiment, where she was shocked to see her eldest nephew, John Bowes-Lyon, in uniform.* 'He suddenly looked exactly like my brother Fergus who was killed at [the Battle of] Loos, & in the same regiment,' she wrote to Queen Mary. 'It was uncanny in a way, & desperately sad to feel that all that ghastly waste was starting again at the bidding of a lunatic.' John was killed fighting against a joint Italian-German force in Egypt. Another nephew – her sister Mary's eldest – was captured by the Nazis and sent to the notorious Colditz prison.[1]

---

* She was honorary colonel-in-chief of the regiment from 1937 until 2002.

Back in England, the Queen's youngest brother David helped lead what he called 'one of Britain's secret armies'. David, who turned forty in 1942, had helped found a secret department called the Political Warfare Executive, whose acronym prompted its nickname, 'Pee-Wee'. Although politically David Bowes-Lyon was slightly to the right of Cleopatra, he partnered in leadership with a Labour politician, Hugh Dalton, who proudly described himself an anti-monarchist 'in every country but my own'. Together, they worked to set up nineteen pirate radio stations for 'a group of German socialists who are calling on other German socialists to join them in their fight'. Pee-Wee requisitioned the Duke of Beaufort's country estate, from which they broadcast these messages into the heart of Nazi-occupied Europe.

Elizabeth's father Claude passed away at Glamis on 7 November 1944, a few months before his ninetieth birthday. Princess Elizabeth was particularly upset at her grandfather's death. The 1940s were times of transition for the family, as the princesses became teenagers and then adults. The King referred to his wife and daughters as 'We Four' or 'Us Four', a happy unit, and he struggled as the princesses matured. The Queen, the more pragmatic of the two parents, reminded her husband, 'They grow up and leave us, and we must make the best of it.' Princess Elizabeth wanted to volunteer for the war effort on the grounds that 'I ought to do as other girls of my own age do.' The Queen supported her request – and the Princess eventually trained as a mechanic – but not before the King dragged his feet and urged her to enjoy what was left of her childhood. The Queen also set up a Girl Guide troop based at Buckingham Palace so that Princess Margaret could have regular contact with friends her own age.

In the first two decades of her marriage, Elizabeth had frequently met European royalty. The onslaught of the Nazi armies in the early 1940s sent many more crowned heads into her company. Several exiled monarchs fled to London, including Queen Wilhelmina of the Netherlands, arriving at Paddington Station with nothing more than a shopping bag and a tin hat. Young King Peter II of Yugoslavia was welcomed by the British royals, though they were less fond of his Romanian mother, the Queen Mother Maria; Princess Marina asked Elizabeth not to invite Queen Maria to a weekend at Windsor Castle because she was 'a bore, a lesbian, and an *intriguante* [schemer]'. There was a great deal of sympathy in Britain for the Dutch and Norwegian royals but almost none for Greece's King George II, whom Tommy Lascelles thought would be happy enough to lose his throne permanently if it meant he could spend the rest of his life at London's beautiful Brown's Hotel – 'his spiritual home', as Lascelles put it.

A private memorandum to the British Prime Minister noted, 'I observe that the Nazis both in Norway and in Holland made a desperate attempt to capture the Royal Family; no doubt they will do the same in this country if they can.' The Nazis' seizure of the Belgian, and later Danish, royal families was a worry for the Allies, since the imprisoned figureheads might be used as a tool to manipulate the local resistance, whereas the Dutch and Norwegian monarchs proved effective in galvanising anti-Nazi organisations. Sir Winston Churchill, who became Prime Minister in 1940, was determined that the British royals would become neither prisoners nor pawns.

Despite his concerns for her safety, Elizabeth did not initially have much affection for Churchill. (Tommy Lascelles described her as 'very anti-Winston'.) She distrusted his ambition and his love of the limelight, and she resented the support he had given to Edward VIII, before and after the Abdication. Nonetheless, by the time she, the King and Churchill stood on the Buckingham Palace balcony to celebrate Allied victory over Nazi Germany in 1945, she had come to respect Churchill's skills as a wartime leader and as an orator. She was as surprised as anybody when, on 5 July 1945, two months after victory, he lost the General Election by a landslide, in favour of a Labour government with Clement Attlee as the new Prime Minister. The British electorate saw Churchill as a man better suited to lead in war than in peace. Attlee hiked taxation on the upper classes, particularly the aristocracy, which did not prevent him forming a friendship with the King, although the pro-aristocracy Elizabeth was appalled. Attlee defended his fiscal policy by saying that 'a juster distribution of wealth was not a policy to soak the rich or to take revenge, but because a society with gross inequalities of wealth and opportunity is fundamentally unhealthy'. The coalmines, the railways, the gas, the electricity, then later the iron and steel industries were all nationalised, while the Labour government also helped preside over British imperial withdrawal from India and created a National Health Service, whereby British taxes were used to fund a 'cradle to grave' service of free and universal healthcare.

41. Lizzie, Get Your Gun

By 1940, the Wehrmacht had swept through most of western Europe, and Britain seemed set to be next. In preparation for the expected Nazi invasion, Elizabeth took shooting lessons with pistols and rifles in the gardens of Buckingham Palace, sometimes using as her targets the scurrying rats who were representatives of the large rodent community set loose on London's streets as buildings collapsed in the air raids. Elizabeth was intent on putting up a good fight and she said that she planned to take as many Nazis as possible out with her before she was killed or captured. 'I shall not go down like the others,' she declared, in a rather unsympathetic take on the other royal refugees flocking to London at the time.

The government wanted the princesses Elizabeth and Margaret sent abroad as soon as possible to remove two possible targets for the Nazis. The Queen refused, famously saying, 'The children will not go without me. I won't leave the King. And the King will never leave.' Nonetheless, Churchill continued to plan for evacuation in the event of an invasion. A Tudor-style mansion on Vancouver Island was secretly purchased as a Canadian Buckingham Palace to serve if Britain fell and a government in exile had to be established to continue the fight. Five officers, leading 124 men from the Household Cavalry and Brigade of Guards, were ordered to smuggle the royals out of London the moment the Nazis landed. Four obscure safe houses were picked along the route between London and Liverpool, where the royals would be put on a ship for Canada – forcibly, if need be. The Coats Mission, named after its commander, Major James Coats, were warned to expect hefty resistance from the Queen, who in several conversations had stressed, 'I should die if I had to leave.' She told an equerry, 'The King had no intention of abandoning Britain. We would have seen it out to the bitter end. You do not abandon your country.'

In the end, the German invasion of Britain never materialised. And thus, neither did the final image of Queen Elizabeth charging down the Mall, firing off her gun like a suicidal yet regal Annie Oakley.

42. Ah, a German!

When their cities were bombed, thousands of British children were evacuated to surrogate homes in the countryside. The princesses went to Windsor Castle, an eleventh-century fortress on the outskirts of London, substantially renovated in the nineteenth century, and subsequently one of the British Royal Family's favourite homes. During the war, the King and Queen spent their nights there and their days at Buckingham Palace, which kept them safer after the bombing attacks shifted predominantly to night-time. In the early stages of the aerial raids on British cities, known then and afterwards as the Blitz, it had made little or no difference; in the summer and autumn of 1940 in particular, bombs were dropped by German aircraft during the day as often as they were by night.

At the start of the Blitz, when the bombs had hit nowhere in London save the East End of the city with its factories, industries and predominantly working-class neighbourhoods, the King and Queen had been booed and jeered during their visits to attacked areas. An angry resident explained, 'It's all very well for them traipsing around saying how their hearts bleed for us and they share our suffering, and then going home to a roaring fire in one of their six houses.' Class tensions were at an all-time high at that stage of the war, not helped by disgusting stories of luxury hotels in the West End installing air raid shelters complete with dance-floors so their upper-class patrons could keep enjoying their night as the city burned above them. As a precaution, rather less plush air raid shelters were also installed in Buckingham Palace.

On the morning of 13 September, shortly after they had arrived in London from Windsor, the Queen heard the air raid sirens and went to find the King to walk down to the shelter together. Before they went, he asked her to help him take out an eyelash, when they heard the whirring propellers of a Luftwaffe bomber.

They looked at each other and said, 'Ah, a German.'

Elizabeth wrote later that day that there followed 'the noise of an aircraft diving at great speed, that we had only time to look foolishly at each other, when the scream hurtled past us, and exploded with a tremendous crash in the quadrangle. I saw a great column of smoke & earth thrown up into the air, and then dashed like lightning into the corridor.' A second bomb exploded nearby. 'It is curious how one's instinct works at these moments of great danger,' she continued, 'as quite without thinking, the urge was to get away from the windows. Everybody remained wonderfully calm, and we went down to the shelter. I went along to see if the housemaids were all right.'

Someone nearby shouted for bandages for three labourers who had been strengthening the foundations beneath the chapel when the bomb went 'through the floor above them. My knees trembled a little bit for a minute or two after the explosions! But we both feel quite well today, tho' just a bit tired. I was so pleased with the behaviour of our servants.' Remembering that the palace kitchens had a glass ceiling, the Queen went to check on the staff, where she found a chef still carrying on as if nothing had happened. When she asked if he was all right, the chef dismissively referred to the bomb in French as 'a little something in the corner, a little noise'. He 'took the opportunity to tell me of his unshakeable conviction that France will rise again!'*

The King, the Queen and the other occupants had lunch in the palace air raid shelter. The all-clear sounded at about 1.30, which meant they did not have to cancel their trip to the East End. 'The damage there is ghastly,' the Queen told Queen Mary. 'I really felt as if I was walking in a dead city, when we walked down a little empty street. All the houses evacuated and yet through the broken windows one saw all the poor little possessions, photographs, beds, just as they were left. At the end of the street was a school which was hit, and collapsed on top of 500 people waiting to be evacuated – about 200 [bodies] are still under the ruins. It does affect me seeing this terrible and senseless destruction. I think that really I mind it

---

* The northern half of France had been occupied by the Nazis earlier that year.

much more than being bombed myself. The people are marvellous ... We must win in the end.'[2]

43. A wee touch of the imp

Elizabeth was preparing for a visit to Northern Ireland in June 1942 when her eighteen-year-old goddaughter, Elizabeth Vyner, died of meningitis while serving with the Women's Royal Naval Service (popularly nicknamed the 'Wrens').

The news arrived in a letter from Elizabeth Vyner's grieving mother, Doris. The Queen called it:

> *your wonderfully brave and beautiful letter ... [I] can only say how I am thinking of you all the time, and praying with all my heart that your great courage will take you through these terrible days ... As you say, it is wonderful that Elizabeth had her heart's desire, and happiness and laughter, and that she will not know sorrow or despair ... I pray God that I may be allowed to share in the inspiration of your tremendous courage and hope and faith. Your letter was like a shining light in a dark world, and I feel absolutely confident that your great spirit will take you through all this. Darling Doris, if only loving thoughts could help. I am thinking of you & Clare & the boys all the time. Later on, let me know when you feel like seeing me & I will come so gladly.*
>
> *With all my love & everything I have, Elizabeth.*

The visit to Northern Ireland went ahead as scheduled. Unlike the other parts of the United Kingdom, from 1922 until 1972 Northern Ireland had its own prime minister, who dealt with local matters of government. In 1942 the post was held by John Andrews, whose brother Thomas had helped design – and drowned on – the *Titanic* thirty years earlier. Prime Minister Andrews, with his whole cabinet, was waiting on the quay as the King and Queen arrived; a royal official described Andrews as 'inflexible as granite' against the idea of Irish reunification.

This was the first visit to Northern Ireland for the King's Private Secretary Tommy Lascelles, who was surprised by the extent of the Royal Family's popularity in the region. It is worth noting by way of historical context that, this time, the King and Queen were taken only to areas that strongly supported Northern Ireland remaining part of the United Kingdom. They began with the industrialised quarter of east Belfast, where they visited shipyards and military aircraft manufacturers. From there, to the governor's residence at Hillsborough Castle, then to the Parliament buildings at Stormont in Belfast and to the port town of Bangor. Here Lascelles witnessed 'a really remarkable demonstration of loyal enthusiasm, which I have never seen surpassed in my twenty years' experience. We were mobbed by a boisterous but thoroughly well-mannered crowd … Considering the strict secrecy that had necessarily been observed about the visit until that morning, the streets were remark-ably crowded, and always deafeningly vociferous.'

One of those cheering on the Belfast streets in 1942 remembers, 'We sort of suspected they were coming or *somebody* was coming. The men in the factories could just tell from the way their bosses were carrying on in the days leading up to it. And sure, you could never hide anything from an east Belfast housewife, they knew everything. Anyway, when we heard the Queen was coming, the streets were bunged to cheer them. Oh, we loved her! The King was such a good man, of course, I wouldn't say a word against him, but – *the Queen*. I adored her. I still adore her. Belfast had been flattened by the Nazis, but we were still standing – and there they were. And she, the Queen I mean, didn't stop smiling that whole day. She respected the people of Belfast enough to turn up and show them she was enjoying her time there. Doesn't matter if you're tired or miserable sometimes; you put a smile on your face and your best foot forward!' A pause, then, 'But do you know one of the reasons I always had such a soft spot for her? You just knew she had a wee touch of the imp to her. You could tell she'd be a great laugh with a couple of whiskeys in her. Great woman. Tough as nails. I still love her.'

44. The Windsor brothers

While Winston Churchill's affection for the former Edward VIII survived the Abdication crisis, it did not survive the war. The Duke and Duchess of Windsor had been in Paris when the German army invaded France. There were fears in London that Hitler hoped to capture the Duke of Windsor and use him as a Nazi puppet, parading him as a rival king to his brother George VI, then put him on the British throne to legitimise a Nazi occupation. Joachim von Ribbentrop, the former German ambassador to the United Kingdom, was explicit about this: 'Germany is determined to force England to peace by every means of power and, upon this happening, would be prepared to accommodate any desire expressed by the Duke, especially with a view to the assumption of the English Throne by the Duke and Duchess.' Hitler offered to put 50 million francs into a Swiss bank account for the Duke and Duchess's use, if they would publicly distance themselves from the British Royal Family. The Duke then gave an interview to an American magazine in which he strongly implied that Britain could not win the war against Germany; this infuriated Churchill, whose goal was to convince America to join the war as Britain's ally. He wrote to the Duke of Windsor to tell him in no uncertain terms that his 'language, whatever was meant, will certainly be interpreted as defeatist and pro-Nazi ... I would wish, indeed, that your Royal Highness would seek advice before making public statements of this kind.'

As the Nazis closed in on Paris, the Duke of Windsor disobeyed a direct order from his brother to return to Britain. For the former king's growing number of sceptics, it looked like he wanted to be 'captured' by the Nazis. Since the roads north towards England were blocked by the Wehrmacht, the British government decided to evacuate the Duke and Duchess south to Spain, which, although then ruled by the crypto-fascist dictator General Francisco Franco, remained officially neutral. The couple finally left France, only to again reject orders in Spain, sent via the British embassy in Madrid. As bombs rained down on British cities and children were being evacuated in their thousands, the Duke refused to co-operate until Wallis was recognised as Her Royal Highness. 'My wife and I must not risk finding ourselves once more regarded by the British public as in different status to other members of my family,' he informed Churchill.

Churchill replied, 'Your Royal Highness has taken active military rank and [so] refusal to obey direct orders of competent military authority would create a serious situation. I hope it will not be necessary for such orders to be sent. I most strongly urge immediate compliance with the wishes of the Government.' The King approved this telegram to the Duke, who not only dug in his heels but upped his conditions with the demand that both he and his wife be received at an audience at Buckingham Palace by the King and Queen, an event that should be included in the Court Circular, the daily printed record of the Royal Household's engagements. While the Duke and Duchess have many admirers even today, it is hard to find anything admirable in the Duke's priorities in 1940. He stood like a Windsor Nero in a Huntsman suit, fiddling as Europe burned in front of him, obsessing over trivialities and his creature comforts as millions were displaced and armies mobilised.

The British had to get him out of the Nazis' way. There was already a great deal of suspicion about his meandering 'escape' from Paris, and Madrid was too easily accessible for kidnappers, especially since the Duke was unlikely to resist. He gave the impression that he would rather be in Berlin with his wife treated as an HRH than in London where she wasn't. Churchill felt they had to give the former king something to do. The governorship of the Bahamas was suggested, an idea that Elizabeth strongly but unsuccessfully opposed. She argued with justification that her brother-in-law had shown himself beyond unreliable throughout the war. With far less justification, she also claimed that 'the Duchess of Windsor is looked upon as the lowest of the low'. Churchill, armed with reports from the British intelligence services, agreed with the Queen on the former point and wrote, 'The activities of the Duke of Windsor on the Continent in recent months have caused [His Majesty] and myself grave uneasiness as his inclinations are well known to be pro-Nazi.'

Despite Elizabeth's preference that the Duke be left to twiddle his thumbs or play golf in Spain, the Bahamas was far enough from the major theatre of the war to keep him out of trouble, and so the Duke was appointed governor. He moved to Portugal in preparation for boarding a

British warship to the Caribbean. Here too, however, he delayed by refusing to embark until he received 'many of our things that we shall need in the Bahamas and which we are trying to recover from France'. Given that Paris had just fallen to the Nazis, shipping the Duke and Duchess's furniture was likely to prove a little tricky.

The Duke and Duchess were eventually persuaded by their friends to board the warship and they spent most of the war years living in the governor's mansion in the Bahamas. They complained; everybody else was envious. In October 1945, five months after the end of the war, the Duke asked for a new position, one that strikes a chill. He wanted to be made Britain's ambassador to Argentina. The Queen and Tommy Lascelles swooped in to veto this; Lascelles gave a three-point rebuttal, the second item of which was a study in understatement: 'The Duke has certain disagreeable personal skeletons in his cupboard … all proven German agents,' many of whom were fleeing to Argentina in the aftermath of Nazi defeat or seeking papers to help them do so. It is worth noting that the King told everything to his wife in those years, including the content of intelligence reports; when discussing Edward VIII later with the historian Kenneth Rose, Elizabeth said, 'I wonder whether he really liked England. I am certain, however, that he did want to come back as King.'

Due to the war, the Duke of Windsor had not been able to return from the Bahamas for the funeral of his younger brother, the Duke of Kent, who was killed in a military air crash on 25 August 1942. Only seven weeks earlier, Princess Marina had given birth to their third child and second son, Prince Michael. At the funeral, the Queen had to help Marina to her feet after prayers, during which the King and his brother Prince Henry, Duke of Gloucester, wept. Afterwards, as the mourners filed out, the Dowager Countess of Oxford and Asquith spotted the playwright Noël Coward, to whom she said, 'Very well done, wasn't it?' Which Coward thought sounded 'as though she had been at a successful first night. I thought this offensive and unforgivable.'

As mentioned in the previous chapter, there were long-standing rumours in London theatre circles that Coward and the Duke of Kent had been romantically involved with one another. It was believed by people who knew one, or both, well, and it was never denied by Coward, although

London's rumour mill is a thing of its own, so a dose of caution should be maintained with most of its offerings. Chips Channon, who himself seems to have been in unrequited love with the Duke of Kent for years, cryptically referred to Kent's sexuality in his diaries: 'Of course he had a secret of which he rarely talked and was ashamed.' Channon thought that Kent and Marina 'must have been the most beautiful and dazzling couple in the world'. He remembered the days just before the Abdication, when he memorably heard of the scandal while standing bare-legged in leder-hosen as the Duke arrived in distress at his apartment just as Channon was about to leave for a costume ball at the Austrian Legation. That night, the Duke had told Channon that both he and Marina had decided they would prefer to see Wallis as queen, or princess consort, rather than Elizabeth, 'as they both like her better'. Mediatisation suddenly mattered less for Princess Marina.

The relationship had somewhat improved in the six years between the Abdication and the Duke of Kent's tragic death – Elizabeth greatly admired Marina's care for her three children – and the King wanted to help the widowed Princess with her finances by asking the government to exempt her from inheritance tax. War widows were, generally, excused from death duties but Tommy Lascelles persuaded the King not to lobby on Marina's behalf, since to do so in wartime would be disastrous in terms of public relations given the Princess's unique privileges and wealth. 'Taxation no doubts leans as heavily on his widow as it does on the rest of us,' Lascelles concluded, 'she surely ought to be able to jog along with what she's got; and if she can't, she has a number of very rich in-laws who could quite well help her without any embarrassment to themselves.'

45. Hi, Your Majesty!

Shortly after the Duke of Kent's funeral, Elizabeth was floored for two weeks by another bout of the flu. Thus commenced her lifelong belief in homeopathy, as she was treated at Balmoral by Sir John Weir, first President of the British Faculty of Homeopathy. Tommy Lascelles was also unwell, though for very different reasons, after drawing a card that read 'a St Bernard' during a game of charades at Buckingham Palace. The barking he had embarked upon to win the point had exacted a hefty toll on his vocal cords. The Queen played on the same charades team as Eleanor Roosevelt, who was visiting London after America's entry to the war in late 1941; Churchill attended the party but declined to join the game. Lascelles, quite unnecessarily, summarised in his diary that the First Lady 'looks like a she-camel, and is tough; but I like her, and see dignity, and even greatness, in her'. Roosevelt was surprised by the strictness of the rationing and the meagre standard of the food offered even at the royal table.[3] This was the situation only in London. In the countryside, the King, the Queen, and their entourage ate better, since there was no rationing of game or fish, both of which were plentiful on their estates.[4]

In October 1940, before America joined the war, Elizabeth had written despondently, 'There is not a bright spot anywhere.' The tide seemed to have turned by 1943 when, during the King's visit to the armed forces in Malta, the Queen and the Duke of Gloucester carried out the monarch's functions on his behalf. There were fewer bombed-out sites for the Queen to visit as the Luftwaffe's capabilities had begun to falter. At the worst stage of the Blitz, Elizabeth had found each visit profoundly moving and privately told her elderly mother-in-law, who had been evacuated to live with a niece in the countryside, that 'I feel quite exhausted after seeing and hearing so much sadness, sorrow, heroism and magnificent spirit.'

When the first bomb hit Buckingham Palace, Elizabeth was almost relieved, remarking that she finally felt she could look the people of the East End in the face. It certainly seems to have marked a change in attitudes to the royals when they visited affected areas. This quote however, famous in the 1940s, has since been sharply critiqued as an example of privileged cluelessness, since even with the bomb attack on 'dear old BP' Elizabeth had been able to recuperate that night in the luxury and comparative safety of Windsor Castle. Elizabeth was not stupid, and elsewhere in her letters she makes it clear that her troubles could not compare to those of working-class communities. She also strongly resented those in the upper class who continued to dance the night away throughout the Blitz. Her comment articulated that she did not feel her family should remain unscathed, rather than any mistaken belief that her sufferings were now equal to those of the people she met in the East End. It is not, however, a quote that has necessarily dated well.

In terms of what to wear to the bombed neighbourhoods, the Queen's wardrobe was again devoid of black. As with the French visit of 1938, it was felt to send too depressing a message. Instead, she wore lilacs, pinks and blues, usually one colour, even one hue. None of these colours were traditionally associated with despair, and they would not show the dust from the bomb sites. Churchill's government stipulated that her clothes should neither look too shabby, as it suggested defeatism, nor too ostentatious, which suggested her being out of touch.

The relationship between Elizabeth and the East End came to be one of the most special to her from her time as Queen. Every year on her birthday until the end of her life, a residents' group representing East End survivors of the Blitz sent a birthday cake to the Queen Mother's residence. Aged eighty-seven, she visited the Queen's Head pub on Flamborough Street, where she asked the landlord, Vic Jones, if he would teach her how to pour her own pint. 'I was told three months before that it was happening,' Jones said about the 1987 visit, 'and I was warned not to tell anyone until ten days beforehand. My family had been in the trade since 1881 – they ran the Bull's Head in Duckett Street. But the Blitz hit us badly. We lost twenty-two members of the family – grandfather, uncles, cousins. So it did feel relevant when the Palace approached me about her visit. The Palace bloke said: "Don't worry. She will make you feel at ease." I didn't believe him. But he was right. She was terrific. You have to remember she was an old lady. I shook her hand and she felt like a sparrow and I was so scared I might crush her. I asked her what she wanted to drink and she asked for a pint of Special. She poured it herself and she knocked back at least three-quarters of it. I have to say I was impressed.'

Charles Friend, who later became the Pearly King of Poplar and the Isle of Dogs, remembered when Elizabeth visited his street after it was hit by the Luftwaffe: 'I was about thirteen, and it is a day I will never forget. She had a word for everybody. She came and chatted as if she had known them all her life. It was a real morale booster to the East End. My mother and her friends were in tears, something I had never seen before. She was fabulous. We never forgot her and she never forgot us. She was the greatest royal favourite there has ever been, and she would always be Number One.'

During these visits, Elizabeth broke with protocol and held babies while their mothers showed them around their homes. She put her arms round people as they sobbed, and said, 'Perhaps I can try. I'm rather good with dogs,' as she coaxed a family's pet out of a half-collapsed house, from which the terrified pup refused to budge. Bill Bartley, who also met Elizabeth at the East End bomb sites, recalled, 'There was still an air raid on when she walked through the rubble. I always thought the world of her. She doesn't sit back pompous-like. I remember her putting her arm round people covered in blood and grime and consoling them.' Elizabeth repeated this behaviour whenever she visited cities targeted by the Luftwaffe. Lord Harlech, the Civil Defence Commissioner for the North-East of England, told a friend, 'When the car stops, the Queen nips out into the snow and goes straight into the middle of the crowd and starts talking to them. For a moment or two they just gaze and gape in astonishment. But then they all start talking at once. "Hi! Your Majesty! Look here!"'

46. Grinning Liz

Around the dinner party tables of the capital, the Queen's popularity with the middle and working class counted against her. In the sepulchral gloom of dining rooms with their windows resentfully blacked out to confuse the Luftwaffe, a diner sensed a mood of 'eighteenth-century malice' when the Queen's name came up in conversation. Eyebrows arched and lips curled in a milieu where Elizabeth's weight gain was judged a more damning indictment than her in-laws' fascism. As the port was passed, you might hear the views of the Welsh newspaper tycoon, Lord Kemsley, who thought the King and Queen reeked of 'ineptitude, incompetence and lack of all imagination', although he dared not attack them in his newspapers for fear of a public backlash. To the discontented remnants of the Appeasement brigade and their friends, the King 'sounds almost idiotic' because of his speech impediment. At a similar party, you might find Bertie's youngest sibling, the Duke of Kent, laughing with

Chips Channon at his brother's middle-class financial habits: 'Do you know what Bertie does with his money?' the Duke asked Channon. 'Why, he *invests* it!' At another, one might have heard the exiled Crown Prince of Greece sneering to his friends about Queen Elizabeth's manners. Did you know, she hadn't kissed him or his brother on the cheek by way of greeting? Maybe she had not learned how to be truly royal yet, mused the Crown Prince.

Seeing only each other, talking to nobody who thought any differently to themselves, this group distracted themselves from their own dwindling relevance by predicting that it was only a matter of time before the King and Queen, perhaps even the monarchy itself, lost its appeal. After all, Elizabeth was 'treacherous and snobbish for all her charm'. Being called snobbish by this set was hypocrisy on the scale of being called prejudiced by Mussolini. Elizabeth's smiles while visiting people were mocked by baroquely named nonentities such as the Vicomtesse de Janzé, a British socialite married to a French aristocrat, who gave the Queen the derisive nickname 'Grinning Liz'. It stuck. Even the Duke of Kent started using it, behind her back.

47. The worst mistake of my life

Two years after the Second World War ended, and just before dinner, the Queen handed a Bible to Jan Smuts, Prime Minister of the Union of South Africa. The Bible had once belonged to Paul Kruger, Afrikaner President of South Africa until he was defeated by the British during the Second Boer War in 1902. A British soldier had stolen the Krugers' family Bible as a spoil of victory. Forty-four years later, his widow heard that the Royal Family were going on a state visit to South Africa, so she wrote to the Queen with the request that she bring the Bible back to its homeland.

On the tour, the royals met a surviving veteran of the Boer War, who told Elizabeth that they would never forgive the English for what they had done. To which the Queen smoothly replied, 'I understand perfectly. We feel very much the same in Scotland, too.' She shocked her hosts by walking over to talk to inmates from a local leper colony and quickly recovered her balance seconds before becoming airborne when the red carpet she was walking upon was found regrettably to be still attached to the train slowly easing away behind her. During an expedition to an ostrich farm, the King was invited to clip the tail of one of the birds. There was a moment's awkwardness when everyone could see he had performed the task incorrectly, whereupon the Queen swooped in to spare him any embarrassment and whacked the right amount off in one go. 'We do a lot of gardening at home,' she beamed, scissors aloft. 'The King is good at digging and weeding. It is I who concentrate on the secateurs.'

The King initially seemed to be on excellent form. A gentleman in the crowd had slathered a huge amount of brilliantine gel into his hair. On the positive side of things, this holds the hair intact like a slab of marble, but it also suffers the somewhat negative side-effect of attracting bees, quite a few of whom emerged as he doffed his cap to bow to the King. George VI told him not to worry because it is better to have bees in the bonnet than ants in the pants.

Behind the scenes, the King was struggling. He lost a stone in weight over the course of the South African tour and, onboard their train, he seemed exhausted. Before he left Britain, the Prime Minister, Clement Attlee, had emphasised to the King how important it was that the visit be a success. Since 1910, in the aftermath of British victory in the Second Boer War, South Africa had technically been a monarchy, operating as a self-governing protectorate of the British Empire. Many in the Boer community, which consisted mostly of the white Afrikaans-speaking descendants of Dutch colonists, were still strongly anti-British and anti-monarchy. The royals' visit came just before a general election in South Africa at which the Afrikaans-led National Party was expected to make major gains. The National Party's two principal aims were to create an independent South African republic and to introduce a system of rigid racial segregation: Apartheid.

Before sailing to South Africa with her parents, Princess Margaret, then sixteen, told her grandmother Queen Mary that she had never met anybody who was not white before. Upon arrival, Margaret wrote, with some surprise, that the white people did not seem very nice in South Africa. This view was shared by the Prime Minister's representative to the royal party, who described 'disgusting behaviour' from 'a large percent of the so-called top-notchers of either Cape Town or Port Elizabeth'. Adding to the opposition from the Afrikaans community to the royals visiting in the first place, there was almost a diplomatic incident over the King's insistence on personally pinning medals on black war veterans; the pro-Apartheid movement claimed that white people had to be kept completely separated from other races, even invoking absurd 'medical' conspiracy theories to promote their claims. Neither, when the King and Queen were overheard referring to the South African police as 'the Gestapo', were their comments well received by white South African nationalists.

The constant supervision, interference and criticism, as well as the dawning realisation that the tour was not going to do enough to bolster support for the pro-British faction in South Africa, contributed to the King's depression. Although they had flown to Belfast for the victory celebrations at the end of the war in 1945, the Queen remained nervous about aeroplanes, which perhaps explains why all their travel within South Africa was by rail or road. During their drive to Johannesburg, the King snapped: he launched himself into a confused and confusing tirade, shouting directions at his baffled chauffeur. The Queen tried to soothe her husband, while his daughters attempted to cover up their father's panic by making good-natured jokes. As the chauffeur became more and more unsure, the King's equerry, a war hero named Group Captain Peter Townsend, turned round from the front passenger seat to shout at the King, 'For Heaven's sake, shut up, or there's going to be an accident!' That evening, the King came to Townsend to apologise: 'I am sorry about today. I was very tired.'

Two high-profile public royal murders in Elizabeth's lifetime had taken place in motorcades – those of Archduke Franz Ferdinand of Austria in 1914 and of King Alexander I of Yugoslavia in 1934 – and she worried over her husband's safety. As they were being driven through cheering crowds in Pretoria, Elizabeth saw a man from the Zulu community slip past the police lining the royal route. They began chasing after him as he ran towards the car, shouting something they could not hear over the crowd and the cars' engines. When he reached the door of the slow-moving royal automobile, its top down, Elizabeth threw herself in front of her husband, raised her parasol and smacked the man with it. He stumbled back and was caught by the police, who took him away. Days later, Elizabeth was horrified to hear that the man had been shouting, 'My Princess!' (some sources say it was 'My King!') and he was carrying a card that he wanted to give to the Princess Elizabeth for her twenty-first birthday. The South African police had dragged him away as the motorcade drove on and they then beat, punched and kicked him until he lost consciousness. Decades later and in old age, Elizabeth still referred to the events of that day as 'the worst mistake of my life'.

After the National Party's victory, Elizabeth would not meet a South African head of state until she had tea with President Nelson Mandela in 1996. In the years between, Mandela had spent twenty-seven years in prison as the most famous opponent of the Apartheid that Elizabeth's 1947 visit had so spectacularly failed to prevent.

48. Philip Mountbatten

Elizabeth might have liked to see her eldest daughter marry a British aristocrat. The younger Elizabeth was set on one candidate, and one only – Philip, a prince who had been born on a kitchen table in Corfu as his parents fled the political turmoil that swept his uncle King Constantine I from the throne of Greece. The exiled Philip had been educated initially in Germany and then in the United Kingdom, where he joined the Royal Navy and served in the Second World War. There had been a great deal of tragedy in Philip's early life. His mother was institutionalised for years as the result of a nervous breakdown, culminating in a possible misdiagnosis of schizophrenia. Philip left Germany when his Jewish headmaster, Kurt Hahn, was forced to flee and set up a new school in Scotland; Philip was among its pupils, to the discomfiture of several of his German brothers-in-law who joined the Nazi Party. One of them, travelling with Philip's pregnant sister Grand Duchess Cecilie, was en route to a family wedding in England when their aeroplane crashed in fog. Cecilie had apparently gone into labour as the aeroplane plummeted, for her remains and those of the baby were found in the wreckage with those of her husband, her mother-in-law and Cecilie's two sons, aged six and four at the time of their deaths. Initially, Cecilie's only surviving child was her infant daughter Princess Johanna, too young to fly with the family in 1937, but who then died of meningitis two years later.

Love and support for Philip were offered by his mother's Mountbatten relatives, including his cousins Patricia and Pamela, who adored him, and by his uncle 'Dickie', Lord Mountbatten, who was Supreme Allied Commander of the South-Asia Theatre during the Second World War. Stability was provided by Gordonstoun, the Scottish boarding school founded by Philip's exiled German headmaster. Philip and Princess Elizabeth met briefly on several occasions in the 1930s and, by the tail end of the war, romantic feelings had developed. Lord Mountbatten was thrilled, so much so that Philip had to ask him to take a step back from meddling.

Neither the King nor the Queen were quite so enthusiastic. The King did not want to see the family unit break up just yet, while the Queen harboured reservations about Philip's suitability and Mountbatten's enthusiasm. She worried that Philip leaned left in his politics and that Lord Mountbatten was a little too fond of publicity – and far too fond of the Duke and Duchess of Windsor. Princess Elizabeth held her ground and, after Philip was invited to join the Royal Family at Balmoral, he reassured his putative mother-in-law with a letter in which he reflected, 'I am sure I do not deserve all the good things which have happened to me. To have been spared [death in] the war and seen victory, to have been given the chance to rest and re-adjust myself, to have fallen in love completely and unreservedly.' The night before the Westminster Abbey wedding, the King created Philip His Royal Highness the Duke of Edinburgh, Earl of Merioneth and Baron Greenwich; from his honeymoon, the new Duke wrote to his mother-in-law, 'Lilibet is the only "thing" in the world which is absolutely real to me and my ambition is to weld the two of us into a new combined existence that will not only be able to withstand the shocks directed at us but will have a positive existence for the good ... Very humbly, I thank God for Lilibet.'

In the King's letter to his eldest daughter after her wedding, he wrote, 'I have watched you grow up all these years with pride under the skilful

Glamis Castle, which has belonged to Elizabeth's family since the fourteenth century.

'The one who got away'? Elizabeth's beau, Captain James Stuart, who married her friend Lady Rachel Cavendish on Elizabeth's birthday.

Elizabeth's wedding day in 1923. From left to right: her parents Lord and Lady Strathmore, Elizabeth, 'Bertie' the Duke of York and his parents Queen Mary and King George V. Smiling was not en vogue in formal photographs.

Elizabeth, in 1932 when she was still Duchess of York, with her six-year-old daughter, the future Queen.

As queen, visiting London's Great Ormond Street Hospital for Children in 1938.

Elizabeth with her family during her Silver Wedding celebrations. Her critics, nicknaming her 'Grinning Liz', claimed she never missed a chance to steal the limelight.

The King, the Queen and Princess Margaret. Both women were shattered by the King's death, aged 56.

In Scotland in the early 1970s, the Queen Mother greets her grandson Prince Edward, the future Earl of Wessex, and the Queen.

The Queen Mother with Princess Diana, Prince William and Prince Harry at the Trooping of the Colour in 1989. The two women's relationship was about to implode, for a variety of reasons.

'Is it just me or are the pensioners getting younger these days?' was one of the Queen Mother's frequent questions in the 1990s.

In 2022, the Queen recalled, 'My mother always gave me support and encouragement. She had an infectious zest for living and an extraordinary capacity to bring happiness into other people's lives.'

The Queen Mother leaving church with her great-grandson, Prince William.

Waving to the crowds at Clarence House for her birthday celebrations.

A quick glass of champagne, offered by buggy-side members of the Toastmasters Guild on her 101st birthday.

direction of Mummy, who as you know is the most wonderful person in the World in my eyes, & I can, I know, always count on you, & now Philip, to help us in our work. Your leaving us has left a great blank in our lives but do remember that your old home is still yours & do come back to it as much & as often as possible. I can see that you are sublimely happy with Philip, which is right.'

49. Wedding times and conga lines

The Queen's nickname of 'Grinning Liz' flourished, as shown by a guest's account of Princess Elizabeth's wedding when he spotted the mother of the bride in her orange dress – 'Grinners herself looked like an inflated tangerine … She looked IMMENSE, and even her grin dampened to the minimum by the gigantic contours of her face, it was like the sun trying to shine through clouds.' A year later, on a royal visit to Paris, a spectator described the Queen's appearance as that of a 'balloon about to take off, covered in two-way stretch dove-grey with very padded-shouldered box jacket … The Queen gets very pink in the face. They say she puts a lot back.'

Elizabeth's fondness for food and drink augmented her penchant for a good time, especially now that the war was over. At parties in Buckingham Palace, she persuaded her husband, and even Queen Mary, to join her and their guests in a conga line. Elizabeth and the King celebrated their twenty-fifth wedding anniversary in 1948 and the crowds outside Buckingham Palace called for them so intensely that the King and Queen went out eight times to acknowledge their cheers. For her critics, this was yet another example of Grinners' love of the limelight.

After balcony call number seven, the King sighed, 'Why can't they leave us alone?'

Elizabeth looked at him and replied, 'One day they might *not* want us.' Grin in place, waving arm aloft, she went back out to the crowds.

VI

Widow
(1950–1960)

In the years following their silver wedding anniversary, the King's health went into rapid decline as he struggled with lung cancer. He and the Queen became grandparents when their daughter the Princess Elizabeth, Duchess of Edinburgh, gave birth first to Prince Charles in 1948 and then to his sister, Princess Anne, in 1950. They were indulgent and affectionate grandparents; as Elizabeth admitted, 'Half the fun of being a grandmother is being able to spoil your grandchildren.' On her father's orders, his deteriorating health was kept from the Princess during her pregnancies.

There was a political changing of the guard in 1951 when the Conservatives won the General Election, which brought Winston Churchill back as Prime Minister. The Queen had hoped that peace would bring an easier schedule, certainly a less worrying one, for the King. It was not to be. When a mutual friend told her that he had recently seen the Duke of Windsor, who looked so well rested, the Queen replied, 'Yes, who has the lines under his eyes, now?' The King, who put himself under a great deal of pressure to fulfil his constitutional duties, had a temper, which Elizabeth calmed by taking his wrists as if she needed to take his pulse, while saying, 'Tick, tick, tick,' until the King laughed or relaxed. He worried over the country's economic downturn after 1945 and he continued to smoke heavily, although the health implications of that were not fully understood at the time.

While she focused on her husband's recuperation from various, and increasingly frequent, bouts of ill health, the Queen felt betrayed by her children's former governess, Marion Crawford, who signed a book deal with an American publishing house to write about her experience working for the royals. Elizabeth was enraged by 'Crawfie's' new venture. As Princess Margaret reached her eighteenth birthday and no longer needed a governess, Crawfie had been granted a cottage in the grounds of Kensington Palace, the decoration of which was paid for, as a retirement gift of sorts, by Queen Mary.* Queen Elizabeth begged 'my dear Crawfie', in person and by letter, not to publish:

> *I do feel, most definitely, that you should not write and sign articles about the children, as people in positions of confidence with us must be utterly oyster, and if you, the moment you finished teaching Margaret, started writing about her and Lilibet, well, we should never feel confidence in anyone again. I know you understand this …*
> *Having been with us in our family life for so long, you must be prepared to be attacked by journalists to give away private and confidential things, and I know that your good sense & loyal affection will guide you well. I do feel most strongly that you must resist the allure of American money & persistent editors, & say No No No to offers of dollars for articles.*

The resulting book, *The Little Princesses*, was an affectionate piece of fluff that became an international bestseller. Given what came later in terms of royal tell-alls, *The Little Princesses* reads like a love letter, the gentle wholesomeness of which could comfortably pass censorship by a Sunday School teacher. Elizabeth did not care. Its tone did not concern her; its existence in the first place was an invasion of her family's privacy. She was aghast at reading details like what her daughters had eaten for breakfast as children or what kind of nursery games she and the King had played with them. According to Lady Astor, the King was also upset by the book, and 'Princess Elizabeth is deeply shocked & hurt & furious'.

---

* Called Nottingham Cottage, it was a grand retirement gift. From 2011 to 2013, it was the home of William and Catherine, Duke and Duchess of Cambridge. From 2013 to 2019, it was Prince Harry's residence, where he proposed in 2017 to his then-girlfriend Meghan Markle. The Duke and Duchess of Sussex left for Frogmore Cottage in 2019.

Crawfie was never forgiven or received back into court circles. While Queen Elizabeth's displeasure is to some degree understandable, she did not seem to realise the extent to which Marion Crawford had been pressured by her editors, who changed whole passages 'word by word, line by line' in her manuscript, or by her new husband, Major George Buthlay, a manipulative womaniser who encouraged his wife to do whatever the publishers asked. Under Buthlay's influence, Crawfie said yes to every offer for a paid article that came her way. This continued until she wrote an article in which she purported to have been an eyewitness at an annual royal event in London and sent the article to an American magazine who published it, only to find out that the event had been cancelled at the last minute due to a national strike. After that, Crawfie's credibility was somewhat less than unassailable.

50. Sissinghurst

As of 1947, Elizabeth had spent more of her life being royal than otherwise. As time went on, this led to increasingly ridiculous moments. Within the monarchy's property portfolio, there were various properties, like Crawfie's cottage, which were either gifted or offered at a reduced rental rate to serving or retired courtiers and servants. Elizabeth suggested that one in Windsor Great Park be offered to Captain Oliver Dawnay, her Private Secretary from 1951 until 1956.[1] When Dawnay and his wife went to see the proposed house, they were shocked by how large it was and wondered how much it would cost to heat such 'a barracks of a place'. They declined Elizabeth's offer with the respectful ruse that the house wasn't quite right for their two small children. She nodded sympathetically as she said, 'Yes, I knew it would be too small.'

The Queen lunched with Vita Sackville-West and her husband Harold Nicolson, after Nicolson received the commission to write the official biography of Elizabeth's late father-in-law George V. They hosted her at Sissinghurst, their once-dilapidated Tudor manor house in Kent, which they had lovingly restored. She had a wonderful afternoon, as she told

Tommy Lascelles: 'What I particularly liked was that the Nicolsons had gone to no special trouble for me – it was just like a cottage meal!'

'No special trouble' was an interesting take on the Nicolsons' preparations. They had decorated their table with their best dinner service and enough huge bouquets of flowers to shame an Easter parade in Rotterdam.

51. I'll see you in the morning

'I must tell you that we were ideally happy, due to the King's wonderful kindness & goodness and thought for others. I never wanted to be with anyone but him, & during the last ten terrible years, he was a rock of strength and wisdom & courage. So that in thanking you for your letter, I thank you also for the advice you gave the King in 1922.' Shortly after her husband died, aged fifty-six, in February 1952, Elizabeth wrote these words to a friend who, thirty years earlier, had encouraged Bertie to propose to Elizabeth one last time.

George VI's last day alive had been a happy one. He, Elizabeth and Margaret were at Sandringham. A week earlier, they had gone to London Airport to see Princess Elizabeth and the Duke of Edinburgh off on tour to Australia and New Zealand. The original plan had been for the King and Queen to go, until his doctors advised against it, and so the Edinburghs left Charles, aged three, and Anne, not yet two, in the care of the King and Queen as they set off, via Kenya, for Australia. The Pathé newsreels at the airport captured the Queen blowing a kiss to her daughter. Contrary to the cheerful optimism of the newsreader who told listeners and viewers that 'it is wonderful to see His Majesty looking so well', the King looked gaunt and exhausted.

On 5 February, the King went shooting on the Sandringham estate during the day and, after dinner, looked over new paintings with the Queen and Princess Margaret. Mother and daughter had been visiting friends all afternoon, including the artist Edward Seago, from whom the Queen had commissioned the paintings a few months before. '[The King] was enchanted with them all,' Elizabeth wrote, 'and we spent a very happy time looking at them together.' After dinner, the King listened to the BBC news before going to the kennels to check on Roddy, his golden retriever, who had cut his paw in the fields earlier that day. The King grabbed a copy of *Country Life* magazine, said to his wife, 'I'll see you in the morning,' and went to his bedroom on the ground floor, where he had been sleeping following an operation to remove part of his lung. He opened his window for a little fresh air, went to bed, and passed away while asleep. Elizabeth was having morning tea in her bedroom when the King's equerry arrived to inform her that she was a widow.

After seeing her husband's body, Elizabeth ordered that there be someone on vigil throughout so that he would 'not be left alone'. She went to the Nursery to see their two grandchildren.

'Don't cry, Grannie,' three-year-old Prince Charles comforted, before he was told that his grandfather was gone. The news that she was Queen Elizabeth II was sent to the former princess in Kenya, from where she immediately returned home with her husband, as Prime Minister Winston Churchill delivered a moving tribute to George VI via radio.

'When the death of the King was announced to us yesterday morning there struck a deep and solemn note in our lives which, as it resounded far and wide, stilled the clatter and traffic of twentieth-century life in many lands, and made countless millions of human beings pause and look around them,' he began. Churchill praised the late King's 'example as a husband and a father in his own family circle, his courage in peace or war – all these were aspects of his character which won the glint of admiration, now here, now there, from the innumerable eyes whose gaze falls upon the Throne'.

To his radio audience of millions, Churchill reflected on the king he had come to know during the Second World War:

His conduct on the Throne may well be a model and a guide to constitutional sovereigns throughout the world today and also in future generations. The last few months of King George's life, with all the pain and physical stresses that he endured – his life hanging by a thread from day to day, and he all the time cheerful and undaunted, stricken in body but quite undisturbed and even unaffected in spirit – these have made a profound and an enduring impression and should be a help to all. He was sustained not only by his natural buoyancy, but by the sincerity of his Christian faith.

During these last months the King walked with Death as if Death were a companion, an acquaintance whom he recognized and did not fear. In the end Death came as a friend, and after a happy day of sunshine and sport, and after 'good night' to those who loved him best, he fell asleep as every man or woman who strives to fear God and nothing else in the world may hope to do ... No Minister saw so much of the King during the war as I did. I made certain he was kept informed of every secret matter, and the care and thoroughness with which he mastered the immense daily flow of State papers made a deep mark on my mind ...

Let me tell you another fact. On one of the days when Buckingham Palace was bombed the King had just returned from Windsor. One side of the courtyard was struck, and if the windows opposite out of which he and the Queen were looking had not been, by the mercy of God, open, they would both have been blinded by the broken glass instead of being only hurled back by the explosion. Amid all that was then going on, although I saw the King so often, I never heard of this episode till a long time after. Their Majesties never mentioned it or thought it of more significance than a soldier in their armies would of a shell bursting near him. This seems to me to be a revealing trait in the royal character.

Just before announcing 'God Save The Queen' for the first time since the death of Victoria half a century earlier, Churchill turned his attention to the widowed Elizabeth: 'May I say – speaking with all freedom – that our hearts go out tonight to that valiant woman, with the famous blood of Scotland in her veins, who sustained King George through all his toils and problems, and brought up with their charm and beauty the two daughters who mourn their father today. May she be granted strength to bear her sorrow.'

52. The House of the Northern Gate

The famous 'Three Queens' photograph, captured by photographer Ron Case, showed Elizabeth's face, in the depths of grief behind her mourning veil, a few days after her husband's death. It became one of the most famous photographs of the decade, and among the most renowned royal photographs of the century; in it, Elizabeth stands next to her mother-in-law Queen Mary, who in turn is next to the new Queen Elizabeth II. Princess Margaret, out of shot, was with them as they waited for the King's coffin to be brought to its lying-in-state at Westminster Hall where, over the next three days, 304,000 people filed past to pay their respects. As Queen Mary, herself in poor health, watched the King's cortège pass by the windows of her home at Marlborough House, a lady-in-waiting heard her whisper, 'There he goes.'

In the months after her husband's funeral Elizabeth, now the Queen Mother, struggled. Lionel Logue recommended a medium, who was allegedly blindfolded before being escorted from her home in Wembley to meet the Queen Mother. Less relatable was Elizabeth's unhappiness at vacating Buckingham Palace to move into Clarence House, a nineteenth-century mansion within walking distance of the palace and originally built for King William IV, who had been Duke of Clarence before his accession. Elizabeth II had to put her foot down to her mother's entreaties that she be allowed to continue living at Buckingham Palace, in defiance of the usual etiquette for widowed queens.

There was an avalanche of condolence letters. Among those she answered personally was one from the former Prime Minister, Clement Attlee, who was so shocked by the King's death that Labour Party colleagues thought he arrived at a meeting 'looking like he had a stroke' on the day the news broke. Attlee's subsequent tribute to the King in the House of Commons was one of the few times, by his own admission, that he ever struggled to keep his emotions in check in public. Churchill had once joked that Britain was the only country to have a government led by socialists who were in favour of a monarchy.

Queen Mary had been right, in the 1920s, when she concluded that Elizabeth would be the making of Bertie. He was an inherently good man, kind, diligent and dutiful, yet he was painfully insecure, prone to intense anxiety that in its turn fuelled self-doubt, occasional outbursts of ferocious bad temper, and depression. His stammer and lack of confidence were especially debilitating in a monarch who took the throne at the dawn of the media age, when photographers, newsreel cameras and radio made it impossible to hide such issues as had many leaders in the past. Elizabeth had tirelessly encouraged her husband to see therapists to help him, and she had kept going until they found the right one in Lionel Logue. She had calmed Bertie, encouraged him, loved him, and they seemed to have a wonderful time in each other's company. With the benefit of hindsight, and even from the vantage point of a more cynical time, it is hard to imagine a king and queen better suited to their duties during the war years. Despite knowing that her husband was ill, Elizabeth had clung to the belief, on increasingly slender evidence, that she had years left with him, a mistake which added shock to grief. With the King gone, she also felt isolated, as one of her ladies-in-waiting reflected: 'Loneliness is the hardest thing to bear, not having by you the one person to whom you can say anything and everything.'

Still in mourning, the Queen Mother went home to Scotland. There she was asked to stay with Commander Clare Vyner and his wife, Doris, at their home in Caithness, which bore the glorious name 'The House of the Northern Gate' and offered views towards Orkney, just over a dozen miles across the sea. Lady Doris's friendship with the Queen Mother had begun in childhood and they had remained close throughout Elizabeth's time as queen.

Of the Scottish 'whirly wind' that blew in off the sea, the Queen Mother hoped, 'It'll blow the cobwebs away!' She and the Vyners took long walks along the 'rugged glory of a magnificent coastline', where her hosts showed Elizabeth the near-derelict Barrogill Castle, with its erratic distribution of roof tiles through which rain and sea-spray had added a sheen of green mould to the crumbling staircase. Built for the 4th Earl of Caithness during the reign of Mary, Queen of Scots, when it was called the Castle of Mey, Barrogill's best days seemed long behind it. The castle had been requisitioned by the army during the war and then returned to its amiably eccentric owner Captain Frederic Imbert-Terry, who could not afford to pay the rates. It looked set to be demolished until the Queen Mother saw it for the first time in 1952 and declared, 'Never! It's part of Scotland's heritage. I'll save it.'

Captain Imbert-Terry offered the castle to her as a gift, since he felt he could not justify charging anyone for it, given its state of disrepair. The Queen Mother refused, on the grounds that members of the Royal Family cannot legally receive gifts in that manner nor of that magnitude. He then set the nominal fee of £100 and Barrogill became the Queen Mother's home in what she lovingly called 'the most remote part of the world'. She changed Barrogill's name back to the Castle of Mey and began plans for its restoration.[2]

The Queen Mother's purchase raised alarm bells in London, where Churchill worried it would function as a sort of retirement home for her. He felt, considering the Queen Mother's popularity, that it would be a great mistake for her to retreat into a widowhood in which she undertook few public appearances. He was just about old enough to remember how unpopular isolation had made Queen Victoria after the death of her husband Albert. None of Elizabeth's three predecessors as widowed queens consort had completely retired from public life or duties and, as Elizabeth herself often said, 'Traditions exist to be kept.'[3] Churchill considered the matter important enough that he flew to Scotland to speak with the Queen Mother in person. 'Your country needs you, Ma'am,' was only part of Churchill's conversation with Elizabeth, but it was the crux. The Queen Mother eventually agreed with the Prime Minister that she still had a duty to the monarchy.

During her grieving, the Queen Mother was sent a book of verse by her friend, the actress Dame Edith Evans, who had just filmed her soon-to-be-iconic turn as Lady Bracknell in the film adaptation of Oscar Wilde's *The Importance of Being Earnest*. (Anyone who has heard Evans' delivery of 'A handbag?' will not forget it.) During one of her walks in Scotland, the Queen Mother took Evans' gift with her to read and later wrote to her friend:

It is giving me the greatest pleasure. I took it out with me and started to read it sitting by the river. It was a day when one felt engulfed by great black clouds of unhappiness and misery. I found a sort of peace stealing round my heart. I found hope in George Herbert's poem 'who could have thought my shrivel'd heart could have recovered greenness …' And I thought how small and selfish is sorrow. But it bangs one about until one is senseless and I can never thank you enough for giving me such a delicious book wherein I found so much beauty and hope, quite suddenly one day by the river.

Elizabeth said later that walking in Scotland, with a face red and slightly stinging from the elements, was among the things which made her happiest. Grief, for her, was not overcome so much as managed by doing things, even if it was initially nothing more than very long walks. For months after her husband's death, she was bereft, crying in front of her daughters and expressing to her friends the bewilderment that comes from bereavement. She was fiercely protective over her husband's legacy for the rest of her life, consistently emphasising his contribution to their success when it was increasingly attributed by historians solely, or largely, to her: 'It was not me,' she said, more than once. 'We did it together.'

Still wearing mourning, her return to public appearances began three months after the funeral with an inspection of the Black Watch regiment, in which her brothers had served and her brother Fergus and nephew John had been killed. Her speech, delivered as the Black Watch was preparing for deployment to the war in Korea, was short and she referred to the regiment as 'so dear to my heart and to many of my family'. There was a relapse in her grief a few weeks afterwards and it was the end of 1952 before she returned to a public schedule that would remain busy until 2001.

'I love life,' she reflected later, 'that's my secret. It is the exhilaration of others that keeps me going. Quite simply, it is the people who keep me up. I love talking. Meeting people is good for me.'

There were various options as to what to call Elizabeth now that she was a widowed queen.* She felt that including the word 'dowager' in her

---

* A brief note on the different titles appropriate to a British queen is included in the Author's Note.

new title would make her sound as old as God's governess, so she rejected it. The suggestion of 'queen mother', first used for Charles II's mother in 1649, was proffered and accepted.* Elizabeth became, officially, Queen Elizabeth the Queen Mother. Her critics speculated that Grinners had managed to score a title whereby she was referred to as a queen twice as much as anybody else.

53. Prince Paul's chocolates

The Queen Mother held a strong set of beliefs pertaining to chocolate. Specifically, that the posher a box of chocolates were, the greater the risk to their taste, as there was a tendency to concoct a series of dubious flavours, all of which sounded elegant and none of which had any business being wedged into a chocolate shell. Then, everyone pretended to like them lest they be mocked for an unsophisticated palate. The Queen Mother wrote effusive thank-you notes to her friend, Prince Paul of Yugoslavia, when he sent her reassuringly cheap, or reasonably priced, boxes of chocolates, into which she could safely plunge her hand without nervously consulting the menu – as she resentfully had to do with a collection sent to her from a very prestigious department store, which she had come to loathe after biting into a chocolate filled with a cream called rose petal and lavender – which, as she pointed out on several occasions, were the same ingredients as bath salts. She was back on the issue of sub-par posho-chocs in another letter to Prince Paul about his chocolates, when she wrote, 'The extraordinary thing is, that they are _all_ good! I have never had a box of chocolates before which didn't have pink flavoured bath-salts, or nougat made of iron filings & sand, and it is so exciting to _know_ that yours are all delicious!'

---

* For clarity's sake, for the rest of this book, 'Queen Elizabeth' and 'the Queen Mother' will be used to refer to the main figure, while 'the Queen' or 'Elizabeth II' refers to her daughter. From 1952 to 2002, when courtiers or British writers referred to 'Queen Elizabeth' they typically meant the Queen Mother, since The Queen became her daughter, Elizabeth II.

54. Group Captain Townsend

Group Captain Peter Townsend had been one of George VI's favourite equerries. Handsome, polite, a devout Protestant and a decorated Royal Air Force veteran, Townsend was one of Churchill's 'Few', having taken part in the aerial Battle of Britain during the worst days of the Blitz, when the RAF's victory prompted Churchill's famous remark, 'Never in the field of human conflict was so much owed to so many by so few.' Following George VI's death, the Royal Family came to value Townsend so much that the Queen Mother invited him to join her household as its Comptroller. Long working hours had often taken Townsend, by then in his late thirties, away from his wife Rosemary; news of her subsequent affair soon trickled through the Royal Household's gossip mill, where it elicited sympathy for Townsend until rumours began that he seemed very fond of the Queen Mother's youngest daughter, Princess Margaret.

Margaret, in her early twenties, was devastated by her father's death. Like her mother, she seemed to have clung to the hope that the recent operation on her father's lungs had bought him a reprieve, perhaps by a span of years. A year after the King's funeral, Margaret and Townsend told the Queen Mother that they were in love and planned to marry once Townsend had divorced Rosemary. According to Townsend, Queen Elizabeth seemed calm and sympathetic to their situation. 'Seemed' being very much the operative word.

There was a sixteen-year age gap between the princess and the pilot. The more significant gap from the Queen Mother's perspective lay in the relatively short window between her father's death and Margaret's announcement that she wanted to marry his former confidant. She asked Tommy Lascelles to come to see her. Lascelles, who had delayed his retirement to stay on as the monarch's Private Secretary for the transitional first year of Elizabeth II's reign, recalled that the Queen Mother wept as she told him Margaret's news. Lascelles did not feel moved to confess that he had in fact known about the liaison for months, having tried to warn Townsend during a visit to Balmoral six months earlier, when 'I told him that it was being commonly, and widely, said that he was seeing too much of Princess Margaret.' He had spoken to Townsend again at Christmas, two weeks before the Queen Mother was informed, by which point Margaret had told her sister and the Duke of Edinburgh.

The Princess agreed to her family's request that she wait and seek advice, which from the government was not encouraging, although far less damning than is usually presented. Attitudes towards divorcees' remarriage had softened between 1936 and 1953, and the British public were mostly supportive of the Princess's romance with a Battle of Britain hero. Ultimately and notoriously, the couple did not marry, officially because Townsend's divorce made him an unsuitable husband for the Queen's sister.

Decades later, one of Queen Elizabeth's employees told a historian: 'The Queen Mother also thought that it was a terrible mistake that everyone had made such a fuss over Princess Margaret wanting to marry Group Captain Peter Townsend. She thought that if they had been allowed to marry, her younger daughter's life might have been much happier.' That is not, however, even remotely reflective of what the Queen Mother thought in the early to mid 1950s. Both of her daughters' initial failure to keep her in the loop meant that she assumed the worst, and did not so much leap to the wrong conclusion as toboggan into prophecies of doom. Pinpointing precisely what Elizabeth did is difficult. Some felt she did the greatest harm to Margaret's cause by doing nothing, 'ostriching' until, all of a sudden, she was roused to action and began grimly citing every possible catastrophe that the couple might face. In an echo of what had happened with her own James Stuart thirty years earlier, Townsend was suddenly found a job abroad. In his case, the post was as an attaché in the well-bred somnolence of the British embassy in Brussels. Margaret was not told about her fiancé's demotion until she too was abroad, thousands of miles away in southern Africa, as her mother's companion. Frustrated, Margaret allegedly once threw a book at her mother's head.

Once back in Britain, the Queen Mother continued to oscillate between silence and terrible warnings. She believed that the Townsend marriage would cost Margaret not only a place in the line of succession, but her Civil List salary from the government, her right to reside in the royal residences, her protection officers and her public duties. During a fraught family conversation, the Queen Mother asked where on earth Margaret was expected to live if she married Townsend, to which the Duke of Edinburgh impatiently asked his mother-in-law if she knew that, 'it is still possible, even nowadays, to buy a house'. The Duke's sarcasm, and accuracy, did not land well with an already irritated Queen Mother who left, slamming the door as she went.

Noël Coward, subsequently as good a friend to Princess Margaret as he was with the Queen Mother, recorded the atmosphere in a diary entry for July 1953:

> *During the last week a journalistic orgy has been taking place over poor Princess Margaret and Peter Townsend. He has been posted to Brussels and she is in South Africa[4] [sic] with the Queen Mother. She is returning tomorrow, poor child, to face the* Daily Mirror *poll which is to decide, in the readers' opinion, whether she is to marry a divorced man or not! It is all so incredibly vulgar and, to me, it is inconceivable that nothing could be done to stop these tasteless, illiterate minds from smearing our Royal Family with their sanctimonious rubbish. Obviously, the wretched Peter Townsend should have been discreetly transferred abroad ages ago. Now it is too late and everyone is clacking about it from John o' Groats to Land's End. One can only assume that the 'advisers' at Buckingham Palace and the Lord Chamberlain's Office are a poor lot. A welter of pseudo-religious claptrap is now swirling around the feet of the poor Princess and the unfortunate young man … I suspect she is probably in love with him but, whether she is or not, it should never have been allowed to reach the serious stage.*

Two years later, Margaret issued a statement announcing that she would not marry Townsend. We can only speculate whether this was a result of the enormous pressure placed on her or because, after so many delays, the romance, which began in difficult circumstances, had simply 'Petered out'. Margaret was far more pious in her Anglican faith than is usually supposed – she took a great interest in the Church's teachings and its liturgies – and it may be that some of her words, citing religious concerns, had more than just a grain of truth in them. As with most things in life, her decision was likely the result of a combination of factors. Noël Coward characterised the public's response to her decision as 'half the world religiously exulting and the other half pouring out a spate of treacly sentimentality. I hope she will not take to religion in a big way and become a frustrated maiden princess.'

55. Dropping out for Dior

By the end of their visit to France, the Queen Mother felt she had to apologise on her youngest daughter's behalf to Lady Cynthia Jebb, wife of the British ambassador from 1954 to 1960. Mother and daughter had arrived to stay at the embassy on their way home from an official visit to Italy and Princess Margaret had stepped off the plane to Paris seemingly the worse for wear after a heavy night out in Rome with friends. The embassy had organised a busy itinerary for the Queen Mother and the Princess, despite Lady Jebb's suspicion that the only reason that a tremblingly hungover Princess Margaret was there was 'to get her hair done by Alexandre, and to fit a Dior dress'. Her feelings towards the 26-year-old Princess did not improve throughout the visit, by the end of which Lady Jebb had concluded, 'Princess Margaret seems to fall between two stools. She wishes to convey that she is very much the Princess, but at the same time is not prepared to stick to the rules if they bore or annoy her, such as being polite to people. She is quick, bright in repartee, wanting to be amused, all the more so if it is at someone else's expense. This is the most disagreeable side of her character.'

Lady Jebb's suspicions – that finding time to meet Christian Dior and the mononymous celebrity hairdresser Alexandre were the main reason for Margaret's sojourn in Paris – were confirmed when the Princess suddenly announced she could not join her mother at an official meeting of French schoolchildren. Regrettably, Margaret had developed a terrible cold. She sniffed sorrowfully and loudly as she delivered this sad news. Lady Jebb was then accidentally informed by a maid – innocent in the Princess's ruse – that they had managed to book Alexandre to visit

Princess Margaret that afternoon. As requested, the appointment would take place when everybody else was at the children's meet-and-greet.

After that and her fitting with Dior, Princess Margaret decided to fly to England a day earlier than her mother. As she curtseyed goodbye to the departing Princess, Lady Jebb said, 'I'm so glad, ma'am, that having your hair shampooed did not make your cold worse.'

56. Her Excellency?

At the end of the 1950s there were rumours, quite possibly birthed by a bored journalist, that the Queen Mother would be the next Governor General of Canada, succeeding Vincent Massey on his retirement. Although members of the Royal Family had held the post before, the majority felt Massey should be replaced by a fellow Canadian. The Queen, when asked about this new role for her mother, laughed and put the story to bed with her reply, 'What a novel idea. I'm afraid we would miss her too much.'[5]

A new decade brought a new rumour, specifically that the Queen Mother might marry again, even that she might add another crown to her portfolio with a wedding to the widowed King Olav V of Norway. Olav, whose Swedish wife Crown Princess Märtha had died of cancer in 1954, laughed at the gossip, unlike poor Arthur Penn, a friend since Elizabeth's debutante days, who was mortified by tabloid speculation that he had proposed to her in the spring of 1960. Penn, who lost his own battle with cancer seven months later, found press intrusion into his life 'most odious', especially as there was no truth in rumours of a renewed romance.

Elizabeth had no inclination whatsoever to marry again. As much as she had loved her husband, by the 1960s she enjoyed her independence so much that, on waking each morning, her favourite thought was, 'And *what* would Elizabeth like to do today?'

VII

Queen Mum
(1960–1970)

There is a wonderful photograph from the 1960s of Elizabeth Taylor at a wedding, standing behind the Queen Mother's chair, preparing to ask her if she wouldn't mind having a photograph taken together. Affectionately nicknamed 'the Queen Mum' in the British tabloids and by many members of the public, Elizabeth remained one of the Royal Family's most popular members throughout the decade. Her Private Secretary, Sir Martin Gilliat, noticed 'how perfectly poised she always is at public occasions', although sometimes, knowing that she was only shown what people wanted her to see on official visits, she liked to wander off the pre-approved path, breezing through an unmarked door with the question, 'Oh, what's this room for?'

She trusted Gilliat and enjoyed his company, as shown by the fact that he arrived on a trial basis in 1955 which still had neither technically ended nor been reviewed when he died, unretired, in 1993. He was particularly good at putting her guests at ease. On being greeted by Gilliat, they had 'a fortifying drink pressed into their hands. And,' according to Martin Charteris, Elizabeth II's private secretary from 1972 to 1977, 'I may say that dear Martin was as generous in dispensing his own alcohol as he was in pouring Queen Elizabeth's.'

Both Gilliat and Charteris noticed a marked increase in the Queen Mother's 'ostriching' tendency. Gilliat observed 'how she hates being asked to take a decision and will dig in her toes the more she is pressed', while Charteris thought it was how 'she has learned to protect herself. What she doesn't want to see, she doesn't look at.' Elizabeth was by then aware of how she was mocked by many in what she called London's 'Smart Set'. Gilliat thought, 'She is frightened of clever people and always suspects that they are laughing at her.' There were times when she felt quite low. She told the actor Sir Alec Guinness that she had been struggling with feelings of depression. During those spells, Elizabeth spent her evenings eating alone in front of the television.

She offered significant support and advice to the Queen, who usually spoke with her mother by telephone two or three times a day when they were not together. Throughout her first ten years as monarch, Elizabeth II had won a great deal of applause for her tact, diligence and devotion to duty. The historian and columnist Kenneth Rose wrote in his diary in 1966 that the Queen 'misses nothing when ministers discuss their business with her. In twenty years' time, she will be as formidable as Victoria herself.'

As had her mother Cecilia in the 1920s, the Queen Mother kept private the details of a battle with cancer which, in 1966, seems to have resulted in the temporary fitting of a colostomy. Her daughters spent Christmas Day visiting her in hospital and the operation was followed by a series of personal donations from the Queen Mother to the Colostomy Welfare Group.[1] She pressed ahead with her 1967 tour of Canada even though, a year after, the extent of her illness continued to make itself visible. When the Queen Mother and her granddaughter Princess Anne went to the ballet with the 69-year-old King Frederick IX of Denmark, who was on an official visit to Britain with his Swedish wife, Queen Ingrid, another theatregoer thought that the Queen Mother looked 'surprisingly faded'.

57. Dear old Edwina

In February 1960, Lord Mountbatten's globetrotting wife Edwina, Countess Mountbatten, passed away and was buried at sea from the warship *Wakeful*. When told of the funeral arrangements, the Queen Mother mused, 'Dear old Edwina, she always did like to make a splash.'

58. The Countess of Snowdon

When he heard the news that Princess Margaret was engaged to the London photographer, Anthony ('Tony') Armstrong-Jones, the novelist Kingsley Amis was unimpressed, characterising it as a story in which 'a royal princess, famed for her devotion to all that is most vapid and mindless in the world of entertainment, her habit of reminding people of her status whenever they venture to disagree with her in conversation, and her appalling taste in clothes, is united with a dog-faced tight-jeaned fotog [photographer] of fruitarian tastes such as can be found in dozens in any pseudo-arty drinking cellar in fashionable-unfashionable London. They're made for each other.' A guest at the Princess's Westminster Abbey wedding in May 1960 described the mother of the bride as 'a great golden pussycat, full of sad little smiles'. Tony, with a densely populated romantic past, was ennobled as Earl of Snowdon by the Queen, although Prince Philip allegedly thought it unwise or unnecessary, an elevation by which Margaret became Her Royal Highness Princess Margaret, the Countess of Snowdon.

The relationship between Queen Elizabeth and her youngest daughter was sometimes strained, particularly in the immediate aftermath of the Townsend affair. Both could be quite cutting to each other and Margaret resented the ways in which her education had been less thorough than her sister's. Mother and daughter did, however, share a love of singing, mimicry and a drink. Apparently, one Christmas, after a potent number of pre-dinner gins and Dubonnet, the Queen Mother could not easily get the vegetables out of the serving dish and sent two consecutive spoonsful of peas into the air, which caused her and Princess Margaret to dissolve into a fit of giggles.

59. Mitfords, Marchmains and Mosleys

The six Mitford sisters, born into an aristocratic family between 1904 and 1920, have been described as the 'prototype it-girls'. Their mother, Lady Redesdale, complained that every time she saw a scandalous newspaper headline containing the words 'peer's daughter', she assumed one of hers must be involved.[2] Their only brother, Tom, was killed on active service six weeks before the end of the Second World War.[3] His sister Jessica, nicknamed 'Decca' in the family, had escaped life as a debutante to fight for socialism in the Spanish Civil War, while another sister, Unity, had emigrated to Germany to stalk her idol Adolf Hitler by finding out which cafés in Munich he liked and visiting them, day after day, until he noticed her. She later wrote home to British newspapers boasting of the marvellous activities she was invited to by the Nazi high command, such as dinner parties during which elderly Jewish citizens were herded in front of her and forced to eat grass while Unity and her fascist friends laughed at them. She was so devastated when Britain declared war on Germany that she tried to commit suicide by shooting herself in a Munich public garden. She aimed sharply enough to give herself lifelong brain damage but with insufficient accuracy to end her life. She was repatriated to Britain, where she died several years later.

By the standards of her class and generation, the youngest Mitford, Deborah, had the most conventional life of the sisters, marrying Lord Andrew Cavendish, who succeeded his father as Duke of Devonshire in 1950. She was also the family's lone defender of the Queen Mother, admitting 'I'm ¾ in love with her' and, after accompanying her on an official engagement in 1965, asserting that 'She really is *superb* at her own type of superbry.' She unintentionally gave Elizabeth her codename in the Mitfords' correspondence, 'Cake'. The Duchess and the Queen Mother had attended a wedding at which, when it came time to cut and serve the cake, the Queen Mother exclaimed 'Oh! The cake!' with such unfettered glee that Deborah was lastingly impressed by her enthusiasm.

If Deborah gave the nickname affectionately, at least two of her relatives did not use it in the same spirit. Across the Channel in Paris,

Deborah's eldest sister Nancy was one of the Queen Mother's most stri-
dent critics. Nancy, who was author of several best-selling novels about
life in the English upper class, disliked the Queen Mother almost as
intensely as she did Marie-Antoinette, the Austrian-born queen of France
beheaded by revolutionaries in 1793, for whom Nancy evinced not the
least sign of sympathy, thinking 150 years and a decapitation insufficient
reasons to let go of a grudge. Her sisters noted that they dare not even
mention an exhibition about Marie-Antoinette lest it 'set Nancy off'.
Nancy shared her dislike of both queens in letters to her friend, the novelist Evelyn Waugh, agreeing with him that, 'I'm sure the Queen is *awful*,
everything I hear confirms this impression. Probably you can't not be if
you are a Queen, excellent reason for getting rid of them as they have
here. The awfulness of Marie Antoinette surpasses imagination until you
know something about her – dying bravely is not enough & anyway most
people do as we learnt in the late war.'

After the Second World War, Nancy Mitford was joined in Paris by her
sister Diana, who arrived there with her husband Sir Oswald Mosley,
founder of the British Union of Fascists. The Mosleys, who had married
in 1936 at the home of Josef Goebbels, the Nazis' Minister for Propaganda,
had been imprisoned in Britain during the war and had continued to
promote fascism after their release.* It was 1989 before Diana Mosley
publicly conceded that the Holocaust had indeed happened; even then,
she refused to acknowledge that as many as six million Jews had been
murdered, nor that Hitler had anything to do with it. As late as 2000, she
suggested that a good idea for the European Jewish communities before
the Second World War would have been to send them to Uganda, because
it has a nice climate and is 'very empty'. When the evidence proved Hitler's
complicity in genocide, Diana reluctantly concluded that he must have
had a breakdown during the war because the lovely man she knew, with
'mesmeric' blue eyes, could never have done something so horrible.
According to Diana, prior to 1939, Hitler had apparently been nothing

---

* Hitler was guest of honour at the Mosleys' wedding. He brought carnations and
chrysanthemums for the service and the couple presented him with their marriage certificate
as a memento of the day.

but sweetness and light. The only comment from her Nazi-befriending days that she seemed to genuinely regret was the long-standing rumour that she had referred to Adolf Hitler as 'darling Hittles'.

Diana Mosley's dislike of the Queen Mother stemmed in part from her close friendship with Wallis, Duchess of Windsor, who along with her husband the ex-king, warmly welcomed the Mosleys when they relocated to Paris after the Second World War. In contrast to his new friends, the former king seemed almost remorseful over his sympathy for the Third Reich in the 1930s. Publicly, that is. Privately, the Duke of Windsor eulogised Hitler long after his death. At a Parisian supper party, he defended Nazism's policies far more vigorously than did Oswald Mosley, by telling a guest, 'You just don't understand. The Jews had Germany in their tentacles. All Hitler tried to do was free the tentacles.' Diana, who in 1980 published *The Duchess of Windsor*, an admiring biography of Wallis, felt protective of her friends. In 1976, for instance, she wrote to her sister Deborah that she blamed the Queen Mother for the sisters-in-law's feud. Diana objected strongly to 'the time-worn tale that the [Duke and Duchess of Windsor] are blamed because his abdication in 1936 made George VI die in 1953 (or whenever it was) & that being King and Queen not only killed him but half killed Cake ... Well, if Cake hated her spell as Queen I'll eat my hat & coat, & then how about all that Christianity & chat about widows, the dying, & forgiveness of sins, & loving one's enemy etc. Isn't it richly hypocritical?'

There was milder criticism of the Queen Mother from British republicans like Willie Hamilton.* Admittedly, he admired Elizabeth – a 'remarkable old lady' – more than he did any of her relatives. He characterised Elizabeth II as a constitutional 'clockwork doll' and Princess Margaret as 'completely useless' and 'a floosie'. Of the Queen Mother, Hamilton concluded, 'She makes no speeches of consequence. She gets through her public relations by pleasing facial exercises, or by purposely chatting to the "the lads in the back row" and taking a drop of the hard stuff, her native Scotch whisky. Yet, behind the matey tipple and the ever-ready smile, there lurks the mind of a shrewd businessman.'

---

* Labour Member of Parliament, first for West Fife then Central Fife, from 1950 to 1987.

Another sceptic at the cult of 'the Queen Mum' was Stephen Tennant, son of the late Scottish peer, Lord Glenconner. Stephen was a former lover of the famous First World War poet Siegfried Sassoon and one of the possible inspirations for the character of Lord Sebastian Flyte in Waugh's novel *Brideshead Revisited*. In the 1920s, Stephen had been regarded as one of the brightest of the Bright Young Things, the high-living and heavy-partying set at the centre of London Society. From his childhood visits to Glamis, Stephen had known Elizabeth for decades, and he had disliked her for almost as long. Specifically, he had never forgiven her for rejecting the romantic interest of his elder brother Christopher. 'She looked everything she was not,' Stephen wrote of the Queen Mother, 'gentle, gullible, tenderness mingled with dispassionate serenity ... Behind the veil, she schemed and vacillated, hard as nails.' Convinced that Elizabeth must have been to blame for his brother's heartbreak, Stephen felt that, before her marriage, Lady Elizabeth encouraged men to court her simply because she liked attention and that 'she picked her men with the skill of a chess player, snobbish, poised – with a rather charming vagueness. She schooled her intentions like a detective, totting up her chances. I sensed her air of puzzled disdain.'

Increasingly reclusive in later life, Stephen was offended by Elizabeth's continuing popularity with the British public, sarcastically observing, 'Oh, the Queen Mother loves all children & flowers, family love at stifling point. All her days are domestic hours ... All that she clutches turns to gold!' He may have been on to something when mocking how she was described by some of her admirers by the 1960s, for example the right-wing pundit who declared, 'Her Majesty Queen Elizabeth, the Queen Mother, is the supreme mother-figure today in a world tortured by fear, rootless, disillusioned, largely bereft of beliefs. In this bleak era of shaken values, she remains the wise, calm, smiling epitome of motherhood. The national symbol of unselfish love. She typifies Christian values.'

60. Queen of the Mey

On a clear evening at the right time of year, the Northern Lights can be seen from the Castle of Mey. Queen Elizabeth's guests would troop outside to see them, sometimes joined by their 'inspired hostess'. One of them wrote of Mey, 'There is walking and talking (occasionally shouting), swimming and sleeping, eating and feasting – and yes, singing.' Singalongs around the piano at the Castle of Mey were a regular occurrence, as they had been at Glamis decades earlier. Predictable favourites included patriotic numbers like 'Land of Hope and Glory', Scottish ballads such as the Jacobite lament 'The Skye Boat Song', and less predictably, 'She'll Be Coming Round the Mountain (When She Comes)'.

At her Scottish home, the Queen Mother continued to preside over a way of life that had always been rare but which, by the 1960s and 1970s, was hurtling towards extinction everywhere else. The structure and manners of Elizabeth's household still mirrored the Edwardian manners that she had learned at her mother's knee. If a guest had ever sent the Queen Mother a gift, it was truffled out and prominently displayed during their visit. For the smooth running of the kitchen and its staff's convenience, the guests made their choices for breakfast the night before, and it was brought to married women on trays in their bedrooms. The hat that the Queen Mother wore to church would remain in situ throughout Sunday lunch, which was always a traditional roast. She used compliments to forestall awkwardness, or insults, from one guest to another. When a gentleman to her right picked up his bowl to drink from it, she smiled, 'Yes, I always think soup tastes *much* better that way,' before anybody else felt the need to correct him. Since servants sometimes cleared the plates of everybody at the table once the Queen Mother had finished, she tactfully used her salad plate as a delaying tactic. If she noticed a fellow diner who was particularly slow at eating, she would continue to move a fork through her salad until she noticed the last guest had finished, then would set her cutlery down. The salads also came in handy when her temperamental chef went on strike, which he did periodically if colleagues upset him, prompting the Queen Mother to nod,

'Oh, well, he's obviously a bit upset, but I'm sure he'll come round eventually and get back to work. In the meantime, we shall have to eat salads.' Which they did until the storm in the kitchens abated.

Things that delighted her were greeted with 'This is a treasure!' As was a well-made drink, which might also be described as 'made to doctor's orders!' This was code for 'just what I wanted,' in the same way that 'Oh, do you really think so?' said with her head gently to one side as her hands traced her three-strand pearls, meant 'You're wrong,' and 'Do stay for lunch' meant 'and leave shortly after.' Her guests understood that, just as they knew that it was in no way an invitation to extend their stay when the Queen Mother bade them farewell with 'Do you have to leave so soon?', 'Must you go?' and 'So looking forward to seeing you again.'

When she went to Balmoral with the rest of her family, one of the Queen Mother's favourite traditions was the Ghillies' Ball,* hosted at the castle by the Queen for staff and the Royal Family. Her love for the event was shared by most of her relatives – Elizabeth taught Princess Marina the traditional Scottish folk dances called reels for the ball and, years later, Princess Diana had so much fun reeling she tore the hem of her dress. Ladies asked gentlemen to dance at the Ghillies' Ball and the Queen Mother approached a young soldier who, blushing, said he must decline as the Queen had already asked him. As the Queen Mother reeled past him later, she tapped him on the shoulder, said, 'Snob!' and then twirled off, beaming.

61. The Zoo

In July 1965, the Queen Mother accepted her youngest daughter's invitation to visit London Zoo for the opening of a new aviary that had been designed by Margaret's husband, Lord Snowdon. Her erstwhile friend Cecil Beaton was also invited and, according to his diary, he thought the Queen Mother looked 'fatter, dumpier, and more Scotch than ever … her

---

* In Scotland, a person who attends on a fishing, fly fishing, hunting or deerstalking expedition.

head encased in a peasant scarf, [while] Princess Margaret [is] done up like Empress Josephine'. When the Queen Mother laughed, 'from the gut,' Beaton noted, 'the little fat face crinkled, except for two apples in the centre of the cheeks. These remained as round and perfect as always.'

Beaton at least had the decency to confide these observations to his diary, unlike Snowdon who decided to give Beaton some face-to-face advice for his upcoming photoshoot with his wife: 'If you put a strong light directly on her face, she'll close up her eyes just out of tiresomeness and, in certain lights, her face looks fat and pulpy.'

Princess Margaret's marriage ended in divorce in 1978.

62. Save me from good intentions

Despite attempting to keep the news secret, word of the Queen Mother's cancer inevitably got out to the Royal Family's friends and hangers-on. Even those who did not know the precise cause could figure out that she had been seriously unwell and, in the aftermath, their good intentions began to weaken her spirits, in both senses of the word.

She told Princess Margaret that she was having 'very bad luck with the drinks! Perhaps because I am considered a frail invalid, I am always given delicious fruit drinks with so little alcohol that one feels quite sick! Then I ask timidly if I might have just a very little gin in it.'

63. Monsieur de Noailles' cocktail parties

In 1963, the Queen Mother had the first of several holidays as a guest of Charles, Vicomte de Noailles, a French aristocrat who took her on a tour of the Loire Valley châteaux, including the sixteenth-century hunting lodge of King François I at Chambord, with its famous double-helix staircase designed by Leonardo da Vinci, and the river-spanning palace at Chenonceau, which had been given by Henri II to his mistress in the 1540s and requisitioned almost before his body was cold by his widow in the 1550s.

The Queen Mother enjoyed her time with de Noailles as her guide and she appreciated his expertise on French royal and architectural history, as well as his knowledge of the gardens they visited. Madame de Noailles did not join them, as the Noailles' marriage had taken a little bit of a tumble when, not long after their honeymoon, she had caught her husband in bed with his beefcake of a personal trainer. It proved a little tough for marital bliss to recover from that. The Vicomtesse was so miffed at her husband's new royal friendship that she hid in the crowds and tried to start the chant, 'Down with the Queen of England!' as Elizabeth passed.

Although Elizabeth's trips to the Loire were supposed to be private, there was a certain number of dinners and parties that she felt she could not politely decline. Noailles tried to limit the running time so that the Queen Mother could still relax. As the two of them left a cocktail party, guests suspected it was less the royal 'we' and more a tease of her host when, with de Noailles at her side, she apologised with, 'We queens are at the mercy of a very tight schedule.'

64. Going self-service

'She likes all homosexuals. She likes pansies – queers as such,' concluded Sir Isaiah Berlin, Professor of Social and Political Theory at Oxford from 1957 to 1967, coincidentally, the year in which homosexuality was decriminalised in the United Kingdom. Many on the Right, although not all, opposed this decriminalisation and a politician even urged the Queen Mother to send a 'moral message' to the nation by firing any homosexuals on her staff. She replied that, if she did that, she would end up having to go self-service.

At the start of the 1960s Elizabeth's friend Kenneth Rose wondered if decriminalisation would make any practical difference to the discrimination faced by gay people in their everyday lives. He considered it doubtful 'whether one can educate public opinion sufficiently fast to diminish the sense of public repugnance to homosexual behaviour'. Roger Booth, whose friend served the Queen Mother for decades, recalled, 'Even though homosexuality was illegal until the mid-1960s, the royals took a very lordly view of that kind of illegality. They had always known homosexual men – in service and in their families – and couldn't really understand what all the fuss was about.' A dinner companion made the mistake of referring to Queen Elizabeth's absent friend, Prince Paul of Yugoslavia, by some slur. The specific word varies in the retellings, whilst remaining consistent on the fact that it was mocking Prince Paul's youthful affairs with other men. The Queen Mother apparently fixed the speaker with an icy stare before fixing her face into an even colder smile and replying, 'Yes, but *he* is also a gentleman.'

One of her footmen, William Tallon, earned the nickname 'Backstairs Billy' in reference to his growing influence in the household hierarchy and for his many male lovers. Tallon had joined Elizabeth's household when George VI was alive and, barring two years of National Service in the Royal Air Force, he stayed there until her death in 2002. Born in 1935 above his father's hardware shop in a mining town in the north-east, joining the Royal Household in his late teens had allowed Tallon to express his personality and sexuality in ways that could have cost him his life elsewhere. In 1950, he was described as 'classically tall, dark and handsome', with a flair for innuendo and for impressions of people. Having once met the Duke of Windsor, Billy delighted the Queen Mother with his impersonation of him. One of the ghillies noticed, 'The Queen Mother and William were *always* waving and smiling at each other even if they were parting company only for a few minutes – in fact, William's mannerisms and whole demeanour became uncannily like the Queen Mother. One of the footmen used to say, "Billy's the Queen Mother in bloody drag!"'

She appreciated Tallon's ironic sense of humour and struggled to hide her laughter when he whispered, 'O la di da, here she comes!' as a particularly dull gentleman of her household staff plodded towards them. Other jokes landed less smoothly. After one particularly interminable lunch, the Queen Mother said, 'That really did go rather well, don't you think, William? But perhaps we could have a little more gin next time?'

'Perhaps we should have it delivered by tanker?'

'I don't think that will be quite necessary, William.'

65. Communist confetti

Loo rolls billowed into the Queen Mother's path as she walked in procession with Peter Ustinov, who had twice that decade won Oscars for Best Actor in a Supporting Role. He had just been made Rector of Durham University where she, for two years thus far, was honorary Chancellor. As they attended a function at the university, student protesters pelted them with toilet paper; they held one end, then threw the other towards the procession. As one roll landed in her path, the Queen Mother stopped, picked it up, trailed the flailing loo paper back to the protester and smiled, 'Was this yours?'

The student nodded, silently.

'Oh, *could* you take it?' Another nod, as the toilet roll was accepted back from whence it had been thrown. 'Thank you,' followed from the Queen Mother before she pivoted back to Ustinov and the procession.

66. Lochnagar

Dotted throughout the Balmoral estate are small wooden chalets, most of them dating from Queen Victoria's reign, which can be used as bases for picnics or lunches during a day's shooting. During such events, the Queen Mother liked to hire student beaters from the Scottish universities of Aberdeen and St Andrew's. She participated less in the shoots on account of her age, although one of the students remembers her glancing towards the nearby mountains, drink in hand, and enthusing, 'Isn't Lochnagar beautiful today?' Then she would bend down in her seat, flip her head to one side and ask, 'Isn't Lochnagar beautiful, even upside down!'

One rottenly inclement day, the royal party decided to decamp to one of the nearby chalets for lunch. The Queen was confident, though alas incorrect, that the key to said chalet was in her pocket. When they arrived, they found the door bolted and the key nowhere to be found. Fortunately, the Queen could hear somebody moving about inside as rain poured on her mother, her sister, and their assorted guests. She rapped on the door.

'Who the fuck is it?' came a ghillie's gruff voice from within.

'Don't worry,' the Queen Mother trilled merrily in the downpour, 'it's only the Queen!'

67. The Dry Martini flush

In 1969, the Queen Mother attended a concert at the Royal Festival Hall in London. Afterwards, she was cornered by the director's wife who, according to a similarly trapped Cecil Beaton, 'browbeat the Queen Mother into looking at the hall's dreary museum when we were longing for our supper'. The Queen Mother once observed how much of a person's life is spent acting, since manners inevitably require a touch of deceit and self-repression. In that regard, she was a better actor than Beaton, who could not believe how hungry they were by the end of the impromptu tour.

When they finally made it to their supper, Beaton was surprised to hear 'how well' the Queen Mother was openly discussing her political opinions, something she almost never did in public. (The long-standing – and correct – assumption was that most of her sympathies were right-wing.) She believed that the best government for Britain was a Conservative one, with a strong Labour opposition. 'Most surprisingly,' she then proceeded to tell Beaton and Sir David McKenna, Chairman of British Transport Advertising, who was sitting next to her, that she was strongly 'for the Trades Unions and thought them jolly clever fellows'.

Impressed with her articulateness and surprised by her candour, Beaton concluded that the supper had been fuelled by 'masses of drinks of all sorts' and that the Queen Mother, along with several guests, had acquired a gentle glow that he described as 'the Dry Martini flush'.

68. Sprigs of heather

While her sense of fashion was becoming even more of a punchline in the 1960s than it had been in the mid-1930s, Elizabeth defiantly called her clothes 'old friends'. Since 'you never get rid of old friends', she continued to wear, year in year out when she was in Scotland, tartan skirts, a felt hat accented with a feather and jaunty sprig of heather, and a tweed jacket. When outdoors, this Caledonian uniform changed only if she decided to go fishing. One evening, she caused some concern when she did not return home until well after sunset. Suddenly, from the gloom, emerged the Queen Mother, sporting wax jacket and wellington boots and holding aloft an enormous salmon.

'*This* is what kept me!' she beamed in triumph.

VIII

Steel Marshmallows
(1970–1980)

For the Queen Mother, the social life she established in the 1960s continued into the 1970s, as did her public engagements and tours. She particularly enjoyed the social aspect of horse racing, and her friends in the racing world included the retired athlete Colonel William Whitbread, who had a very busy romantic life. He often turned up to races with whomsoever he was dating at the time, introducing the woman in question as his niece to avoid awkward questions.

Spotting Whitbread at the racecourse one afternoon with a new plus one, the Queen Mother asked knowingly, 'Billy! Another niece?'[1]

The Queen Mother's interest in racing began in earnest in 1949 after she was seated next to a jockey at dinner. Her initial investment was to go halfers with her eldest daughter on a horse called Monaveen; from there, her commitments grew until she had a stable of horses, riding in the Strathmore colours and scoring over four hundred combined victories over the decades. She insisted on being kept appraised of the horses' well-being and admitted, 'I've loved horses ever since I was a little girl. Probably one gets too fond of them.' She wept as she watched an American horse-whisperer named Monty Roberts treat one of her nervous fillies, calling his gift 'one of the most wonderful things I've ever seen in my life'. Even from her hospital bed, when she was being treated for cancer, Queen Elizabeth regularly called the stables to check that 'my darlings' were being properly looked after. At one Grand National, her horse, Devon Loch, collapsed near the winning post. According to Michael Adeane and the Duke of Devonshire, both of whom were with the Queen Mother when they heard the groan go up from the crowd, she stood and left, saying, 'I must go down and comfort those poor people.' She then dried the jockey's tears, checked on the horse and went to visit the stable lads, 'who were also in tears'.

'That's racing,' she said. 'There will be another time.'

The Queen, who shared her mother's love of the pastime, once spotted her on television at the Cheltenham races and phoned later that day to urge her to wrap up more sensibly during bad weather. It had been miserably cold, yet the Queen Mother had dressed for the beautiful summer's afternoon she wanted, rather than the gloomy one forecast.

'Don't worry, darling,' she replied. 'I've got my pearls to keep me warm.'

In her private life, by the 1970s Elizabeth was grandmother to six – the princes Charles, Andrew and Edward, Princess Anne, and Princess Margaret's two children David, Viscount Linley, and Lady Sarah Armstrong-Jones. Elizabeth II's Silver Jubilee in 1977 was marked with many celebrations across Britain, organised both by the government and local communities. It was, sadly, the first decade Elizabeth experienced without any of her siblings. Her eldest sister Mary, Lady Elphinstone, had died in 1961; Rose, by then Dowager Countess Granville, passed away in the first half of 1967, and their youngest sibling, David, in the second half.

Cecil Beaton described the Queen Mother as a marshmallow forged on a welding machine. That toughness was passed on to some of her grandchildren, particularly her eldest granddaughter. In 1974, shortly after Princess Anne's marriage to Captain Mark Phillips, their car was stopped by a man with a gun and suffering from severe mental ill health. He shot – though not fatally – her protection officer, her driver and a journalist, then pointed the gun at 23-year-old Anne, ordering her to come with him. 'Not bloody likely,' she answered. The man tried to drag her out of the vehicle, while her husband successfully fought to keep her in the car until a passer-by, boxer Ronnie Russell, rushed over and punched the assailant twice in the head. Enough unwounded policemen quickly arrived to get the patient safely away.

Politically, the issue of Northern Ireland's continued membership of the United Kingdom came to a boil in the most hideous way possible, as the country slid into a generation of political and sectarian violence –

referred to simply as 'The Troubles' – in which many atrocities were committed from 1969 to 1998. The Irish Republican Army (IRA) were forthright about their determination to target members of the Royal Family, which led, belatedly, to a steep increase in their security.

69. Sir Frederick's bathroom

Throughout the 1970s, the Castle of Mey remained Elizabeth's favourite home.[2] Guests invited for the first time might be treated by her to two traditions. The first was a stroll across the lawns, all of which were free from chemical fertilisers as per the Queen Mother's explicit instructions. 'Nobody likes them!' she informed her guests. (She was wrong, if ahead of the curve, as they were very popular in British agriculture in the 1970s.) Past the lawns, she took her debuting guests to see two enormous cannons, pointing out to sea – 'in case Napoleon ever came', Queen Elizabeth explained.

Next on the tour she showed her guests round the castle with its tartan wallpaper which, when it appeared in an American magazine, inspired the designer Ralph Lauren to create tartan and plaid wallpapers for his collections. The Queen Mother liked to inform the guests that her castle was 'either a small big house or a big small house', and to take them up to the turrets from where, in 1621, Lady Elizabeth Sinclair had thrown herself in despair after her father, the Earl of Caithness, locked her in the tower to punish her for falling in love with a local farmhand. Sinclair, known as 'the Green Lady', was said to haunt the uppermost floors of the tower from which she had jumped to her death.

Those who had already stayed at Mey on previous occasions were excused the tour. This was welcome news for one Sir Frederick, who had taken the sleeper train up from London, then grabbed a bite of something questionable for breakfast in a railway café before motoring to Mey, where he arrived while the Queen Mother was showing off to the newcomers the anti-Bonaparte ballistics. One of the servants conducted Sir Frederick to his room, where he bolted to the loo – but did not bolt the door – as he fell victim to 'rather a dicky tum-tum' in consequence of his dubious breakfast. Unfortunately, Sir Frederick had been allocated a bedroom in the turret haunted by the Green Lady and his lavatory window was the one from which, according to legend, she had leapt in 1621. Toilet-trapped by his digestive tribulations, Sir Frederick heard his hostess ascending the stairs while regaling her guests with the tragic tale of Lady Elizabeth Sinclair and her plough-toting lover. Frederick froze – not that he had much choice by way of room for manoeuvre – banking that silence too would spare him any embarrassment. Surely, the Queen Mother wouldn't bring guests in *here*?

Alas. A Green Lady did appear in Sir Frederick's turret, in the form of a tartan, wool and pearl-wearing Queen Mother who cheerfully flung open the door to the lavatory, flanked by four guests. Sir Frederick, *sans culottes*, decided that under the circumstances, bowing to the dowager queen seemed ill-advised. There was a silent beat before the Queen Mother smiled politely and turned to her guests with a regal gesture to announce, 'And *this* is Sir Frederick's bathroom!' Nodding at Sir Frederick, who remarked later that he wished he were dead, Queen Elizabeth sailed off down the corridor with her tour party, all of whom forgot to close the door.

70. The Emperor's visit

In 1971, Japan's Emperor Hirohito arrived in the United Kingdom for the first time in fifty years. Between the visits lay the Second World War, in which the two countries had been on opposing sides. The arrival of the Emperor and Empress was intended to mark a rapprochement, a quarter of a century after the war's end. This was easier for diplomats to promote than it was for veterans to support. Many survivors of the Japanese prisoner-of-war camps, some of them victims of torture, protested against the imperial visit and, as the *New York Times* correspondent noted, the London crowds were eerily quiet as the Emperor and the Queen rode in a horse-drawn carriage towards Buckingham Palace. At a pre-arranged symbol, dozens of former POWs turned their backs as the Emperor passed.

Where the Queen encouraged reconciliation, the Queen Mother marched hand in glove with her own generation. During one of the imperial trips, she was quite prepared to risk a diplomatic incident – and the deliberate humiliation of their guests – by ordering that the Japanese Sword of Surrender from 1945 be included in the objects of interest traditionally laid out for visiting heads of state. The Queen, fortunately for all concerned, swiftly vetoed the idea.

71. Even Hitler was afraid of her

The Queen Mother was a moderately good shot in everything except conversation, where her skill level rose to expert. She certainly did not miss and hit the wall when Prince Charles suggested inviting the Duke and Duchess of Windsor to stay. Prince Charles explained, 'I, personally, feel it would be wonderful if Uncle David and his wife could come over and spend a weekend. Now that he is getting old, he must long to come back and it would seem pointless to continue the feud.' He hoped that it would give him a chance to talk properly with his great-aunt Wallis, since 'it is worthwhile getting to know the better side of her'.

The Queen Mother did not think there was a better side, either to her sister-in-law or to the proposed invitation. Her relationship with her eldest grandson was a close and loving one – Princess Margaret told her mother she had never seen a grandchild as devoted to a grandparent as Charles was to her – but no amount of affection could induce the Queen Mother to soften on Wallis and David. Instead, Charles had to visit the Duke and Duchess at their beautiful home on the outskirts of Paris. He left more in sympathy with his grandmother's views, concluding that the Duchess of Windsor was 'totally unsympathetic and somewhat superficial. Very little warmth of the true kind; only that brilliant hostess type of charm but without feeling. All that she talked about was whether she would wear a hat at the Arc de Triomphe the next day. Uncle David then talked about how difficult my family had made it for him for the past 33 years.'

Studying the daily lives of the Duke and Duchess of Windsor after 1945, their existence read like Sartre's *Huis Clos* with product placement by Cartier. It is hard to tell if they were bored by an unending life of privilege with nothing to do in recompense, although Wallis's letters prove that she certainly struggled – often profoundly – with the emotional burdens and intellectual anaesthesia imposed on her by her dim-witted, permanently offended husband. The crown he had given up 'for her' became a punishing weight in Wallis's life. She was painfully aware of pressure to live up to a sacrifice that she had begged him not to make in 1936 but which she spent the rest of his life trying to compensate for. Four decades passed for Wallis of catering to David's every whim, trying to create a life in which sybaritic luxury distracted from the rolling of one pointless year into the next. If Wallis felt any embarrassment at her husband's constant – and absurd – fear of poverty, she hid it masterfully, even during incidents like their being photographed on the decks of the American luxury liner *United States* in return for a free suite across the Atlantic. Blaming himself for anything was as much of an anathema to Edward VIII as a budget. Everything had to be somebody else's fault – usually his family's, and specifically the Queen Mother's. Neither the Duke nor Wallis had thawed with regard to Elizabeth any more than she had with respect to them by 1971, when they were visited by the writer Michael Thornton.

'So,' the Duke began, 'you're planning to write a book about the Queen Mother.' He turned to Wallis. 'Well, we shall have to be extremely careful what we say on that subject, won't we darling?'

Thornton sensibly asked him why, although he presumably already knew the answer.

'I hope your book will tell the truth,' the Duke urged, 'instead of all that guff they dish out about her. Behind that great abundance of charm is a shrewd, scheming and extremely ruthless woman. But, of course, you can't quote that.'

Wallis correctly identified the Queen Mother as the main reason why they had never been welcomed to return to live in Britain, and wondered out loud if 'When we are dead, perhaps she may at last forgive us.' She confided in Thornton that Elizabeth was 'jealous of me' for marrying David, which was less credible; by then, even Wallis wasn't jealous of herself for marrying darling David.

After pushing the theory that Elizabeth must have been secretly in love with him for the thirteen years between her wedding and his abdication, the Duke said, 'My sister-in-law is an arch-intriguer, and she has dedicated herself to making life hell for both of us.'

'I heard even Hitler was afraid of her,' added Wallis, without realising that most people would see that as a compliment. Perhaps one too many evenings of playing Bridge with the Mosleys had dulled Wallis to what the name 'Hitler' meant to the rest of the world.

The Queen called on the Duke and Duchess during a state visit to Paris, but they had not reconciled with the Queen Mother when the Duke died in France from cancer on 28 May 1972. His body was brought home to England for burial and, at the funeral, as protocol demanded for widows, the Queen Mother yielded precedence to the Duchess and walked behind her. Wallis had been extremely nervous about seeing Elizabeth, although she allegedly drew some comfort from Lord Mountbatten, who greeted her at the airport with the reassurance that the Queen Mother 'is deeply sorry for you in your present grief and remembers what it was like when her own husband died'.

While both the Queen Mother and the Duchess of Windsor behaved with great dignity at their first meeting in thirty-six years, there was no warmth. For the funeral, Wallis wore a black gown, coat, hat and veil made personally for the occasion by Hubert Givenchy. The Duchess told friends that the Queen Mother looked ridiculous in a hideous hat and frumpy dress, but that everything had been done properly during her three-day stay in London. There is no record of the Queen Mother bidding her sister-in-law farewell before she returned to Paris.

72. Do you know who I am?

The Queen Mother's public engagements continued at a high volume into her seventies. She had three questions that she could fall back on if conversation dried up – 'And what do you do?' 'Have you come far?' and 'Aren't we lucky with the weather?' Meaning that the nightmare engagement was a rural retirement home on a rainy day.

One of Elizabeth's favourite stories to tell at her own expense came from an engagement she undertook at a retirement home in Norwich, when she walked over to greet an elderly resident.

The Queen Mother smiled, 'Hello.'

'Hello.'

Still smiling, 'Do you know who I am?'

The resident nodded sympathetically and said, 'If you don't know who you are, dear, there's some nice nurses at a table at the end of this corridor who can help you out.'

73. Raspberries

Granny duties became a part even of the Queen Mother's routine.[3] While the Queen and Prince Philip were on a tour of the Commonwealth, the Queen Mother took over the care of her younger grandsons, the princes Andrew and Edward. Andrew, the future Duke of York, was notoriously disliked by the royals' servants, as would become very clear between 2020 and 2022, when the litany of scandals in which he had involved himself absolved many of them of the loyalty, or timidity, that had hitherto secured their silence. One individual memorably went on record for the *Sunday Times* to say, 'He's a total dickhead, an arrogant shit.'[4] Even long before, one of the Queen Mother's equerries had described Prince Andrew as 'a rude, ignorant sod, and [I] felt like decking him' after witnessing how he spoke to his family's employees. During his stay with his grandmother, Andrew irritated a member of the Queen Mother's stable staff until the young man, close to the Prince's age, lost his temper and hit the Prince, thereby knocking him into a pile of manure. Andrew shouted that he would tell his grandmother about this and, the next day, seeing the Queen Mother walking with her corgis, the lad went over to confess to her and offer his resignation. After hearing him out, the Queen Mother waved her hand dismissively. 'You mustn't worry about it. I'm quite certain Prince Andrew deserved it.'

Aged about eight, Andrew would run outside to a guard at Buckingham Palace who had to salute him. Andrew used this as an opportunity to blow raspberries, until the guard snapped and said, 'Look! Get lost.' Andrew did, briefly, then returned with his father Prince Philip in tow.

'I understand you told my son to get lost?'

'I did, Your Royal Highness.'

'Well, why did you tell him to get lost? Come on, tell me.'

'Well, sir, he kept blowing raspberries at me and every time he comes out, I have to salute him and he's come out about twenty times now in the space of a couple of minutes.'

Prince Philip turned to Prince Andrew and shouted, 'Well, you've heard the man: go on, get lost!'[5]

74. Parlour games

When the family were in Scotland, the Queen Mother sometimes stayed at a comparatively small dower house called Birkhall in the grounds of Balmoral. She stuck to the Edwardian tradition whereby men and women separated after dinner, before reuniting for a nightcap if anybody should still be up. She adored practical jokes; after one supper, a gentleman led the other men back into the Drawing Room to see if any of the ladies were still awake. Seeing the room was empty, he turned to his companions and said, 'Thank goodness, they've all fucked off to bed!'

'I'm rather afraid we haven't,' came the Queen Mother's voice from their hiding spot behind a curtain.

75. Devoir and Dubonnet

Elizabeth quietly exhaled the French word '*Devoir*' ('Duty') to her daughters in public if she felt they needed reminding of the guiding principle. The Queen Mother, Elizabeth II and Princess Margaret regularly lunched together, during which occasions they often conversed in French. At one such lunch, the Queen decided she might, on this occasion, have another glass of wine.

'Are you sure that's wise, darling?' The Queen Mother asked. 'You know you have to reign all afternoon.'

'Oh, Mummy!'

76. The Politburo at the Palace

When, one day in the late 1940s, Queen Elizabeth walked into a corridor at Windsor Castle, she saw Anthony Blunt, Surveyor of the King's Pictures, lying on the ground as he prepared to move an enormous painting by the seventeenth-century artist, Anthony van Dyck.

'Oh Anthony, I hope that hasn't got to go. That's one of my favourite pictures,' she said.

Blunt explained that it was off for cleaning by experts. He was being helped in the task of moving it by his boyfriend, Alan Baker, who 'scrambled to my feet and was about to leave' when Queen Elizabeth said, 'Oh no, no, no,' and invited the couple to tea in her apartments. 'She was very friendly,' Baker remembered. 'They were obviously very friendly. He liked her a lot.'

Anthony Blunt – one of the great art historians of the twentieth century – was distantly related to Queen Elizabeth. His mother Hilda was a second cousin of the Queen Mother's late father.[6] Alan Baker was correct that Blunt, who was knighted in 1956 for his services to the Royal Family, liked the Queen Mother, in sharp contrast to his low opinion of her husband, whose intellectual capabilities and social awkwardness were both mocked by Blunt in his private conversations. He had liked, too, her mother-in-law Queen Mary, who attended many of his lectures and shared his love of history. He was trusted enough by the royals that, in 1945, they sent him on a secret mission to Germany to arrange for the repatriation of thousands of letters written by Queen Victoria to her eldest daughter, wife of the German Kaiser Friedrich III and mother of Wilhelm II. By 1945, the documents were held by a German princess who, having lost sons in both world wars, had become fanatically anti-British; it says a lot for Blunt's diplomacy that he persuaded her to part with the late Empress's letters.

The extent of the British royals' trust in Blunt, and his friendship with the Queen Mother, are particularly remarkable in light of the fact that Sir Anthony was a KGB agent. Having been recruited by the Soviets during his student days at Cambridge in the 1930s, he persuaded people in Britain that he had renounced his youthful support for Communism, while remaining active as a Communist spy until the early 1960s. The Queen Mother attended a lunch on the day the scandal of Blunt's espionage broke to the public, thanks to the publication in 1979 of the book *Climate of Treason* by investigative journalist Andrew Boyle. When a fellow guest at the lunch, unable to contain his curiosity, asked her what she thought of Blunt, she coldly shut the question down with, 'Lovely day, isn't it?'

The Queen Mother was strongly anti-Communist in her views. In a conversation with President Eisenhower years earlier, she fully supported the British and American positions during the Cold War, telling the President, 'We must be firm' against the Soviet Union. She was horrified by the enforced spread of Communism into eastern Europe in the years after 1945 and, in a remark that many interpreted as something she hoped would make its way back to Blunt, 'The one person I cannot stand is a traitor.'

Yet, years later, when she was prepared to talk about Blunt, she was surprisingly forgiving, reflecting in a conversation with the prominent anti-Communist philosopher Sir Isaiah Berlin that 'A lot of people made terrible mistakes – one shouldn't really go on persecuting them.'

77. Good old Cake

Deborah Cavendish, Duchess of Devonshire, went to the opera one painfully cold January evening in 1980, the kind of night in London in which we imagine we will see the city looking like an ice-speckled suburb of Narnia when in truth one is hit by a miserable freezing fog that makes you look over your shoulder for Jack the Ripper. The Duchess was nervous about attendance numbers, as the evening had been organised by her husband to raise money for a local hospital. Luckily, the Queen Mother RSVP'd with a yes.

'Good old Cake came & turned it into a gala,' the Duchess wrote to one of her absent friends. 'One forgets between seeing her what a star she is & what incredible & wicked charm she has got.'

Star timing was not, however, the Queen Mother's forte that night. She lost track of it while chatting with the Duchess during the interval. Then, she heard the opening strains of the National Anthem from the orchestra pit.

'Oh God!' the Queen Mother cried and returned to the royal box, trying, aged seventy-nine, to clear the stairs like an Olympic long jumper with something to prove.

'She *flew* up the stairs,' the Duchess observed, 'dropping her old white fox cape & didn't look round to see what would happen to it.'

She just about made it back in time to be seen standing, singing, and smiling as the anthem asking God to save her daughter came to an end.

IX

Glasses Filled with Dubonnet, Gin and Pimm's (1980–1990)

Lady Diana Spencer moved into the Queen Mother's home at Clarence House in February 1981, following her engagement to the Prince of Wales. Both women had a great ability to see the fun in a situation and to put people at their ease. They were from almost identical backgrounds, as earls' daughters from old aristocratic families, although in Diana's case one with long-standing ties to the court. Another key difference was that whereas Elizabeth's upbringing had been so happy that it made her reluctant to marry into the Royal Family, Diana's had much instability, and she was so keen on the idea of marrying a Windsor that, driving past Buckingham Palace in the 1970s, she told a friend how wonderful it would be to marry the future king, 'like Anne Boleyn or Guinevere'. All things considered, those two probably were not the most inspiring examples.

The Queen Mother had known members of Diana's family since she befriended her great-aunt Lavinia as a teenager during the First World War, and it was assumed, then and later, that the Queen Mother had masterminded the marriage between her grandson and Lavinia's great-niece. This was the version of events immortalised – if that's the right word – in 1982's *The Royal Romance of Charles and Diana*, one of the cheerful pieces of televisual fluff that the British royals now receive as an off-registry wedding gift. While the script of *The Royal Romance of Charles and Diana* was not exactly Shakespeare, it could not be faulted on its casting, with its peppering of screen royalty and the real thing. The Queen Mother was played by Olivia de Havilland, Prince Philip by

Stewart Granger, Diana's mother by Holland Taylor, and Diana by Catherine Oxenburg, daughter of a Yugoslavian princess. In the obligatory 'learning to be a royal' montage, de Havilland's Queen Mother gives Oxenburg's Diana a crash course in etiquette and media management.

There were some early real-life tensions. Diana was upset that, at family dinners, Charles would ask the Queen and the Queen Mother what they wanted to drink before he asked her: 'Fine, no problem,' she remembered later, 'but I had to be told that was normal because I always thought it was the wife first. Stupid thought!' At the end of the decade, although her marriage to Charles had deteriorated, Princess Diana spoke warmly of her husband's grandmother, and she wore the Queen Mother's engagement gift during a visit to the White House when she famously danced with movie star John Travolta. Originally, it was an enormous sapphire brooch, until Diana had the sapphire reset into seven ropes of pearls, kept labelled in her handwriting as 'Engagement present given to me by Queen Elizabeth, February 24 1981'.

The 1980s also brought four more great-grandchildren for Elizabeth. Her first, Peter Phillips, had been born in 1977 – Elizabeth called it 'one of the happiest days of my life' – and Princess Anne gave birth to her second child, Zara, in 1981. Prince Charles and Princess Diana welcomed baby William in 1982 and his brother Henry, universally known as Harry, two years later. Prince Andrew's eldest daughter, Princess Beatrice, whom the Queen Mother adored, was born in London in 1988.

Socially, the 1980s proved a time of rapidly changing, and competing, moods. For the entirety of the decade, Margaret Thatcher was Prime Minister, her right-wing policies attracting applause and rage in almost equal measure. It was also the era of the AIDS crisis, in which two of the Queen Mother's relatives, the princesses Margaret and Diana, faced severe criticism for their involvement. After publicly hugging an AIDS patient, Diana was sneeringly dubbed 'the patron saint of sodomy' by hostile journalists. Princess Margaret helped found, opened, and visited London Lighthouse in 1988 as a hospice for those in the final stage of the disease, and she became patron of the Terrence Higgins Trust, a charity that promotes awareness and healthcare surrounding AIDS and all sexually transmitted conditions. Margaret's friend, Lady Glenconner, lost her son

Henry to AIDS, eighteen months after diagnosis, and she wrote later that Margaret was one of the very few people who continued to visit their home and the only friend who put her arms around Henry in a hug.

Apart from her refusal to cancel her visits to a volatile Northern Ireland, the Queen Mother was far less involved in the struggles and tribulations of the Eighties. Various polls confirmed her position as a popular member of the Royal Family, often pipping the Queen and Princess Diana to top position, and she continued to make hundreds of public appearances every year.

78. Old queens

The Queen Mother's drinky-poo was late.[1] Realising that her footman Billy Tallon had become distracted in a quarrel with his on-again-off-again boyfriend and colleague, Reg Wilcox, the Queen Mother wafted towards the staircase to ask, 'Would one of you old queens mind getting this old queen a drink?'

79. Nerissa and Katherine

One of the most notorious incidents surrounding the Queen Mother was the fate of two of her nieces, Nerissa and Katherine Bowes-Lyon. They were two of the five daughters of her late brother Jock, who had died in 1930. Half a century later, the newspapers discovered that Jock's daughters had been institutionalised and that their famous aunt never visited. From that revelation, Nerissa and Katherine's story transmogrified into a latter-day take on the Monster of Glamis, with the subsequent elaboration that the order to lock them away had in fact come from the Queen Mother herself, who was embarrassed by her nieces' condition and, once her husband became king in 1936, had the girls sent away to spare her, or the monarchy, any embarrassment.[2]

Nerissa and Katherine had severe developmental issues at a time when institutionalisation was not limited to the elite. It was, then, standard medical practice across the social spectrum.[3] There is no evidence whatsoever that Elizabeth had any role in, or knowledge of, the decision to institutionalise her nieces. Nor did it take place in 1936. In 1941, five years after Elizabeth became queen, Nerissa and Katherine's mother, Fenella, accepted her doctor's advice that her third and fifth daughters should be permanently hospitalised. After Jock's death, and particularly after Cecilia's, his children had been raised predominantly by their mother's family. Tragically, neither sister recognised their mother, although they knew one another, and so the decision was taken that they must be kept together. They had hitherto been cared for in a country house paid for by Fenella's father, Lord Clinton, and there was a history of serious mental health problems in Fenella's family, the Hepburn-Stuart-Forbes-Trefusises. Fenella's only sister Harriet was also institutionalised by the family and the same decision was taken subsequently for three of Harriet's daughters, Idomea, Rosemary and Ethelreda, all three of whom had spent their childhoods cared for in the same cottage as Nerissa and Katherine.[4]

As their late father's youngest sister, the Queen Mother was not high in the pecking order with respect to decisions regarding medical care. She was not even the sisters' closest royal relative. They had an elder sister, Anne Bowes-Lyon, who in 1950 married Prince Georg-Valdemar of Denmark. After Fenella's death in 1966, it was Princess Anne of Denmark who was Nerissa's senior relative, socially and legally. Along with their sister Diana Somervell, it was she who made decisions regarding Nerissa and Katherine's care – which, by the standards of the time, was considered excellent.

There are nonetheless inconsistencies in accounts of how much the Queen Mother allegedly knew about her nieces in care: specifically, the claim that she lost touch completely with Fenella's side of the family and believed the sisters had passed away. The Queen Mother attended their sister Anne's wedding reception in 1950 and their niece Katherine Somervell is Elizabeth II's goddaughter, at whose wedding Fenella had been a guest. It seems highly unlikely, almost to the point of impossible, that Elizabeth did not know that Nerissa and Katherine had gone into care. However, once it was brought to her attention precisely where the sisters were living, the Queen Mother sent birthday gifts as well as cheques to the institution to provide Christmas gifts and parties for the residents.[5] She was neither author of the decision, nor an objector to it.

The tragedy of Nerissa and Katherine Bowes-Lyon is less a Machiavellian tale of a scheming wicked queen than a glimpse into the fate of thousands, be it their aunt Harriet, their three cousins, or people from every possible background in the United Kingdom who lived through a time – now mercifully passed – when such attitudes towards mental health were prevalent.

80. The ghosts of the Romanovs

In the early 1980s, Elizabeth was overruled by her eldest daughter on a question concerning King George V. Kenneth Rose, a writer whom the Queen Mother liked very much, had been interviewing her in preparation for his forthcoming biography of her father-in-law, when the Queen Mother and various courtiers realised that Rose was planning to drop a bombshell that implicated George V in an act of cowardice that had helped cause a relative's death.

In early 1917, George V's cousin, Tsar Nicholas II, had lost power thanks to the Russian Revolution, which brought down over three centuries of rule by his family, the House of Romanov. A request was made for Britain to offer asylum to the deposed emperor, his wife and their five children. Britain's Prime Minister at the time, David Lloyd George, allegedly vetoed the proposal, on the grounds that as a deposed absolutist the erstwhile tsar did not deserve to receive sanctuary in a democratic country. Denied permission to come to Britain, the former imperial family were stranded, and they were murdered by revolutionaries a year later.* This account was believed for decades by nearly everybody, including the Duke of Windsor and Lord Mountbatten, whose aunt the Tsarina

---

* There is no truth that the Tsar's youngest daughter, the Grand Duchess Anastasia, survived the massacre, nor did any of her siblings. Her bones were identified and reburied in St Petersburg in 1998.

Alexandra had gone to her death at Ekaterinburg alongside her husband and children.

That version of events endured until Kenneth Rose's research for his 1983 biography of George V, which proved that the decision to deny the Romanovs refuge in Britain had not come from the Prime Minister, but from the King. George feared that the Russian royals' unpopularity might prove contagious. He prioritised his crown over their lives, left them at the mercy of their political enemies, and encouraged a five-decade-long cover-up that absolved him of complicity.

Given that she married into the Royal Family five years after the Romanovs' murder, and that even her brother-in-law believed the lie blaming Lloyd George, it is likely that Rose's bombshell was as much of a surprise to the Queen Mother as it was to everybody else. The truth was, however, a secondary priority for her in this instance and she allied with her daughter's Private Secretary, Sir Philip Moore, to have the section on the Romanovs dropped from Rose's manuscript.[6] Efforts first subtle and then firmer were made to discourage Rose. A request was finally made to Elizabeth II that she deny him permission to quote from the relevant documents in the Royal Archives. The Queen refused to be party to the lie and signed on the memorandum 'Let him publish'.

Rose was accused by some in the palace of presenting the Romanov revelation in too sensational a light. It would be tempting to say that the Queen Mother's opposition came from appreciating that the complexities of the 1917 negotiations would be lost in the retelling, which they were. Even today, four decades after Rose's book, George V's failure to help Nicholas II remains one of the most frequently cited criticisms of the King, despite context painting a more complex picture.[7] There were two revolutions in Russia in 1917. The first, the February Revolution, brought down the monarchy to replace it with a democratic republic; this lasted until the second revolution, in October, which brought Communism to power. The request to shelter the Romanovs was made shortly after the first revolution, when they were in no immediate apparent danger. There was also a near total lack of sympathy for them in Britain. To most on the British Right in 1917, Nicholas II was a feeble incompetent who had allowed his 300-year-old empire to disintegrate through poor leadership, while on the Left the ex-tsar was regarded as a bigoted anti-Semitic tyrant, who had decimated the trade unions and seized every available opportunity to limit democracy until he was overthrown by his exasperated subjects. The silent contempt of the Right meant there was no opposition to the protests of the Left who, in 1917, made it abundantly clear that they did not want Nicholas II living in Britain.

There were many other monarchies in the world aside from Britain's, even more in 1917 than today. Geographically and politically, it was far easier to move the Romanovs to Norway, ruled by Nicholas and George V's mutual cousin, King Haakon VII. The British offer was rescinded as royal relatives in Norway, Denmark, Italy, Germany and Spain negotiated about moving 'dearest Nicky' to another country. In the interim, the Russian republic sent the imperial family to a village in Siberia, where they were still living when the Communists took power and ordered their murder.

While concerns that Rose's discovery would be sensationalised through simplification were justified, it is hard to conclude that Elizabeth was guided by these historiographical scruples. She was trying to protect the monarchy and quite simply did not want to see this surprising paper trail brought to the public's attention. The decision to 'let him publish', and posthumously to exonerate David Lloyd George, was her daughter's. A success for the Queen Mother would have been ensuring that Rose's discovery never saw the light of day.

81. Mrs Brown's marriage licence

Had the Queen Mother been able to get her hands on the relevant Romanov documents, she might have torched them. She certainly seems to have taken to privacy-preserving pyromania when it came to another royal mystery, as she revealed in her old age while dining with friends. Conversation turned to a persistent rumour that has long divided historians: after the death of her first husband, Prince Albert in 1861, Queen Victoria had gone into a long mourning during which she suffered terribly from grief, the intensity of which she expected everybody in her family to share. Years later, she recovered through her friendship with a ghillie called John Brown. Rumour had it that the Queen and the ghillie were not just friends but lovers, while others went further and said that Queen Victoria would rather have secretly married a servant than have sex outside of matrimony. The latter theory of a second marriage has long been dismissed as nonsense. However, Elizabeth blithely revealed that she knew for a fact that it was true because, when she was queen, she had found documents at Balmoral that proved that Victoria and Brown had privately and secretly married.

A guest asked her what she had done with this piece of historical gold. Apparently, 'her eyes twinkled in a steely way,' as she answered, 'I burned the documents.'

82. I shall have to look in my book

Hugo Vickers, her future biographer, first met the Queen Mother when he was a teenager in the 1960s and boarding at Eton, from where he volunteered as a guide at St George's Chapel in nearby Windsor Castle. He also began attending Sunday services, where, on a November morning, he met the Queen, holding the hand of her youngest son Prince Edward. The Queen Mother, who hardly ever missed church, billowed into view, accompanied by eighteen-year-old Princess Anne.

Her hand was outstretched as she approached Vickers to ask, 'And who are you?'

'Hugo Vickers, Ma'am.'

'Ah, yes,' with recognition.

Vickers was so convinced by her tone that he tried to figure out who might have told Queen Elizabeth about him. It was only as he began his career as a biographer that he realised that the idea that she had known who he was, was 'nonsense, of course; it was just her way of putting me at my ease and making me feel special'.

At a dinner party in 1982, he noticed more of her linguistic tricks, such as how she kept politely smiling and chatting to a nearly blind nonagenarian French industrialist, who leant ever further in to make his point until he nearly toppled the Queen Mother into the fireplace. As an increasingly diagonal Queen Elizabeth approached said grate, the rubies of her necklace glinting almost as determinedly as her fixed smile, the industrialist asked her if she might like to join them as guest of honour at another dinner.

'Ah!' the Queen Mother replied with 'an angelic smile' and the forefinger of her right hand aloft. 'Now, I shall have to look in my book.' (Vickers correctly translated that to mean 'No.')

Vickers was at that stage working on his life of Sir Cecil Beaton, who had died four years earlier. 'It was difficult for a homosexual to get [a knighthood],' said a friend of Beaton's. 'But finally the Queen Mother fixed it for him. Several attempts by others had failed.' Despite this and the role his photographs had played in solidifying her public image, she did not attend Beaton's memorial service. She had considered him a friend until the publication of his diaries, in which, along with numerous compliments about her, were many snide remarks about her weight gain and the state of her teeth. She was sufficiently hurt – as well as embarrassed and angry – that she refused even to send a proxy to represent her at his memorial.

83. A Talent to Amuse

In purple velvet, with a matching hat, and diamond brooch, the 83-year-old Queen Mother – looking 'splendid, tremendously well and very fit' according to a congregant – went to Westminster Abbey to unveil a memorial to her late friend, the playwright Sir Noël Coward, who had passed away a decade earlier. Like Cecil Beaton, he had been denied a knighthood on suspicion of his sexuality until the royals directly intervened on his behalf. (He was the son of a piano salesman and so the possibility that snobbery also stood in his way cannot be discounted.) The Queen Mother had hosted Coward's seventieth birthday party, at which the surprise was Elizabeth II's query if he would be willing to accept a knighthood from her.

Over the course of their friendship, the Queen Mother visited Coward at Firefly, his villa in Jamaica, where he asked if she would like a serving of his favourite cocktail, a bullshot (cold beef bouillon, Worcestershire sauce, a dash of lemon juice, a small ocean of vodka). She was 'delighted' with two. He joined her for weekends at Sandringham, where they sang duets of music hall hits like 'My Old Man Said Follow the Van' and Coward's patriotic propaganda piece from the Second World War, 'Don't Let's Be Beastly to the Germans'. They had first met in the 1920s, although it was his work writing pro-British movies, songs and articles during the war that really solidified their friendship. Coward had also served as secret operative for the British Security Coordination during the war, along with the children's author Roald Dahl and James Bond's creator, Ian Fleming. In peace, he returned to the high-society comedies for which he was, and remains, famous.

In the 1950s, Coward was photographed by a journalist travelling on the liner *Queen Elizabeth* as he returned from America for a West End revival of his plays. The *Daily Mirror* ran the piece with a brutally mocking commentary on Coward's outfit, archly asking its readers, 'Is the bow-tie too loud? More like Texas than Tooting? Is he showing too much of a rather crumpled silk handkerchief? Are the cuff-links too large, and does a successful playwright *really* wear a leather belt? Is the jacket too long and too colourful?'

At the theatre, on the day that the horrible article had been published, Coward was invited during the interval to meet the Queen, the Queen Mother and Princess Margaret. The Queen Mother walked straight over to him: 'How lovely to see you again. We have been most angry on your behalf. For the press to attack your integrity after all you have done for England, both in the country and out of it, is outrageous, but don't let it upset you.' He wrote a few years later in his diary, 'I have always liked her since we first met in the twenties, and of late years I have come to adore her. She has irrepressible humour, divine manners and a kind heart. My affection for her has gone far beyond royal *snobisme*. She is also, I am proud and happy to say, genuinely fond of me.'

She was. The monument she unveiled to him in Poets' Corner at Westminster Abbey carried his name and dates, and the epitaph he had once joked that he would want for himself: *A TALENT TO AMUSE.*

84. In Friendship, Elizabeth?

Wallis, Duchess of Windsor, died in Paris on 24 April 1986, after a long decline in which she was pulverised by Crohn's disease, quite probably by dementia, and endured elder abuse from her lawyer, Suzanne Blum, who isolated Wallis from those who cared for her. Elizabeth, shockingly, had apparently at last decided to visit Wallis; she told a friend, 'When I was last in Paris, I tried to see her, but she was guarded by a dragon and I was told she saw nobody.' Instead, she sent a bouquet, signed *In Friendship, Elizabeth.*

It is doubtful that Wallis was still cognitively strong enough to register the gesture, even more doubtful that Suzanne Blum would have let her see the flowers, and, of course, equally improbable that Elizabeth meant friendship, even if her attitude had mellowed somewhat since the 1930s and 1940s. In 1968, when the Duke of Windsor was still alive, Elizabeth was touring an exhibition at the National Portrait Gallery when she spotted a large photograph of the couple. After a long pause during which she kept staring at it, Cecil Beaton heard Elizabeth say, 'They're happy and really a great deal of good came of it. We have much to be thankful for.' If the full sincerity of the flowers can be questioned, it is nonetheless a lot more in terms of a thaw than she had ever been prepared to consider in the four decades preceding it. Elizabeth attended Wallis's funeral service with other members of the Royal Family, except Princess Margaret, who told the Queen firmly that she would rather be excused.

85. Blanche, Dorothy, Rose, Sophia and Elizabeth

The Queen Mother was a huge fan of *The Golden Girls*, an American sitcom that ran from 1985 to 1992. Set in Miami, its four main characters were a sarcastic divorced teacher called Dorothy who, with her remorselessly tactless Sicilian mother Sophia, rents a room in a house owned by Blanche Devereaux, a promiscuous widow from the Deep South; the other room is rented by Rose, a naïve Minnesotan grief counsellor. Respectively played by Bea Arthur, Estelle Getty, Rue McClanahan and

Betty White, the show was ground-breaking for showing women over fifty enjoying themselves and at the centre of the storyline – although Blanche, who introduced herself as 'Blanche Devereaux, it's French for Blanche Devereaux,' insisted that she was thirty-nine and told her granddaughter that a fun nickname to call her in public was 'Sis'. The Queen Mother, like millions of viewers, loved it and the four stars were invited to London to perform scenes from the show at the 1988 Royal Variety Performance, a televised charity fundraiser which is always attended by at least two senior members of the Royal Family.

As the skit got under way, it suddenly dawned on Rue McClanahan that they had not cut some of the more risqué dialogue from the script and that the Queen Mother was sitting on the balcony watching them. When Bea Arthur's Dorothy asked McClanahan's Blanche how long she had waited to take a lover after her husband died, Getty's Sophia chimed in with, 'Until the paramedics came.' McClanahan heard the Queen Mother's laughter and relaxed.

Later, the various acts met with the royal party and the Golden Girls stood next to the Dancing Rockettes. Betty White remembered, 'Queen Elizabeth was *lovely*!' as she complimented them on their performance. The five chatted for a few moments about the show and if they were enjoying their time in London. White joked to the Queen Mother that they were now standing next to some very 'lovely girls'. Taking in the sequins of the Rockettes, Elizabeth replied, eyebrow raised, 'Oh, yes, lovely bodies' in an apparently flawless American accent.

86. The Viscount's handshake

Many of the Queen Mother's guests had their own idiosyncrasies, including Lord Slim, a veteran of the Second World and Korean wars. He liked to greet fellow members of the armed forces with a sharp jab to the abdomen.

Spotting her equerry doubled over and clutching his stomach one afternoon, the Queen Mother said cheerily, 'Oh, I see you've met Lord Slim!'

87. Highballs at Hillsborough Castle

The Queen Mother had loved Northern Ireland since her first visit in 1924. In 2019, her grandson Prince Charles told Northern Irish actors Debra Hill and Matt Cassidy that he shared his grandmother's love for a Belfast bap, a chewy white loaf sold in the local markets with a deliberately burned top that, if thrown at your head, is tough enough to do quite a bit of damage. Those whose teeth have a tenuous relationship with their gums are also best advised to avoid it. Beloved without being considered the fanciest of delicacies in Belfast, it also contains enough carbohydrates to lay waste to the best-intentioned diet.

In 1988, Belfast baps were back on the menu as the Queen Mother made an unannounced visit at the height of the Troubles. It had been only nine years since Prince Philip's uncle, Lord Mountbatten, was killed in a bomb attack by the IRA. During her previous trip, four years after Mountbatten's assassination, a stolen copy of Elizabeth's schedule was found in an abandoned car and a 30lb bomb, manufactured by the IRA, was intercepted before it could be detonated in the crowded centre of Ballymena, a town that the Queen Mother's itinerary confirmed she would be visiting. To diminish the chances of another assassination attempt, there was almost no advanced publicity for the Queen Mother's 1988 visit. She was taken from event to event by helicopter rather than travelling on public roads, with their risk of snipers or car bombs.

She carried out several engagements and stayed under heavy guard at the Royal Family's official residence in Northern Ireland, Hillsborough Castle, a walled Georgian mansion ten miles outside Belfast with famously beautiful gardens and portraits of King George III and Queen Charlotte looming at the entrance.[8] The castle had a special emotional significance for the Queen Mother; it had been the home of her sister Rose from 1945 to 1952 when it was the governor's house, until the largely ceremonial post was abolished in 1973.* During the Hillsborough garden parties that

---

* Rose's husband William Leveson-Gower, 4th Lord Granville, served as governor, first of the Isle of Man and then of Northern Ireland.

became a fixture of Northern Irish civil and social life, the Queen Mother would give her security team a fright by deviating from the route round the gardens to instead go into the crowds to mingle with them. It had been during her first visit to Belfast, back in 1924, that Elizabeth had resisted being rushed away from greeting the gathered people. Now, in 1988, she told her handlers, 'I am not in a hurry. I have time. Time is not my dictator; I dictate to time. I want to meet people.'[9]

On her last night before returning to England, the Queen Mother was hosting a dinner in Hillsborough's state Dining Room. A new member of the castle's staff was a young college graduate from Belfast, who was so nervous serving the Queen Mother – her photograph had been on his parents' living room wall for as long as he could remember – that he spilled a scalding sauce down her dress.[10] Seeing the Queen Mother's eyes sparkle with pain, he also saw his boss staring at him from the far side of the dining room, in silent yet palpable fury. Convinced that he was about to be fired, that night his boss found him to say, 'I was about to give you a very firm talking-to, until Her Majesty Queen Elizabeth sent for me and asked if I would apologise to you from her. She says she accidentally nudged your elbow earlier this evening and made you spill.' David Anderson, head of the Household at Hillsborough, told me years later, 'I can tell you, honestly, she did not nudge his elbow and the reason he had a job the next day was because she took the initiative to lie for him.'

The Queen Mother's presence of mind in saving the young man's job was even more remarkable given the pace of her dinner drinky-poos, in which she outlasted several members of the military. As was traditional, the dinner featured a Loyal Toast, when the guests stood to raise their glasses to 'The Queen'. On this particular evening, after joining in the toast to her daughter, the Queen Mother added her own to 'The people of Northern Ireland'. Up the guests' glasses went once more.

Hillsborough Castle, specifically, is located in County Down.

'To the people of County Down!' the Queen Mother toasted.

The glasses rose; their contents diminished further.

By way of an interesting geographical fact, Northern Ireland consists of six counties.

'To the people of County Antrim!' the Queen Mother continued.

By the time she had individually led toasts to all six counties, rounding things off with County Tyrone, the Queen Mother remained clear-headed, while her guests swayed on their feet and one decimated general ended the evening by throwing up in the Entrance Hall's umbrella stand.

X

I Shall Miss Those Laughs (1990–2002)

'Is it just me or are the pensioners getting younger these days?' the Queen Mother asked as she sailed into her tenth decade. 'Only the kind of person who kicks kittens, snarls at babies and denies the existence of Santa Claus,' concluded one of her admirers, 'can resist her jolly face, her utter femininity, her guileless way of steam-rollering through any situation.'

She needed those steam-rollering skills in the Nineties. The period was difficult for the monarchy. The Queen, who had consulted her mother throughout her reign, relied on her particularly in the first half of the decade. Tabloid intrusion into the lives of the younger royals reached such intensity that it contributed to the Princess of Wales's untimely death, two years after her divorce and five years after her separation from Prince Charles. Prince Andrew and his wife Sarah divorced in 1996. Their phone lines hacked, private conversations recorded, and photographers hiding in the bushes to snap them poolside became occupational hazards for the younger generation. Press intrusion was not helped by some of the younger royals' own actions, as they flitted between complaining about the media and arranging sit-down interviews or tipping off photographers about where to find them. A *sotto voce* 'Oh gosh, not this again' from the Queen Mother as she saw yet another headline about her grandchildren or their spouses became a frequent morning occurrence at Clarence House. To avoid the unpleasant, she cut back her regular newspaper reading to the conservative *Daily Telegraph*.[1] Staff would place it at the top of the morning newspapers in Clarence House, along with *The Times* and *The Independent*, the latter of which ironically provided less-distressing headlines for her due to its republican editorial stance, meaning it never ran stories, sensationalist or otherwise, about the royals.[2]

The Queen Mother did not like any of these family matters to be brought up in conversation and she had different tactics for killing the topic. For staff, it was froideur, as an equerry learned when asked her if she had seen Prince Charles's 'tell-all' interview with Jonathan Dimbleby, broadcast the night before.

'The look she gave me could have frozen fire,' he recalls. A second later, she smiled coldly to tell him, very firmly, 'Some things are best not discussed.' If however a guest brought up the latest royal scandal, the Queen Mother chose alcohol and flattery by selecting a topic that she knew interested the questioner, no matter how stultifying she found it personally, and gesturing subtly to a footman as she asked, 'Do let's have another drink, I'm longing to hear about x' or 'You must have another a glass of wine, and won't you tell me all about y?'

One of the pleasures of growing older can be found in nostalgic reunions of friends and animated conversations beginning 'Do you remember …' By the 1990s, there were few to whom the Queen Mother could say this. Excepting her sister-in-law Princess Alice, Duchess of Gloucester, who died aged 102 in 2004, Elizabeth had outlasted nearly all her contemporaries. She outlived her last sibling by thirty-five years, her husband by fifty. Looking exhausted, she surprised fellow dinner guests at the Middle Temple in 1995 with the quite heartbreaking remark, 'I have done my duty all my life and I shall soon be with my husband again.' Her son-in-law Prince Philip thought it must be horrible to live so long and face a catalogue of bereavements. These led to moments in which the elderly Queen Mother could appear heartless. There was a sharp decrease in her visits to sick friends, even the terminally ill, along with cryptic comments that she 'couldn't bear' to think of them like that and preferred to remember them 'as they were'.

Prince Charles was in Scotland, visiting his grandmother, when his dog, a Jack Russell named Pooh, went missing. He had been running on ahead, capered off, then disappeared. Given the terrain, the fear was that

Pooh had fallen down a rabbit hole. A member of the party recalls that they waited for about ten minutes, calling for the dog, before organising a proper search. After a few hours, Prince Charles felt bad for the staff helping him. He was struggling to hold back tears when he said to his grandmother's equerry, 'Look, you go on back and take the staff with you. I'm going to carry on the search alone.'

According to somebody who was there that weekend, Prince Charles stayed out most of the night looking for Pooh, even digging around on his hands and knees trying to find the rabbit hole where he might have fallen and injured himself. At sunrise, the Prince gave up the search, although for days to come he looked distressed as 'he thought of his dog trapped in a hole, slowly starving to death'. There were further searches, none of them successful. Some present thought that the Queen Mother did not handle the situation well. When Prince Charles told her what had happened, her response was, 'Oh, I'm so sorry to hear that. Do have some tea.' Her equerry at the time feels, 'You have to bear in mind that all her friends and most of her family had died, so a dog didn't really register with her.'

It would be wrong to characterise Elizabeth's final twelve years as solely defined by loss and unhappiness. There were still plenty of occasions when she greatly enjoyed life. Spotting her equerry Colin Burgess riding a motorcycle, she called out, 'I think perhaps it's a little too big for me!' or, as she was being driven through the Highlands in a Land Rover, 'Come on, Colin, let's open her up a bit! Come on, Colin, put your foot down!' This might be followed by a firm order to halt if she spotted an open gate – 'Stop the car! We *must* close that gate or the cows will escape.' 'We' lacked accuracy. She smiled encouragingly from inside the warm car as her driver or equerry got out to bolt the gates and save the local farmer's herd from wandering onto the road. At her 101st birthday, she greeted well-wishers from a motorised buggy, beginning with a toddler who handed her a bunch of flowers and who introduced himself as 'Aged Two'. Forty-five minutes later, as the buggy trundled past the child again, the Queen Mother spotted him and waved, 'Goodbye, Aged Two!' as she and her staff beetled back behind the gates of Clarence House.

One of her favourite guests was Nelson Mandela, the President of South Africa from 1994 to 1999. In 1996, President Mandela visited London and came to Clarence House for tea with the Queen Mother, where they chatted for hours longer than scheduled, before she attended a state banquet in his honour.

Her appetite and her sense of humour remained strong to the end. ('People say it's not good to eat butter. People say butter is bad for your heart. Well, I have eaten butter all my life and look at me.') When a group of children were throwing rocks at cars on the Mall, the Queen Mother had her driver stop as she rolled down the window to chide the culprits. 'Whatever *will* the American tourists think?' she asked them, before waving as she drove on.

Given her age, there was an assumption that she must have gone into cognitive decline, something that is firmly rejected by many people who knew her in the 1990s. Prince Michael of Kent, Sir Rocco Forte, the Household Manager at Hillsborough Castle David Anderson, Major Colin Burgess, and the historians Hugo Vickers and Coryne Hall are all consistent on how well informed she was and that there was no sign – even in 2001 when Hall interviewed her – that her powers of recall had diminished. Hall describes her as 'absolutely razor sharp'. However, there were more and more frequent troubles with physical ill health, during which the Queen waged one uphill battle after another to get her mother to acknowledge her growing frailty. Round One, the walking stick push of '93, ended with Elizabeth II giving her mother a special walking stick with the accompanying note, 'Darling Mummy, Your daughters and your nieces would very much like you to TRY this walking stick! … Just at this moment, it would make the two Margarets, Jean and me* very happy and relieved if you would rely on its support!' This was followed by an initial refusal to use the stairlift the Queen installed for her at Sandringham in 1995. She glared in silent loathing at the handrails thoughtfully installed at the Castle of Mey; the staff waited until she went to church to do it, otherwise they knew she would have vetoed the procedure at the first sign

---

* Princess Margaret and the Queen Mother's nieces Margaret Rhodes and Jean Wills, both daughters of her late sister Mary, Lady Elphinstone.

of a hammer. She tried to hide how bad her eyesight was before a cataract operation in 1996 and only yielded the point when the Queen spotted her mother reading a menu upside down whilst enthusing about how delicious everything looked. She broke her hip in 1998 and underwent hip replacement surgery, during a decade that saw her nearly choke to death and break several bones.

She was uncomfortable with the direction in which British society was moving, the values of someone born in 1900 inevitably clashing with those growing to maturity in the 1990s. 'She had many gay friends, whom she adored and protected. She thought the persecution of gay people, especially when she was younger, was "horrible", a gentleman who knew her told me whilst I was researching this book, 'but be under absolutely no illusion that she would have been vehemently opposed to same-sex marriage.' The age of sexual consent in Britain for an opposite-sex couple is sixteen, while for a same-sex couple it was eighteen. In 1998, the government under Prime Minister Tony Blair decided to make the age consistently sixteen regardless of gender, which the Queen Mother opposed so strongly that she allegedly urged the Queen to speak to the Prime Minister about it. She also felt alienated by what she sometimes characterised as a weak and selfish generation. She waxed nostalgic in 1995 on the fiftieth anniversary of victory in the Second World War, when 'at the moment, the events leading up to the anniversary of VE Day bring back many memories of those now far-off days, though sometimes they seem very close, and how close we all were to each other then in this dear old country'.

88. A nip in the air

'Embarrassing?' the Queen Mother asked, upon hearing there was a nudist enclave near her beach hut. 'For whom? I'm longing to see them. Perhaps the corgis will nip their bottoms.'

Her protection officers had tried to warn her of the naked seaside enthusiasts enjoying the bracing delights of the Norfolk coastline, near a beach hut occasionally used by the Queen Mother and built on the orders of the late Thomas Coke, 5th Earl of Leicester. Lord Leicester's daughter

Anne Tennant, Lady Glenconner, had been a lifelong friend of Princess Margaret, who in adulthood had often used Lady Glenconner's role as her lady-in-waiting as a cover to rescue her from the frequently erratic behaviour of her husband, Lord Glenconner.

After tea in the beach hut, the Queen Mother, hat brim flapping in the Norfolk wind, would often walk the corgis in the direction of the nudist beach, to the despair of her protection officers. Fortunately for all the relevant bottoms, there is no record of her ever unleashing the corgis as threatened. Years later, when Camilla, Duchess of Cornwall, went swimming at the same beach with her friend, the actress Dame Judi Dench, Lady Glenconner told them about the Queen Mother's walks near the nudist beach, whereupon the Duchess and the Dame apparently went off to catch a peek and have a giggle.

89. The salmon's revenge

From childhood, Elizabeth had been a keen angler, a hobby that she pursued in Scotland well into old age. Manners are even more impressive when they are inconvenient, which a redoubtable river-wading royalist proved one afternoon when she spotted a fellow fisherwoman opposite. Belatedly realising that said woman in a wax jacket was Her Majesty Queen Elizabeth the Queen Mother, the lady decided, cascading water be damned, that she was going to curtsey. Rod aloft, one wellington-booted ankle behind another, she dipped into the water before dunking herself into it. The current began filling her boots and the pockets of her Barbour, until she swayed under the excess weight of the water.

The Queen Mother, one hand briefly separated from her fishing rod, beamed, 'Good morning, aren't you very kind? What a lovely day. Have you had any bites?'

Sodden, but with her loyalty, and balance, reaffirmed, the lady righted herself to chat about the salmon, the trout, and the impromptu tailgating from the back of the Queen Mother's Land Rover from which she could see bottles of gin, Dubonnet and Pimm's.

Eating what she caught nearly killed the Queen Mother, who had to be hospitalised after a salmon bone was lodged in her throat. Emerging from hospital, she thanked well-wishers and asked them not to worry, as 'The salmon have got their own back!'

90. Major Burgess's rollerblades

'Colin, what did you do to the dogs, they're so exhausted!' the Queen Mother asked her equerry in front of a party of about thirty people, including various Members of Parliament.

'Ma'am, I tied them to the bumper of a car and took them for a drive,' he explained.

A hushed silence ensued among the guests, before Queen Elizabeth's whoop of laughter with, 'Oh, Colin, you are wicked!'

She had tasked Major Colin Burgess with taking the corgis for a walk. They, as ever, were supremely disinclined to move. He threw a stick to encourage them to trot, for which he was rewarded with a stare as if he had taken leave of his senses. So he tied their leads to a car and went for a very slow drive around the grounds. Slow for him, of course; an Olympic sprint for the enraged corgis.

Burgess had joined the Queen Mother's service aged twenty-six in 1994, beating out two fellow comrades from the forces who, unlike him, had gone to public schools. Burgess's final interview, so to speak, consisted of lunch with the Queen Mother at Clarence House. A starter serving of eggs florentine yielded to meat with boiled potatoes and vegetables, followed by a chocolate fondant, accompanied by a bottle and a half of claret. He soon learned that his employer's refrain of 'do let's have another drink' could make lunches last for hours and one conversation run into the next.

'Ma'am,' he said as she suggested another glass over a midweek lunch, 'I can't, I must do some work this afternoon. I have a busy schedule to get through.'

The Queen Mother looked at the Major, her blue eyes conveying mild concern at this strange reply. '*Colin*, you *must* have some wine. How can you not have wine with your meal?'

Colin again, if less confidently, cited his meetings, even as the likelihood of their happening dimmed before his eyes.

'Colin, don't bother about all that. I'm sure they'll understand if you can't meet them or ring them. Now have some wine.'

'I really can't, Ma'am,' he repeated as the wine was poured by Billy Tallon, of whom a regular guest had warned a newbie, 'No use putting your hand over the glass, he pours it through the fingers!'

Burgess entered a household where he was by far the youngest member of staff, since the Queen Mother refused to let anybody go. A footman grappling with a hangover might be stationed on duty in Clarence House's seldom-used lift, where he could sit until he felt like a human being again. Her Comptroller Sir Ralph Anstruther dealt with the early stages of dementia in the Queen Mother's service, turning up every day, immaculately dressed as always, going through a routine as he had since 1961, with longer and longer spells of exhaustion, which he was allowed to sleep through in his office. After a series of strokes, and the advance of cognitive decline, the Queen Mother gently asked him if he might like to spend some more time in Scotland. Billy Tallon recalled, 'I can remember meeting several ladies with walking sticks who claimed they were still maids but it was clear that they were far too frail to do any work at all. It was part of Elizabeth's kindness that she couldn't bear to treat any former servants harshly, especially if they had nowhere else to go.'

The Queen Mother's ladies-in-waiting, companions who also answered the letters, cards and queries sent by members of the public, have been described as a group of nice old ladies, who weren't too snobbish to take the bus and were kind to their servants. The team included Dame Frances Campbell-Preston, who volunteered on eight-hour shifts manning the Samaritans' helpline, from where she emerged to share stories of true problems which put everything in perspective. For instance, 'I had this chap on last night. He was terribly upset. His boyfriend had tried to commit suicide after finding out that most of his heroin had been stolen and this poor chap just didn't know how to handle it. Life's a strange place, isn't it?'

Early on in his time in the Queen Mother's household, Burgess earned the ire of a general who spotted him rollerblading to keep fit, and crisply informed him, 'I don't think it's very appropriate for a Guards officer to be rollerblading.'

The Queen Mother approached with a hello. 'Oh, General! Colin rollerblades in the park. Don't you think it's wonderful?'

In response to this instruction disguised as a question, the General replied, 'Oh, yes, ma'am, I think it's tremendous.'

91. Back to Spencer House

In June 1997, the Queen Mother joined most of the Royal Family for a party to celebrate the Queen and Prince Philip's fiftieth wedding anniversary. It was hosted by members of the Order of the Garter at Spencer House in London where, seven decades earlier, Elizabeth had met her future husband at a tea organised by her friend Lavinia. Among the guests in 1997 were Deborah, Duchess of Devonshire, and the former Prime Minister Margaret Thatcher who, the Duchess thought, looked suspiciously well-rested.

'Oh!' the Duchess said, aiming a compliment to unearth information. 'You do look wonderful.'

'It's America,' Baroness Thatcher replied. 'I like them and they like me and that is never the case in Europe.'

The Duchess was not entirely convinced that this rejuvenation could be attributed solely to American friendliness. She wrote in a letter to her one of her sisters that 'Mrs Thatcher [*sic*] looked 18. I wonder if she's had her face lifted, really incredible.' In contrast, she was shocked by the Queen Mother's frailty, who 'had to ask for a cushion, she has become so TINY'.

92. Chief leper

'His grandmother is always looking at me with a strange look in her eyes,' Princess Diana told a friend, via a telephone conversation that was being secretly taped and was later sold to a tabloid. 'It's not hatred; it's sort of interest and pity mixed in one. I am not quite sure. I don't understand it. Every time I look, she's looking at me, then looks away and smiles.'

The Princess continued, 'It's affection. Affection. It's definitely affection. It's sort of, it's definitely not hostile in any way. She's sort of fascinated by me, but doesn't quite know how to unravel it.'

It had unravelled between the time the conversation was made, on New Year's Eve 1989, and when it was plastered all over the front pages in 1992. Diana did not enjoy herself at the Queen Mother's ninetieth birthday party in August 1990, calling it 'grim and stilted. They are all anti-me. My grandmother has done another good hatchet job on me.' Diana's grandmother Ruth, Lady Fermoy, had been one of the Queen Mother's ladies-in-waiting since 1956 and, initially, Diana seems to have blamed her for turning the Queen Mother against her. She also apparently felt that sometimes the Queen Mother, to an extent she made obvious, preferred William to Harry, until Diana confronted her about it.

The Queen Mother allegedly referred to Diana as 'a liar', while Diana called her 'the chief leper in the leper colony'. The Princess was particularly irritated by the longstanding theory that the Queen Mother had arranged her marriage in conjunction with Lady Fermoy. She tried to correct the record over coffee with Ingrid Seward, a royal expert who subsequently authored biographies of Diana, the Queen Mother, Prince Philip, Diana's brother-in-law Prince Edward, Earl of Wessex, and their sister-in-law Sarah, Duchess of York. Diana told her, 'The Queen Mother was not instrumental in arranging the marriage with Lady Fermoy. Charles and I arranged it. It is a myth it was the Queen Mother. She didn't do anything.' She added, 'She is not as she appears to be at all. She is tough and interfering and she has few feelings.' Diana's once warm relationship with Princess Margaret had also fallen apart, with Margaret referring to Diana, when she had to, as 'the girl who married my nephew'.

Relations had not improved when Diana was tragically killed in a car accident in Paris a few weeks after the Queen Mother's ninety-seventh birthday. The Queen Mother was baffled by the outpouring of grief at the Princess's death, which she thought more effusive than anything she had seen when the city was being pummelled nightly by Nazi bombs during the Blitz. The events of that week have been discussed elsewhere and well;

here it is sufficient to say that the Queen Mother was uncomfortable with a lot of what she saw, and felt that her daughter the Queen was unfairly criticised by newspapers keen to distract from the fact that some of them had been paying the paparazzi who harassed Diana into the tunnel where she lost her life. Princess Margaret felt desperately sorry for Diana's sons, especially the youngest, since it is 'terrible to lose your mother at that age, and with little Harry's birthday only a few days away'. However, she had no sympathy for the public's mood. She told a friend that the reaction was unhinged, 'rather like Diana herself. When she died, everyone got as hysterical as she was.' She complained about the smell of the mountains of decomposing flowers left at the palaces across London, referring to them as 'floral fascism'. Later, both the Queen Mother and Princess Margaret thought there was no need for a permanent memorial to Diana inside the grounds of Kensington Palace; Margaret acidly suggested, 'It will be quite enough of a memorial to restore the grass in front which all these people trampled the week she died.'

93. Prize fighter

The Queen Mother, in Scotland, had eleven guests for dinner, for which she still dressed. After their meal, they decamped into the Sitting Room, where the Queen Mother suggested they relax by watching an episode of *Keeping Up Appearances*, a hugely popular BBC sitcom about pretentious middle-class housewife Hyacinth Bucket, who insists her surname is pronounced 'Bouquet' and schemes to make her way into the local elite through a series of inevitably comic errors. It, along with the Second World War-set sitcom *Dad's Army*, *The Golden Girls* and the BBC soap *EastEnders*, were the Queen Mother's favourite television shows.

'Certainly, Ma'am,' said her equerry, Colin.

He put the video into the player, hit rewind, and turned the television on, whereupon he and the guests were confronted by a boxing match. Cauliflower ears, cut lips and a blood-stained faced were not, he assumed, appropriate viewing for Her Majesty after dinner. Colin apologised and, flustered, tried to change the channel until the video had finished rewinding – until the Queen Mother interjected with, 'No, no. Leave this on, Colin, you *must* leave this on,' as she settled into her armchair to watch the entire bout. Bit by bit, she edged forward. Her diamond bracelet glinted in the light as she began punching the air with her fists, mimicking her favourite boxer's parries. To the astonishment of Colin and the ten others, the 96-year-old Queen Mother shouted, 'Go on!' at the television. 'Hit him again! No, no – look! He's going to get up from that one. Go on, PUNCH HIM!' When the opponent was battered to the floor of the ring, she clasped her hands together in glee as she said, 'Oh, he's not going to get up from that one, is he?'

94. Matins and Martinis

After Sunday service in the Royal Chapel at Windsor Great Park, the Queen Mother liked to invite her chaplain, the Reverend Canon John Ovenden, and his wife back to her house at Royal Lodge for lunch. Pre-lunch drinks began with a generous gin and tonic. Once the Reverend had finished, the Queen Mother suggested her steward refill Ovenden's glass.

The Reverend demurred: 'I can't possibly have a further drink, Ma'am, as I have to take a baptism this afternoon and need to be reasonably in charge of my senses.'

'Oh, well!' the Queen Mother replied merrily. 'If that is the case, then you most certainly should have another drink – as it will help.'

Ovenden surrendered and imbibed a second drink so potent that, in 2022 he joked, 'To this day, I do not know whether I baptised the child with the correct names or not!'

95. The Captain's House

As at Balmoral, Mey had smaller houses in its grounds. One of which, called the Captain's House, is situated on the opposite side of the road to the castle itself. On a summer's afternoon, the Queen Mother was lunching outside the Captain's House with her lady-in-waiting the Countess of Scarborough and Colonel Alastair Bruce,* whose cousin Lord Elgin – when he was the young Lord Bruce – had served as Queen Elizabeth's Page of Honour in the 1930s.† Security was lax at Mey. Nobody really knew where one boundary line ended and the next began. A bus full of tourists appeared. Spotting the Queen Mother's standard flying above the castle, signifying that she was in residence, they began eagerly taking photos while their tour guide told them the story of the Queen Mother's relocation there after the King's death.

Meanwhile, from the Captain's House, the Queen Mother, the Countess and the Colonel stared up at a bus full of backs. Every single person faced away from them and towards the castle. The Queen Mother's eyesight was deteriorating again, so she gamely waved until Colonel Bruce said, 'To be perfectly honest, ma'am, they're not looking this way. They're all looking towards the castle.'

'Oh, how amusing!'

There is always one person on a tour who's not interested in the stately home or the guide's ruminations. And on this tour, that disaffected soul was rewarded by turning away to look out the window towards the sea and spotting the Queen Mother at lunch al fresco. From within, the cry went up. It was the Queen Mother! The tourists turned almost en masse and the Queen Mother asked to be helped to her feet to wave at them as they waved at her. The tour guide didn't have a single thing prepared in their script for this eventuality.

---

* Latterly Governor of Edinburgh Castle.

† The ties between the families went further. Along with both being members of the Scottish nobility, Elizabeth had first met Marion 'Crawfie' Crawford when she visited the 10th Earl and Countess of Elgin, for whose children Crawfie had been governess.

96. William, Harry and a very cunning plan

In 2020, footage surfaced on the internet of the Queen Mother being asked an impromptu question in the 1990s by a journalist. She had not given such an interview since her engagement in 1923, which had earned her a swift reprimand from her father-in-law. The author and socialite Basia Briggs was in the room when the microphone suddenly appeared in front of the Queen Mother, who was asked what advice she would give to her great-grandchildren William and Harry.

Basia, who described the journalist as 'a grovelling little worm [with] no manners', fortunately released the video decades later for the historical record. You can watch it on her Instagram account, where you can also spot the nanosecond described by Briggs when the Queen Mother's 'good nature turned to steely-eyed irritation'. The smile is back almost before you notice, but her eyes could freeze mercury as the Queen Mother says, 'Oh, I never give advice.' The journalist pressed. The Queen Mother said, 'Well, I hope they will all be brought up to put their country first. Whatever happens. It is one's duty to one's country, isn't it?' She then extended her arm to distance herself from the microphone as she turned away with a courtier, saying, 'I'm sure they will be brought up that way.' The journalist was never invited back to Clarence House and Basia recalls, 'We all wanted to dive under the furniture. I had strong words with him later and said if he had ambushed my Granny like that I would have punched him in the face.'

Prince William's favourite photograph of himself and his great-grandmother 'is a picture of me aged about nine or ten, helping the Queen Mother up the steps of Windsor Castle. I remember the moment because she said to me, "Keep doing that for people and you will go a long way in life."' There are also adorable photographs of a young Prince Harry, in his suit and coat, holding an umbrella over his great-grandmother as they left church together.

She was apparently a dab hand at impressions of characters from the comedy series *Blackadder*, including of Baldrick, a lugubriously unlucky servant played by Tony Robinson who was always concocting another disastrous 'cunning plan', and Miranda Richardson's Queenie, a send-up of the Tudor monarch Elizabeth I, in which she is reimagined as a ditzy yet terrifying tyrant. She also learnt catchphrases from the comedian Sacha Baron Cohen after walking in to find princes William and Harry laughing at his show on television. She tried the catchphrases out on the Queen at Christmas lunch.

In 2001, she threw a farewell lunch at Birkhall for Prince William before he started at St Andrew's, the oldest university in Scotland. As the 101-year-old waved him off, she said, 'Any good parties, invite me!'

'There was no way,' Prince William said later. 'I knew full well that if I invited her down, she would dance me under the table.'

97. My Old Man's a Dustman

After lunch with His Eminence Cardinal Cormac Murphy-O'Connor, Archbishop of Westminster and the Pope's deputy as leader of the Catholic Church in England and Wales, the Queen Mother joined the Cardinal for a singsong. 'He's a very good pianist,' she told Lord Norwich* a few days later, at another lunch, 'and all afternoon we played the piano and we sang the old musical hall songs. And I found I remember all the words and I haven't sung them for sixty years!' They started with songs popular during the Second World War, until the Queen Mother tickled the ivories with an unfamiliar tune.

'I have never heard that one,' the Cardinal said.

'You wouldn't,' the Queen Mother trilled. 'It was a hit tune in 1910!'

When her equerry went in search of them at about four o'clock, quite some time after the Queen Mother was due to have departed, he found the pair singing Lonnie Donegan's 1960 hit, 'My Old Man's a Dustman', belting through the lyrics: 'Oh, my old man's a dustman, He wears a dustman's hat.'

'Most extraordinary afternoon,' the Queen Mother continued to Lord Norwich a few days later. 'And, do you know, I like a *little* Dubonnet

---

* John Julius Cooper, 2nd Viscount Norwich (1929–2018), better known as the author John Julius Norwich.

before lunch …' ('Putting it rather mildly,' Norwich thought.) 'Do you think it might have been spiked?'

Lord Norwich considered it a tad unlikely that someone in the Cardinal-Archbishop's household had spiked the Queen Mother's afternoon drinky-poo.

'I think it must have been spiked,' the Queen Mother concluded.

98. Lord Warden of the Cinque Ports

Since 1978, Queen Elizabeth had been Lord Warden of the Cinque Ports, a ceremonial honour the origins of which date back to the eleventh century; the first incumbent being an Earl of Wessex who was appointed in 1045.[3] In 1999, Colonel Alastair Bruce had published his book *Keepers of the Kingdom: The Ancient Offices of Britain*, a first edition of which he presented to the Queen Mother. Her eyesight was once again giving her difficulty – she perused most of the book while holding it upside down – but it was still sharp enough to spot her absence from the section on the Lords Warden of the Cinque Ports.

'Why am I not in your book?' she asked.

Bruce, who had been told by the Palace before he started writing that no member of the Royal Family would be collaborating with the book, answered, 'Well, to be perfectly honest, ma'am, we weren't allowed to have you in the book.'

'Well, I should be in your book. I have one of the greatest appointments of all – Lord Warden of the Cinque Ports.'

This needed to be rectified. She did not like being managed, or excluded. For the next edition, she would go down to have her photograph taken at the Lord Warden's official residence, Walmer Castle, a sixteenth-century fort built in Kent on Henry VIII's orders. Bruce and his photographer went to scout possible locations at the castle; his first choice was the magnificent castle terrace overlooking the sea, with the cannons still pointed out towards France as they had ever since the invasion scare of 1539. Since Elizabeth was 100 years old, they offered two other locations at Walmer, one of which was inside. Bruce then wrote to the Queen Mother to ask which of the three settings she would prefer.

Her handwritten reply was, 'My dear Alastair, between the cannon pointing at France, of course!' She then offered them choices of her wearing pink, blue or yellow, depending on which would be best for their photograph. She insisted the author appear in some of the photographs with her. It was a beautiful day. She wore blue. And indeed the only being who proved difficult was Minnie the corgi who, no matter which way she was positioned, would ostentatiously shuffle round to present nothing but her back and bottom.

99. The Old Icon

'Hello, Coryne! Look – no dogs!' beamed 'Backstairs Billy' Tallon as he welcomed historian Coryne Hall to Clarence House in December 2001. Hall, then working on the first biography of the last Tsar's eldest sister Grand Duchess Xenia,[4] had nearly cancelled her meeting with the Queen Mother thanks to her phobia of dogs. Two fellow biographers, Theo Aronson and Hugo Vickers, encouraged her to let the Queen Mother's staff know of her fears.[5] The Household wrote back to assure her it was not a problem: the rambunctious corgis would go into a courtier's office until Hall had left. 'I've been asked to do a lot of things in my life,' the Queen Mother said, 'but I've never been asked to put my dogs away.'

Hall was touched and surprised by the gesture, as she was by the fact that the audience was offered in the first place. She had not expected to be invited to Clarence House when she wrote to the Queen Mother, again on the advice of a friend. Grand Duchess Xenia was born in St Petersburg in 1875 and died in England in 1960, having been evacuated from revolutionary Russia by her British relatives in 1919. She spent the rest of her life in Britain where, during the Second World War, she was nearly killed when her new home was narrowly missed during the Nazi air raids. After the near-miss, Xenia was invited north to a house in the grounds of Balmoral and, while Hall was researching that part of her biography, a colleague suggested she write to the Queen Mother, who might have some memories of Xenia from her own wartime sojourns at Balmoral. Hall hoped for a letter back from Clarence House, perhaps with a Queen Motherly quote on Xenia that would go nicely in the biography. Instead, there arrived an invitation to meet Elizabeth in person.

Hall had known Billy Tallon for years, hence his ribbing over the dog embargo, and he escorted her through Clarence House for a how-do-you-do with the Queen Mother's Private Secretary Sir Alastair Aird, an equerry, and one of her ladies-in-waiting. The Queen Mother, true to form, was running late and so Hall had time to chat. She thought the team were 'absolute past masters at putting you at your ease'. The lady-in-waiting asked, 'Can you do a decent curtsey?' and would have offered to show Hall, who had no need since she had sixteen years of ballet training under her belt. As the Queen Mother's first meeting ended, the jollity stopped as Hall thought, 'Hang on, I'm just about to meet the Queen Mother!'

She was escorted by equerry Ashe Windham into the Morning Room, where the Queen Mother was standing with the aid of two walking sticks. Hall recalls that her first thought was, 'She's so tiny that I'm going to have to make a *really* low curtsey here to make it count. Thank God for the ballet training.'

A rumour doing the rounds at the time was that the Queen Mother had excised any photographs of Diana, Princess of Wales, from her rooms. However, as she curtseyed, Hall spotted a prominently displayed photo of Diana, holding her eldest son.

'I hope I can remember something useful about Grand Duchess Xenia for you,' the Queen Mother said, inviting Hall to sit. She recalled going for carriage rides through the Balmoral grounds in the 1940s and stopping to sing as they passed Xenia's house. 'My daughters and I used to sing "The Volga Boat Song"* in tribute to the Russians! Do you know it?'

Hall did not, so the Queen Mother burst into a rousing chorus of the Tsarist-era river song. She hoped that, when it came to writing her book, Coryne would include the mushroom-picking trips they had all gone on together at Balmoral during the war. Then Elizabeth's mind went back even further to those meetings at Sandringham in 1923 with Xenia's

---

* Also known as 'The Song of the Volga Boatmen', first printed in 1866 but extant long before.

mother, the Dowager Empress Marie, and with Bertie's grandmother Queen Alexandra. 'She was anxious to say what she could remember, while she was still there,' Hall feels. 'That was the impression I got. I think it was the fact that nobody had ever asked her about this. She was asked questions all the time but never about Xenia or about that time in her life.' The Queen Mother offered to speak to the Factor at Balmoral on Hall's behalf, to see if he could find anything that would help with her research. It was a biographer's dream, as Hall put it. 'She was ever so nice. It was very fun, to be honest.'

Their audience, too, ran late, which meant the Queen Mother was very tardy to lunch. Hall curtseyed and exited through the Morning Room door, which had been kept open throughout their interview. That was not standard practice at Clarence House and it reflected the household's growing concerns about the Queen Mother's health. More audiences were due in a few weeks' time when the Queen Mother went to Sandringham for Christmas, but as events would have it they were cancelled. Coryne Hall's was thus the last audience of the Queen Mother's career, during which Elizabeth had been able to look back to one of the first, seventy-eight years earlier.

100. Princess Margaret's Marigolds

'Hard luck having to exercise the dogs on a day like this,' a guard said to his two companions as they trudged out of Windsor Castle with the corgis in the pouring rain. The two were a heavily wrapped-up Queen Mother and Princess Margaret.

Mother and daughter, despite many moments of tension, remained close. They liked to go out in the afternoon, disguised in sunglasses and headscarves, for a spin in the sports car owned by Margaret's son David, Lord Linley.[6] On at least three occasions in that final decade, there appeared the unlikely sight of a Marigold-wearing Princess Margaret as she went through hundreds of her mother's letters, put them into black bin bags and burned them. We know this from the testimony of one of the staff members she asked to help her and because the Princess told her friend Kenneth Rose, 'I have already filled two big sacks, and the servants are so pleased at my cleaning up the mess.' Rose felt his soul as a historian shrivel at Margaret's claim that she had burned every letter her mother had ever received. Fortunately it turned out to be a wild exaggeration.

Rose voiced his concerns to one of the Queen Mother's ladies-in-waiting, Lady Prudence Penn, who 'realises how much more valuable it would be for the QM's ultimate biographer to read both sides of the correspondence'. Lady Penn confirmed that among the victims of Princess Margaret's deep clean was every single letter ever written to the Queen Mother by the late Diana, Princess of Wales, along with many innocuous ones spanning nearly a century.

Margaret attended her mother's 101st birthday in August 2001, by which time Margaret's health had disintegrated after a series of strokes and operations. Rose wrote in his diary of his pain at seeing her that day: 'In a wheelchair, she is scarcely recognisable, wrapped in a rug, her arm in a sling, wearing huge dark spectacles against the sun and, worst of all, a face grotesquely swollen. Oh, the pity of it.' The Queen Mother prayed that Margaret would not have to endure the trauma of another stroke and, in the end, that prayer was granted as the last one ended the Princess's life, with her two children by her hospital bedside, on 9 February 2002. Prince Charles went to Sandringham to comfort the Queen Mother. Despite her own infirmities, the Queen Mother, in black with a small veil suspended from her hat, insisted on walking at her daughter's funeral at Windsor. Fifty years before to the day, Margaret's father had been buried in the same place. Her ashes were later laid next to him.

101. Tay Bridge

'Have I died again?' was the Queen Mother's wryly amused query every time a news outlet misreported news of her departure. Mock broadcasts were practised at the BBC in preparation for the inevitable day and members of her household went to regular meetings to co-ordinate her state funeral. Guessing where they were, the Queen Mother got a bit of a kick out of asking them what they had been up to that day and then watching their hibiscus-tinged embarrassment.

She had gone over the preparations herself and once visited a rehearsal at Westminster Abbey to thank the seamstresses and the abbey staff for their work. As she was shown the candles selected for the ceremony, though, she smiled, shook her head, and asked, 'Oh, do you mind *very* much if I bring my own?'

The codename for the Queen Mother's funeral was Operation Tay Bridge, while in conversation with the Earl of Airlie she euphemistically referred to dying as passing on to 'greener pastures'. Still devoutly Christian, she read the Bible and prayed daily, as her mother had taught her to do a century earlier and as she, in her turn, had taught her daughters. She went to the Castle of Mey in August 2001, from where she wrote to Prince Charles, 'Here the sun is shining, the sea is shining, and lovely white clouds are floating about. Of course in five minutes the whole scene can change, angry waves, leaden sky, and a howling wind, not to mention the sea birds and growling of seals. I do hope that Birkhall is being its own dear self, and with endless gratitude for your wonderful present,* From your always loving, Granny.'

That November, in a purple dress and hat, with two walking sticks, she attended the recommissioning of the *Ark Royal*, a light aircraft carrier that she had launched twenty years earlier. She was frail and would have toppled over had the ship's captain and an admiral not been on either side of her. She said, 'Thank you,' then kept on going. She stood to give her speech in a clear and firm voice, which ended with the joke, 'Captain, splice the mainbrace!' – a discontinued Navy term once indicating that the captain should give each crew member a portion of rum. She sang the hymns and the National Anthem and stopped to talk to an officer's daughter, who gave her a bouquet of flowers: 'What age are you? … Aren't these lovely? … Thank you so much.' She was introduced to the youngest member of the crew; she asked him questions about where he was from,

---

* Prince Charles had bought her a huge bath towel, which the Queen Mother described in the same letter as 'heavenly. Thank you a thousand times, they are just what I needed.'

what he hoped to achieve with his life, and told him about the first time she had flown in a military plane, six decades earlier.

That was her last official public engagement.

Towards the end of her life, she said to Billy Tallon, the footman who had been in her service for half a century: 'We're two old dears, really, aren't we, William? But we have had some fun.'

EPILOGUE

Queen Elizabeth the Queen Mother died at Royal Lodge, her house in Windsor Great Park, on 30 March 2002. The Queen was at her side, as were her niece Margaret Rhodes and her chaplain. I was in Edinburgh with my family for the Easter school holidays when the television suddenly dimmed and my father looked up to say, 'I think this might be the Queen Mother.'

I remember every channel diverting to BBC One for Peter Sissons to announce, 'The Queen Mother has died, peacefully, at the age of one hundred and one.' Within minutes, crowds 'young and old had gathered' outside Buckingham Palace and Clarence House. There was scandal among royal watchers at the BBC's failure to provide Sissons with a black tie for the broadcast. Given the years of rehearsal, with newsreaders trained to race upstairs to the cupboard housing black ties and back to the cameras with minimal panting, this was a curious oversight. Sissons, who had to defend himself from unfair insinuations that any oversights were in consequence of 'a decision made by the presenter', later revealed that there had been a quick meeting, in which the conclusion was reached that black ties should only be donned to announce the death of a monarch.[1] Shortly before he went live, a producer whispered in his ear, 'Don't go overboard. She was a very old woman who had to go sometime.'

There were others who felt that pressing Margaret Rhodes on air for details of the moment her aunt had died was in questionable taste. She subsequently told a journalist that she thought there had been too many questions under the circumstances, before adding that she nonetheless

205

felt the criticism was unwarranted and that 'Poor Mr Sissons no doubt had a horrible day'. In the interview itself, Mrs Rhodes said of her late aunt, 'She was a wonderful, wonderful person … One can hardly believe that somebody who grew up in the horse age has seen people landing on the Moon and all the things that happen now.' In 2002 in the Queen Mother's bedroom at Clarence House, there still hung a *Madonna and Child* by Raffaelino del Garbo, left to her by her grandmother Caroline, while on either side of her bedhead were two little angels that she had bought in a marketplace in Bordighera, when she was eight years old, Italy still had a king, oceans were crossed by ships, aeroplanes were funny things that looked like cigars, and nobody knew what a tank or a gas mask was, much less televisions or rockets or the internet.

Just over two hundred thousand mourners filed past her coffin as it lay in state at Westminster Hall. They included Coryne Hall, who queued for six hours to pay her respects and curtseyed to the coffin. She had just found out from Billy Tallon that hers had been the Queen Mother's last private audience. The Queen and the Prince of Wales both gave televised tributes, Prince Charles's emphasising how much 'she meant to my whole family, particularly The Queen, to whom she was such a stalwart and sensitive support when my grandfather died, when he was only two and a half years older than I am now. For me, she meant everything and I had dreaded, dreaded this moment along with, I know, countless others. Somehow, I never thought it would come. She seemed gloriously unstoppable and, since I was a child, I adored her … She wrote such sparklingly wonderful letters and her turn of phrase could be utterly memorable. Above all, she saw the funny side of life and we laughed until we cried – oh, how I shall miss her laugh and wonderful wisdom born of so much experience and an innate sensitivity to life. She was quite simply the most magical grandmother you could possibly have, and I was utterly devoted to her.' As per the Queen Mother's stipulation, her death was not allowed to alter any plans for her daughter's Golden Jubilee celebrations later that year.

Queen Elizabeth the Queen Mother was buried next to her husband and the ashes of their youngest daughter at St George's Chapel, Windsor.

FURTHER READING

In the decade immediately after her death, Queen Elizabeth was the subject of two excellent biographies. The first, Hugo Vickers' *Elizabeth, The Queen Mother*, was the product of forty years' research and was published in 2006. The second, released in 2009, was the Queen Mother's official biography, written by William Shawcross.

Elizabeth was also the subject of biographies by Lady Cynthia Asquith, Lady Colin Campbell, Helen Cathcart, Dorothy Laird, Ann Morrow, Elizabeth Pakenham, Countess of Longford, Penelope Mortimer and Ingrid Seward, most of which were written during Elizabeth's lifetime. Lady Colin Campbell's was written after the subject's death and was released in 2012; Ingrid Seward's *The Last Great Edwardian Lady* was updated with a new preface following the Queen Mother's passing.

There are several books dealing with specific periods or episodes in Elizabeth Bowes-Lyon's life. Her childhood is the focus of Grania Forbes's *My Darling Buffy: The Early Life of the Queen Mother* (1997), with its foreword by Queen Elizabeth's grand-nephew Michael Bowes-Lyon, 18th Earl of Strathmore and Kinghorne. The relationship between Lionel Logue and King George VI, as well as Elizabeth's pivotal role in arranging the therapy, is dealt with in *The King's Speech* (2011), a book co-written by Peter Conradi and Logue's son Mark. The disintegration of her relationship with the Duke and Duchess of Windsor is covered in Andrew Lownie's *Traitor King: The Scandalous Exile of the Duke and Duchess of Windsor* (2021) and in Anne Sebba's *That Woman: The Life of Wallis Simpson, Duchess of Windsor* (2011). There is also Graham Viney's *The*

Last Hurrah: The 1947 Royal Tour of Southern Africa and the End of Empire (2019), and memoirs by Elizabeth's niece Margaret Rhodes, *The Final Curtsey: A Royal Memoir by the Queen's Cousin* (2012) and by her equerry Major Colin Burgess, *Behind Palace Doors* (2006), both of which include much on the Queen Mother's final years.

William Shawcross edited many letters sent by Queen Elizabeth over the course of her life, which can be found in *Counting One's Blessings: The Selected Letters of Queen Elizabeth the Queen Mother* (2013).

Many of Elizabeth's contemporaries left behind memoirs, diaries and letters, and I am particularly grateful to, and can recommend, those edited by Simon Heffer, Charlotte Mosley, D. R. Thorpe and Hugo Vickers.

LIST OF ILLUSTRATIONS

Integrated images:
p.4: (UtCon Collection / Alamy)
p.18: (Classic Image / Alamy)
p.36: (IanDagnall Computing / Alamy)
p.61: (Ray Jelliffe / Cartoonstock)
p.64: (© Cecil Beaton / Victoria and Albert Museum, London)
p.96: (Popperfoto / Getty)
p.118: (Hulton Deutsch / Getty)
p.136: (Everett Collection Inc / Alamy)
p.152: (Keystone Press / Alamy)
p.166: (Trinity Mirror / Alamy)
p.182: (Brian Purdy / Alamy)

Plate section images:
Glamis Castle: (Shutterstock)
Captain James Stuart and Lady Rachel Cavendish: (Chronicle / Alamy)
Elizabeth's wedding day: (The History Emporium / Alamy)
Elizabeth with her daughter, the future Queen: (Classic Image / Alamy)
Elizabeth at Great Ormond Street Hospital: (Daily Herald Archive / Getty)
Elizabeth with her family during her Silver Wedding celebrations: (PA Images / Alamy)
The King, the Queen and Princess Margaret: (The National Portrait Gallery)

The Queen Mother, Prince Edward and the Queen: (Trinity Mirror / Alamy)

The Queen Mother, Princess Diana, Prince William and Prince Harry at the Trooping of the Colour: (Tim Graham / Getty)

The Queen Mother in sunglasses: (John Shelley Collection / Getty)

The Queen Mother with the Queen: (Hulton Royals Collection / Getty)

The Queen Mother with Prince William: (Trinity Mirror / Alamy)

Waving on her 90th birthday: (Georges De Keerle / Getty)

A glass of champagne from members of the Toastmasters Guild: (Tim Graham / Getty)

ACKNOWLEDGEMENTS

I had for a long time considered writing a book on Queen Elizabeth the Queen Mother, but the idea crystallised, appropriately, over a gin and tonic on a beautiful summer's day in the south of England. I had sworn it would be the start of some time off from writing, but my willpower proved pathetic. I must thank wonderful Jasper Waller-Bridge, Michelle Dockery and Saul Goldberg for that conversation, which inadvertently started this project, and Arabella Pike who, two days later over a lunch in London, said 'Let's do it' to the idea. She, and my US editor Trish Todd, have my thanks not just for saying yes to *Do Let's Have Another Drink* but for encouraging me to have fun with it. The same is true of my friend and agent, Brettne Bloom.

I am more grateful than I can say that in 2014 I mentioned my hope to one day write something about Queen Elizabeth to David Anderson, who, with the immense kindness that was his dominant characteristic, shared many priceless memories of his time with her. David's death in 2017 was a shock and his friendship is profoundly missed. My thanks too to Lord Astor of Hever, Dr David Bell, Basia Briggs, Major General Alastair Bruce, Matt Cassidy, Anthony Cheetham, Kitty and Dominic Colchester, Magda Czyż, Dr Sophie Duncan, Andrew Elgin, Dr Owen Emmerson, Lydia Forte, Sir Rocco Forte, Coryne Hall, Aoife Herity, Debra Hill, Susan Hunnisett, Laura and Tom Hunniwood, Robert Jackson and Camilla Woodward, Leanda de Lisle, Dr Lauren Mackay, Kate McCaffrey, Dr Hannah McCormick, Ashley Montgomery, Tracy Murrell, the Reverend Canon John Ovenden, Julian Ovenden, Alison Palmer, Dr

Estelle Paranque, Mike Poirier, Luke Redgrave and Shaun Woodward, Alexa Reid Smith and Olivia Auerbach, Antonia and Archie Sebag-Montefiore, Anne Sebba, Paul Storrs and Mari Sveistrup. It is worth reiterating that any opinions on individuals or events are my own.

Lastly, as always, I must thank my wonderful family, whose support has been unfailing.

Gareth Russell
Hampshire, Summer 2022

REFERENCES

Author's Note
1. 'Queen Mother' was used for queens Alexandra and Mary in the prayer books and as the title for Marion Crawford's 1951 biography of Mary.

1: East or West, Home Is Best
1. They were made Lords Glamis in 1445 by Scotland's James II, James VI made a Patrick Lyon Earl of Kinghorne in 1606, and Strathmore was added by King Charles II in 1667.
2. J. Wentworth-Day, *The Queen Mother's Family Story* (London: Robert Hale, 1967), p. 15.
3. Lady Cynthia Asquith, *Queen Elizabeth* (London: Hutchinson, 1937), p. 44.
4. It has since been merged with its next-door neighbour to become business offices.
5. Streatlam had belonged to the family before it was gifted to John Bowes, illegitimate son of the 10th Earl. After his death, in 1885, it reverted to Elizabeth's side of the family.
6. Elizabeth later told one of her footmen, Billy Tallon, that she might have been born in a horse-drawn ambulance, a fact that her parents may have omitted since giving birth outside the home, even in a hospital, was considered faintly déclassé by the aristocracy in 1900.
7. For a good summary of the debate, see Grania Forbes, *My Darling Buffy: The Early Years of Queen Elizabeth the Queen Mother* (London: Richard Cohen Books, 1997), pp. 2–9; Hugo Vickers, *Elizabeth, the Queen Mother* (London: Arrow, 2006), pp. 1–2; Jane Dismore, *Princess: The Early Life of Elizabeth II* (London: The Lyons Press, 2018), p. 40, and cf. Lady Colin Campbell, *The Untold Life of Queen Elizabeth the Queen Mother* (London: Dynasty Press, 2012), pp. 11–22.
8. Interestingly, 1921 was also specified in the private correspondence of the Bowes-Lyons' guest Sir Shane Leslie as the year when the business of the Monster 'was officially brought to a close'.

2: War Wounds

1. He may also have been wounded in a game played several years later. My thanks to Dr Hannah McCormick for discussing the medical evidence with me.

2. Even years later, Elizabeth could spot the Glamis war-time alumni in crowds waiting to greet her and she kept in touch with many of the veterans via letter. She sent help to them where and when she could, and she employed some of those who had fallen on hard times in the years since 1918. She had first met Ernest Pearce as a patient at Glamis during the First World War, when he was a 23-year-old corporal of the Durham Light Infantry and sent to Glamis after his right shoulder was shattered at the Battle of Ypres. Although he preferred life in the countryside, after the army Pearce had worked in a shipyard, a job he lost during the Great Depression. Elizabeth sent money for groceries and new clothes for his children and she then offered him a job as one of her gardeners at Royal Lodge, along with accommodation in a small cottage for him and his family. Pearce kept the job until his death in 1969, by which point his niece Mary Ann had also been working for Elizabeth, for twenty-three years, in her kitchens, becoming head cook until her retirement in 1981.

3. Homeland of George V's grandfather and Queen Victoria's husband, Prince Albert of Saxe-Coburg-Gotha (1819–61).

3: The Delightful Duchess

1. Bertie's sister, Princess Mary, married the heir to the English earldom of Harewood in 1922 and their cousin Princess Maud married Lord Carnegie, heir to the Scottish earldom of Southesk, in 1923. Marriages with British subjects had hitherto been slightly more common for princesses than for princes. Two princesses, both called Louise, one of whom was Queen Victoria's daughter and the other King Edward VII's, had married Scottish dukes. The three British princes who had attempted to flout the practice – two sons and a grandson of King George III – were either pressured into annulments or denied the right to share their titles with their wives.

2. When the relationship became sexual is debated; it seems to have ended in 1928. Three fascinating and longer volumes of Channon's diaries, edited by Simon Heffer, have been published between 2021 and 2022 and the quote here is taken from Channon's diary entry for 22 February 1928, in Simon Heffer (ed.), *Henry 'Chips' Channon, The Diaries: 1918–38* (London: Hutchinson, 2021), p. 312.

3. This was later confirmed by Prince Paul's eldest son in conversation with Elizabeth's biographer, Grania Forbes.

4. Mary, along with her unlikely allies Kaiser Wilhelm II and Queen Victoria, believed that the relationship had been non-consensual, see James Pope-Hennessy, Hugo Vickers (ed.), *The Quest for Queen Mary* (London: Zuleika,

2018), pp. 36–7 and Pope-Hennessy's meeting with the Duke and Duchess of Beaufort, 22 November 1958, cit. p. 301n.

4: Queen

1. There was also a crypto-fascist government in Austria, headed by Chancellor Engelbert Dollfuss, from 1932 until he was assassinated by Nazis in 1934. Four years later, Austria was absorbed into Nazi Germany.

2. Seidler initially shelved the George VI project to concentrate on his next movie, *Malice in Wonderland*, a luxuriously camp drama inspired by the rivalry between two gossip columnists, played by Elizabeth Taylor and Jane Alexander, during the Golden Age of Hollywood.

3. *The King's Speech* was the second production about the couple, the release of which was delayed until after the Queen Mother's passing. The other, *Bertie and Elizabeth*, was a British television movie, in which they are played very well by James Wilby and Juliet Aubrey, with Dame Eileen Atkins as Queen Mary, a role she reprised for the first season of the Netflix series, *The Crown*.

4. James Pope-Hennessy, 'A General Note Upon the Duke of Gloucester (May 1957)', in Pope-Hennessy and Vickers, p. 175.

5. Greece had officially been neutral during the war until it joined the Allies in 1917. Its royal family were, however, dogged by rumours of divided loyalties, particularly in light of the King's marriage to the Kaiser's sister.

6. While writing this book, a friend from Mississippi joked with me that Wallis would have been able to spot Elizabeth's politesse – 'Wallis was from the South, believe me, she knew a *bless your heart* lady a mile away.'

7. The Queen softened on Emerald Cunard when Princess Olga of Yugoslavia, Prince Paul's wife, spoke to her on Emerald's behalf, after which Lady Cunard was invited to the Palace for tea.

8. Leaving aside the likelihood or otherwise of the Hohenzollerns re-gaining their throne, Friedrich-Georg seemed an unlikely future emperor, as he was the fourth son of the last Crown Prince. Many German monarchists believed the Crown Prince had been disgraced by his alleged cowardice at the end of the Great War and that the monarchist cause would be best served by keeping him as far away from it as possible. Friedrich-Georg's eldest brother had renounced his rights in order to marry a commoner, the second brother had spent a great deal of time living in America and (wrongly, as it transpired) was expected to mimic his eldest brother, and the third, Prince Hubertus, had joined the Nazi armies in 1934. By quite a stretch, this allegedly left Friedrich-Georg as the most 'natural' candidate to become Kaiser after Nazism's anticipated implosion.

5: The Most Dangerous Woman in Europe

1. The future Lord Elphinstone was later joined in captivity at Colditz by the King's 21-year-old nephew George, Lord Lascelles.

2. There was a second attack on Buckingham Palace, during which the King and Queen came far closer to death than the government was prepared to admit at the time. The windows imploded into the room as the King and Queen were flung against the walls.

3. Propagandists in both Britain and America wanted to capitalise on the friendship between the Queen and the First Lady, which presented problems as both women were averse to being manipulated into doing anything with which they felt uncomfortable. Both declined a suggestion from the *Ladies' Home Journal* to publish an imagined conversation between them, in which they extolled the virtues of hard work in the factories to help the war effort. Elizabeth expressed her discomfiture with the idea in conference with Tommy Lascelles, who agreed with her concerns that 'the UK will dislike their Queen being involved in such an obvious bit of machine-made propaganda.'

4. Even there, other rationing laws were in place, right down to the amount of bathwater allowed, and fireplaces were abandoned in favour of small electric heaters.

6: Widow

1. In the year he joined the Queen's service, 31-year-old Dawnay attracted the press's attention when he jumped into the River Blackwater to help five people trapped in an overturned car. He rescued Mrs Ann Cameron-Know and her three children, although sadly the driver had been killed on impact.

2. The circumstances surrounding the purchase of Mey were sensitively portrayed in the eighth episode of the first season of the Netflix series *The Crown*, in which the grieving Queen Mother is brilliantly played by Victoria Hamilton, the Vyners by Caroline Goodall and David Yelland, and Captain Imbert-Terry by John Standing.

3. These were Queen Mary, George V's widow from 1936 to 1953; Queen Alexandra, Edward VII's widow from 1910 to 1923; and Queen Adelaide, William IV's widow from 1837 to 1849. All three were less visible than they had been as consorts, but it is not true, as is often stated, that British dowager queens retired from public life until the custom was changed for Elizabeth in the 1950s.

4. This was a mistake on Coward's part. The Queen Mother and Princess Margaret were in Rhodesia, now Zimbabwe.

5. Massey was instead succeeded by Georges Vanier, the first Quebecois citizen to serve as Governor General.

7: Queen Mum

1. They were joined by Prince Charles and Princess Anne.

2. It was either them or the 'Golden Guinness' sisters.

3. Tom Mitford was a guest of the Astors at Hever Castle in May 1929, when Elizabeth returned there for the first time since her marriage. Along with

Bertie, other guests included Elizabeth's brother David, their cousins Rachel Bowes-Lyon and Alice Cavendish-Bentinck, and J. M. Barrie, author of *Peter Pan*.

8: Steel Marshmallows

1. Sir Michael Oswald to Hugo Vickers, in Vickers, *Elizabeth the Queen Mother*, p. 453.
2. This is one of my favourite stories about the Queen Mother. It has also been told about a guest staying at Royal Lodge. On the balance of probabilities, it seems more likely that it took place at Mey. I have compiled it from three different sets of recollections, which happily all agreed on the main details.
3. This anecdote has been told to me over the years by four different people, but with significant deviations. Three of them identified the lady involved as the Queen Mother, while another thought that it was the Queen. The story told by the three-to-one majority was that it was the Queen Mother – this was the version told to me by David Anderson, head of the Household at Hillsborough Castle from 1984 to 2009.
4. The article, by Roya Nikkhah, was published in *The Sunday Times* on 10 October 2021.
5. This story was recounted twice, with no significant variations, by two former employees – in conversation between the author and David Anderson, 18 October 2014, and in Major Colin Burgess, *Behind Palace Doors: My Service as the Queen Mother's Equerry* (London: John Blake, 2006), pp. 162–3.
6. Their friendship is included in the BBC mini-series *The Cambridge Spies* (2003), in which the Queen Mother is played wonderfully by Imelda Staunton, in one of the few dramatisations to depict her sense of humour, and Blunt by Samuel West.

9: Glasses Filled with Dubonnet, Gin and Pimm's

1. This story has been told many times and it is perhaps one of the most famous anecdotes about Queen Elizabeth. An equerry who worked for the Queen Mother is fairly confident that it is apocryphal, although he is at pains to point out that he cannot be certain.
2. This version of events was dramatised in the seventh episode of Season 4 of the Netflix series *The Crown*, in which the Queen Mother was played by Marion Bailey, Princess Margaret by Helena Bonham Carter, Nerissa Bowes-Lyon by Pauline Hendrickson, and Katherine Bowes-Lyon by Trudie Emery.
3. Bertie's younger brother, Prince John, who died in 1919, also had developmental concerns as well as epilepsy, and it says much for the positive changes in attitudes to mental health that, today, the isolation of Prince John, 'the lost prince' kept away from public view, is regarded as cruel, tragic and unnecessary; whereas, at the time, some doctors thought

Queen Mary was soft for having him live on the estate in a cottage rather than sending him to an institution.

4. It was Fenella who later described her daughters as dead when submitting information to a new edition of the social dictionary, *Burke's Peerage*, although there is some evidence that, by that stage in the 1950s, she too was struggling with her mental health.

5. There has been one claim from a former staff member at the hospital that the Queen Mother did privately visit the sisters in the 1980s, but I have not been able to confirm this.

6. From 1986 until his death in 2009, Lord Moore of Wolvercote.

7. A full picture of the negotiations has only recently become clear thanks to the research of Helen Rappaport in her 2018 book *The Race to Save the Romanovs*.

8. This arrangement of portraits was changed with the renovations conducted by Historic Royal Palaces after 2014.

9. Recorded by the MP for Antrim North, *Hansard*, 11 July 2000.

10. A similar story is told about a dinner party, this time in England, although it seems quite possible that it happened more than once. David Anderson, in conversation with the author, remarked that he heard 'Queen Elizabeth regularly did things like that to help cover up mistakes.'

10: I Shall Miss Those Laughs

1. This meant that Queen Elizabeth was mirroring her late father's morning reading routine. The *Telegraph* had merged with Claude's staple *Morning Post* in 1937.

2. From its founding in 1986 until the late nineties, *The Independent* avoided royal stories, feeling that the rest of the British press covered them in sufficient, or excessive, detail.

3. The title has changed several times; however, it can be traced back to the constables of Dover Castle.

4. John van der Kiste and Coryne Hall, *Once a Grand Duchess: Xenia, Sister of Nicholas II* (Stroud: The History Press, 2004).

5. Theo Aronson was friend and biographer of Princess Margaret (1997) and Hugo Vickers, since his biography of Cecil Beaton mentioned in Chapter 9 of this book, had authored lives of Vivien Leigh (1988), Greta Garbo (1994) and Prince Philip's mother (2000). His biography of Queen Elizabeth the Queen Mother was published in 2006, and was followed five years later by his life of the Duchess of Windsor.

6. After his father's death, the 2nd Earl of Snowdon.

Epilogue

1. Perhaps in response to the criticism in 2002, black was worn to announce the death of Prince Philip in 2021.

INDEX